HOLLYWOOD A GO-GO

Andrew Yule
HOLLYWOOD A GO-GO

An Account of The Cannon Phenomenon

SPHERE BOOKS LIMITED

Sphere Books Ltd
27 Wrights Lane
London W8 5TZ

First published 1987
Copyright © 1987 Andrew Yule

Set in Linotron Imprint by
Rowland Phototypesetting Ltd,
Bury St Edmunds, Suffolk
Printed and bound in Great Britain by
Cox & Wyman Ltd, Reading

ACKNOWLEDGEMENTS

My grateful thanks to the British Film Institute library in London, the Museum of Modern Art's Film Department and the Lincoln Centre Library for the Performing Arts in New York, together with their patient staff, to *Screen International*, *Hollywood Reporter* – and in particular, the inestimable 'Show Business Bible' itself, *Variety*, to the various financial institutions and their representatives who gave so freely of their time and insights both on the East and West Coasts of the USA, and in London, and to the various critics who have commented on Cannon's movies over the years. A special 'thank you' also to Eunice Sweeney, my endlessly patient secretary.

A.Y.

LIST OF CHAPTERS

INTRODUCTION

Every author needs a fairly compelling reason to undertake a book —
mine was the need to explain the Cannon phenomenon. Over the
years there have been clues scattered regarding the company's
success, but Cannon continually reminded me of a little outfit
named Commonwealth United in the old conglomerate days, and
then of Sir Lew Grade's Associated Communications, for both
organisations had kept on producing and announcing more and
more films despite the puzzling fact that no-one went to see the
pictures that got made.

When Cannon announced in February 1986 that they intended
to seek further money from the public through another securities
offering, which went on to yield them $207m, I decided that a
closer look was warranted. For although as new movie moguls
Menahem Golan and Yoram Globus had some features in common
with the old Hollywood bosses, movie-making skills were not
amongst them. Nor was being in touch with public taste, except
when they pandered to the lowest common denominator, and even
then they often got it wrong. The list of films produced since

Cannon's formation arguably includes some of the shoddiest fare ever foisted on the public.

Golan functions as the flamboyant front man for the organisation, working mainly on the 'creative side', as he would term it. Globus' function is financial – he is the company's master of deals and head number cruncher. Together, they claim to make 'one perfect man'.

For anyone fascinated by the Indian rope trick, here we have the Israeli version. How did they get it up in the first place? Will it stop defying gravity and fall back to earth? Fellow-fakir Lew Grade's moment of truth came when Kermit the frog and his Muppet pals collapsed under the weight of his LONE RANGER and TITANIC masterpieces. In the case of Commonwealth United, conglomerates went out of fashion and the whole mess rolled over backwards.

Cannon's rope trick long ago ceased to be a side-show attraction and for a while they were fashionable on Wall Street and with the public at large. They are occasionally rumoured to have received financial underpinning from home, although they protest that they have done it all by themselves, vehemently denying association with anyone, especially the Mafia.

If it took hits to keep a film company going – and it seems to take just that for everyone else – then Cannon would have folded up their tent and disappeared into the night long ago. Instead their shares climbed steadily from 20 cents in 1979 to a peak of $45.5 in July, 1986, when the company's worth was put at $371m.

So is Cannon an overleveraged house of cards? Has it all been done with mirrors? I hope the following account of the Cannon phenomenon will provide a few clues.

Chapter One
THE WORLD MINUS ISRAEL

Menahem Golan was born Menahem Globus in 1929 in Tiberias, a town that boasted two synagogues and two cinemas. The son of Polish immigrants, he grew up absorbed in Hollywood movies, for which he would work and fight to get ticket money. 'Like for millions in other countries these movies provided something beyond every day life,' he recalls. 'They gave us kids our music, our haircuts, our dreams.' Eventually he befriended one of the projectionists and was able to sneak in to see films for free. 'Everybody was rich in these movies,' he remembers. 'Everybody was sexy. Even the gangsters were sexy and good.'

Although he flunked English at school and was regarded as the class wimp due to his having no aptitude for sports, he was in charge of the school drama class when he was twelve. At the age of eighteen during the 1948 war of independence he listened to Ben Gurion's call that everyone should take Hebrew names to help create a nation, and took his surname from the nearby Heights, going on to become one of Israel's first military pilots. According to Golan, he dropped hand grenades from a Piper Cub in between acting as a junior reporter for an air force magazine. Three years later he enrolled at the Old Vic Theatre School in London – not quite the Old Vic itself, as later hand-outs would claim – and ostensibly trained as a theatre director. In actual fact his training was as a stage manager, not a director. It was true that the course was in stage management and production – but it was a two-year course and since the school was being shut down, Golan only got the stage management portion. Undeterred, he returned to Israel to direct legitimate theatre, or at least his version of this. He reckons to have introduced Israeli audiences to American dramas and musicals like *A Street Car Named Desire* and *The Pajama Game*. By 1960 he had had enough of the restrictions of theatre work, as he recalls, 'I was bored with the theatre. I was bored with four walls, with the limited scope. My imagination went much further. I had loved the cinema from my childhood – for me it still works better that the best play by – what's his name? The best British playwright. I was at the peak of my career, I was directing for every theatre in Israel between the ages of twenty-one and thirty, but eventually I couldn't take it any further and I just went and quit. I went to New York with my family.' His family at this time consisted of his wife Rachael and the first of his three daughters. At the same time as representing the film, radio and TV department of the Israeli Embassy in New York, the enterprising Golan enrolled himself in New York City College Film Institute to study film making. 'But I was bored in school,' he now says. 'Even the teachers told me that the best way to learn film is just to go ahead and make it.' Armed with this advice, he briefly joined Roger Corman's production team as a humble, or maybe in Golan's case not so humble, grip apprentice on the European location shoot of *The Young Racers*, recalling, 'I heard that Roger Corman was giving opportunities to students. I wrote him a letter, and he invited me to come to Monte Carlo. He said, "On 15th June come to Monte Carlo. This is the hotel: I'll be there, and I'll give you $100 a week. You will drive the car, you will feed me, you will be a grip and you will work on a film. And you will pay the hotel bill and all expenses!"

'So, I went there and did the movie with Roger Corman. There was another student in the same crew called Francis Ford Coppola: he had this little Nagra and a microphone and he was doing a film, which was terrible. Another guy there was Robert Towne, who is now a top director and top writer. He was a grip too. The budget, I remember, was $90,000 and we were shooting at every race-track in Europe. It was a great experience because of the people who were making it. After a week nobody was on set by 8 o'clock in the morning: they all slept in until 9 o'clock. So Roger said, "I'll give $10 to anybody who can get me the crew tomorrow at 8 o'clock." I started picking Francis and everyone up, got them to work, got the $10 and he made me his assistant. He kept elevating me. But I was also his driver. I remember one day, while I was driving him, I was telling him about a play I directed in the theatre in Israel, which was a big hit, called *El Dorado*. I said, "This will be a great movie about gangsters, hookers, the underworld and so on." He liked it and said, "How much?" I said, "$30,000. You give me $30,000 and I'll give you the world minus Israel." He agreed.

'Unfortunately for the project, I was silly enough to tell everyone how proud I was to get $30,000 to do my first picture. And that bastard Francis Ford Coppola heard about it and went to Roger and said, "How can you give this Israeli $30,000? Give *me* $30,000 and I'll make an *American* film for you." Roger said, "Do you have a script?" Coppola said, "Of course I have a script!" And, from that night on, he didn't sleep. He was in a room near me and he was typing all night. Then, from Aintree, he went over to Ireland and came back with a deal from the Irish studio to finance the rest of the movie, Francis Ford Coppola's first movie titled *Dementia 13*, and I lost the financing for *El Dorado*. Francis had the nerve to ask me to work for him for chicken shit as his assistant. I said, "No way: you stole my financing! You stole my movie!" Anyway I went to Israel and found financing there – I did my first movie in Israel. But it was one of the great experiences: I think I learned more with Roger than from anywhere.'

On Golan's return to Israel he signed Hayim Topol to star in *El Dorado*, financing the film through the Israeli government and in partnership with his young cousin Yoram Globus, with whom he had formed Noah Films Ltd. Far from being close, the families had in fact been at complete loggerheads for years until a reconciliation was effected at Menahem's *bar mitzvah*.

Yoram Globus was born in 1941 in a small village called Motzkin, then his family moved to Haifa, the chief seaport of

Israel, where his father bought a cinema. 'I was practically born in the cinema,' says Globus. 'I remember, as a child, I used to correct the photographs hanging in the theatre if they were crooked. I would give away theatre tickets to my friends. I didn't realise that the tickets had a value of money. Then when I was in High School, I gave my father a condition – I will be in High School if I can be the projectionist at night. I did it, but it was very difficult doing both.'

After he had served his time in the army his cousin Menahem paid for him to go to business school and then when he had graduated Noah Films was born and the two of them were into production and distribution. Globus came to Golan with an extraordinary grasp of figures and deals, and was the business brain behind Noah. At the same time he was totally devoid of any artistic flair and his detractors would maintain that this was something he was never to acquire. The two of them formed an incongruous pair – Golan was a big extrovert slab of a man, Globus was small and introverted. What they shared – apart from a professed love of cinema – was a thick Israeli accent when speaking English, that could be cut with a knife. Even then their dream was that one day their films would break out of the Israeli market and they would score a world-wide hit, but they had a long way to go and several setbacks to face before this was to happen. A side-trip to Hollywood in 1964 made another lasting impression on Golan. He spent several fraught and frustrating weeks sitting in a cheap Hollywood hotel while trying to sell major studios the idea of financing a low-budget spy movie he wanted to make in Israel. 'It was my first encounter with the system,' he recalled. In the end, after being given the run around all over town he turned in desperation to Samuel Z. Arkoff at American International Pictures. To Golan's astonishment and gratification, Arkoff read the script overnight and reached the decision the next day as he and his right-hand man stood shoulder to shoulder in American International's executive urinal. Golan got his cheque and claims, 'It was my first great teaching experience of Hollywood.' The movie emerged as *Trunk to Cairo*, before promptly disappearing.

That same year Golan produced *Sallah*, directed by Ephraim Kishon, again starring Topol, which was nominated for an Academy Award in the Best Foreign Film category. It didn't win, but it was a milestone for the young team. It didn't travel too well either, the *Spectator* being of the opinion that the title role was played by Topol with 'grizzly self indulgence'. The *Guardian* asked, 'Surely not made for export?' John Russell Taylor concurred: 'To put it kindly, the film bears every mark of being for home consumption only.' Even then they decided to opt for quantity rather than quality, a harbinger of things to come, churning out deathless epics with titles such as *Eagles Attack at Dawn*, *The Great Telephone Robbery*, *Daughters, Daughters*, *The Miracle*, *The Highway Queen* and a total of forty odd shoestring films. Their one deliberate – and hugely expensive – stab at the international market, *Escape to the Sun*, for which they retained the services of Laurence Harvey, misfired badly, flopping even in Israel. Dominate the Israeli film industry they did, but hardly a ripple reached the world audience they dreamed of.

Two of Noah's early films were reviewed in New York's *Village Voice* by Robert Gross. He described *Lupo* and *Margo* as 'two travesties – insults both to Corman's ability as a teacher and to Israelis in general.

'Golan seems to have incorporated a million different obnoxious styles in these vain attempts at comedy, where even the few funny moments get smothered by over acting and sloppy camera work. They are neither specifically Jewish nor ethnically viable, tending to border on the banal to just plain awful. In *Lupo* the low point of the film occurs when Lupo's horse gets run over by a car, eliminating the best actor in the film. In *Margo* (the actors) go through exaggerated grimaces, and dialogue that borders on the retarded at every picture-postcard place of interest – until you feel you are watching an El Al commercial. Golan degrades both the Arabs and the Oriental Jews in Margo's town by picturing them as stereotyped morons.'

Golan felt frustrated – okay, they were making movies, but for a very small audience, for their Hebrew black-and-white Bs were not widely exported commodities. Looking back Golan recalled, 'How could we conceive of competing with the American movies to which the mass audience streamed? Sometimes a Swedish, French or Japanese movie acquired an artistic reputation, but for the market-place American productions were so far advanced we didn't have a chance.' Unlike the way the duo now tell it, and even despite the undoubted popularity of some of their product in their native

7

Israel, all did not run smoothly even then. Lines may have formed for many of their releases, but there was a reaction against what many saw as their profound influence over trends in film-making in Israel and the media often blamed Golan personally for the low standards in the home-grown film industry. He let it be known that he felt the media and his peers were not being objective and were denying him due credit for galvanising Israeli film production.

Often Golan's contemporaries would be angered by his buccaneering make-or-break techniques, but there was general agreement about one thing – his indefatigable energy and high level of initiative. A colleague in those early days who worked with them, fell out with them, then worked with them again, recalls, 'I knew them when their arse was hanging out of their trousers. Above all they were fighters and fearless – or daft. They put everything on the line for their passion and when they went broke, knew only one way out – make another film.'

Itzhak Kol, now head of Cannon Productions in Israel, vividly recalls Golan in these early days: 'After I became to know him well I found out that he is far too soft. People who say he is ruthless, I think that they don't know him. They don't know the man. I remember once Menahem and Yoram, they were my clients when I had the lab and the studio here in the country. So they wanted to take the answer print of one of their pictures and I told him, "Menahem, I am not going to give you the print until you are paying me in front." I tried and then Menahem came and said, "Look, I don't own anything. I don't have car, I don't have a frigidaire and I don't even have a house or an apartment. The only thing that I have is a wife and daughters. If you can put a mortgage on my wife and my daughters it's okay with me. And if you are not going to give me the answer print you are ruining me absolutely." So – he started to cry and even the people are saying that *I'm* ruthless. I became soft and I gave him and I am not sorry for that.'

At one time the duo were forced to mortgage their houses to keep their productions going, then both found themselves yanked before the authorities in Israel for non payment of taxes. Later Golan had his old car confiscated, but each time they picked themselves up again to make one more movie, convinced that eventually the breakthrough had to come.

In 1968 they hocked everything they owned to finance the production of *Teyve and His Seven Daughters*, their most expensive film to date. A European producer, Arthur Brauner, had been sufficiently taken with their work to suggest a co-production deal on *Teyve*, on which the musical, *Fiddler on the Roof*, was later based. Golan collaborated on the screen play with writer-poet Hayim Hefer. It was chosen as the first Israeli film to be entered for the coveted Golden Palm award at Cannes, prompting the raising of further funds for a make-or-break publicity bash. When revolutionary students closed the festival and threatened to burn down the theatre in which *Teyve* was due to be shown, Golan bustled into the theatre and grabbed the precious reels of film, then throwing them under his coat, he ran for his life. It seemed like the end, until Jack Fishman asked to see *Teyve* and acquired the rights. Saved by Fishman's cheque, Noah was back in business and the film went on to become a modest hit. Fishman recalls their meeting at Cannes: 'I believe they can't be understood without knowing their set-backs, sacrifices and slights. You have got to be exceedingly careful when you do business with them, but only because they want to make money to make more films, not because they are your movie egomaniacs trying to swagger and dominate.'

The year after Cannes the two of them flew to New York on December 31st, $100 in their pockets and with another film to hock around. A cheap hotel near Times Square was where they saw in the New Year, and as they toasted each other with hot cups of coffee to ward off the bitter cold, they vowed that the 70s would be better. This time they were determined to make it, but once again they had to return to Israel and more Noah films to bail them out. In 1972 they turned out *The House on Chelouche Street*, which was nominated for the Best Foreign Film, like *Sallah* before it. Also like *Sallah* it didn't win, but it represented another step up for the team. In the same year, in one of the strange company decisions which occasionally bedevil a major studio, MGM decided to pick up their *Kazablan*, a musical about a Moroccan immigrant. As produced and directed by Golan, with Globus as executive producer, the movie had broken all box-office records in Israel. Unsurprisingly, MGM did not enjoy the same success in the US market. In the UK Tom Hutchison for the *Sunday Telegraph* described it as a 'Naive oddity. Everyone keeps saying "My life" and "Already" and at the end I found that I had enjoyed it all despite myself and almost despite the film.'

Golan was next signed by the British independent outfit Tigon Films to direct local comedian Norman Wisdom in *What's Good for the Goose*. It sank without trace, even in Britain, and virtually wrote 'finis' to Wisdom's hitherto flourishing career. Undaunted – or perhaps a little bit daunted – Golan nevertheless went on to direct what he again hoped would be the international breakthrough, a little number called *Diamonds* in 1975. It starred Robert Shaw, Richard Roundtree and Shelley Winters. It looked big but it wasn't big – flopping even in Israel, although it pulled in a few customers in Italy.

Now it was back to Hollywood, where Golan directed *Lepke* with Tony Curtis at the old Selznick studios, Golan recalling that *Lepke* was made for $900,000 and claiming it was sold to Warner Brothers for world-wide distribution for $1,750,000. Warners got no bargain, for the film did a quick fold. *Variety* wrote that 'Apart from the minor novelty of being about a Jewish gangster, the picture is a stale rehash of stock gangster pic situations, without originality of theme or treatment.' Golan looks back on the visit with mixed feelings. 'Israel didn't allow you to take money out. So, I swear to you, we came like that – jackets, trousers, a little valise. We came to America, and we didn't have a dollar. We got a two-week visa and somehow we started our little production company called AmeriEurope. We had one secretary and a telephone when we decided to try and put *Lepke* together. Then we wanted to buy a big company – we wanted to buy Allied Artists which was bankrupt, but we didn't have any money.'

In 1977, back in Israel again, Golan co-wrote and directed the last of the three films based on the Entebbe Raid, entitled *Operation Thunderbolt – Raid on Entebbe*. Although business was still only modest, the picture garnered yet another Best Foreign Film nomination for the team without actually gaining the award. This time opinion was split critically, right down the middle. David Robinson in *The Times* described it as 'Certainly the best of the screen versions of the Israeli raid on Entebbe,' while Alexander Walker for the *Evening Standard* described it as 'The worst'.

Now they were ready for their big breakthrough, though not quite internationally. In 1977 they produced *Lemon Popsicle* in

Israel. As directed by Boaz Davidson, it was the first in a series of films about teenagers coming of age, which mixed youthful sex with a 50s rock-and-roll soundtrack – a Hebrew rip-off of *American Graffitti*, no less. It sold a million tickets in Israel in a fifteen-theatre release, then broke out in the German market. By the time the Cannes Film Festival of 1978 arrived, Golan and Globus could claim their first international success – excluding the US, where they claimed it was sold, but where it nevertheless remains unreleased to this day.

Flushed with its success, the duo stated at Cannes that they would be spending $10m in all in 1978 on four features to follow up *Lemon Popsicle*'s success. The *Uranium Conspiracy* had already completed filming just weeks before the festival, on locations in Israel, Germany and Italy on a claimed $2.5m budget. These were the days when it suited them to exaggerate their budgets; that way people thought of them as bigger than they were and it helped to justify their claim even then to be 'a major independent'. Negotiations were stated to be still on for *Conspiracy* with an English distributor, but since it never appeared in Britain, presumably the negotiations broke down. Golan asserted, 'We have $1m sales already – minimum guarantees between theatrical and video sales, and that is not counting the US where we hope to rake in another $2m.' This was among the first of Golan's ongoing over-estimates and claims.

Next up was to be *Savage Weekend*, a pick-up which had been filmed in New York State before being taken over by Golan/Globus and rushed to Israel for post-production. The print had arrived from Israel two days after the festival had started, then was smuggled past the French customs to avoid delays, before being promptly screened – and sold to six territories, according to Golan.

It's a Funny Funny World – from the *Lemon Popsicle* team – was due by July, then would come the really big one from Golan that the world was supposedly waiting for, an item called *The Magician*, Golan's pet project, the script being based on the novel by Isaac Bashevis Singer. Golan explained that the rights for *The Magician* had been bought originally by Walter Reade. Laurence Harvey was to have played the lead with Milos Forman due to direct from a script by Wolf Mankowitz – in fact it had been Harvey who brought the project to Golan's attention when they had been filming *Escape to the Sun*. However, both Harvey and Reade died before the film could be started and it took Golan two years to clear the rights, then a further two years to get what he called a 'snappy script'. He stated that this was one project he was not pre-selling, although he had received 'tremendous offers'.

The movie was shot in West Berlin with an Israeli, British and German cast and crew, financially underpinned by the Munich-based tax shelter company Geria, and with a loan from the German government who were anxious to encourage filming there. Golan was described on the set as being aware of every prop, every point of continuity, every camera movement, and orchestrating technicians and actors in a search for continual high points – which he then pursued with tactless enthusiasm, the drama being further heightened by the fact that everything had to be conducted in Hebrew, German and English, with Golan the only bridge between all three, having taken on direction of the movie after Milos Forman dropped out. The star-studded cast he had recruited included Alan Arkin, Louise Fletcher, Valerie Perrine, Lou Jacobi and Shelley Winters. The film was released as *The Magician of Lublin* to withering reviews, contrary to Golan's later claims. It was considered to be an A-1 stinker – worse, it did no business wherever it was shown. Nigel Andrews in the *Financial Times* wrote that 'It keeps charging forward with reckless disregard for the subtler nuances of Singer's tale and gets from Alan Arkin his crudest performance in memory.' *The Spectator* wrote, 'It takes an interesting theme and proceeds to ruin it with a combination of woodenness and sentimentality. The direction is so rudimentary, the script so banal . . .' David Robinson in *The Times* said, 'It's one of these films which is so far from the original that it is hard to see why the director even bothered to adapt it. The mystical and metaphysical elements of Singer's novel quite escape Golan. Instead he interpolates his own kitsch and frightful invention.' Derek Malcolm in the *Guardian* stated, 'I'd like to draw a veil over Menahem Golan's awful version.' David Castell in the *Sunday Telegraph* wrote, 'The picture is yet another indiscriminate product of tax shelter money.' Eric Shorter lamented, 'A respected novel has been rearranged in the manner of a Broadway musical comedy, but without wit or music.' Philip French summed it up as he wrote, '*The Magician of Lublin* is the worst film to be adapted from a major literary work for years.'

Quick as a flash *It's a Funny Funny World* was transmogrified into *Going Steady (Lemon Popsicle II)* and there were some sighs of relief as the cash-flow resumed. Both the '*Popsicles*' were directed by Boaz Davidson and although the pictures were far from master-pieces, at least they had wide appeal – except, unfortunately, in the US.

Among the other Golan/Globus features 'lined up' for 1979 were to be the musicals, *The King and the Cobbler*, described by Golan as a 'Biblical rock musical' and another called *Discomania*. Like many other features that were announced, these never appeared and from the sound of them perhaps it was just as well.

Next to roll was another Golan 'special' that he would direct himself, *The Apple*, billed as a 'futuristic rock musical fantasy'. If only the artist in Golan could have been held down for a time, things would have been much better for them, as this was to be another total disaster, ravaged by the few critics allowed to see it and deemed to be totally unreleasable. After a title change it surfaced in Britain as *Star Rock*. A shocked Tim Pulleine wrote in *Monthly Film Bulletin*, 'This cut-price extravaganza plummets to a new low in opportunistic inanity.'

Meantime a New York based film production company called the Cannon Group Inc was in deep financial trouble. Founded in 1966 by Denis Friedland and Christopher C. Dewey, Cannon had sought to produce low-budget movies aimed at a teenage audience, hopefully to emulate the success of Samuel Arkoff's American-International Pictures. After some years of strictly *schlock* produc-tion that nevertheless paid the rent, Cannon released *Joe*, starring Peter Boyle. Directed by John Avildsen, who would go on to helm the original *Rocky*, the film was Cannon's biggest hit to date and in 1973 they had gone public, trading stock over the counter and gaining an additional source of capital. Success continued with the *Happy Hooker* series and items such as *Maid in Sweden*, *Cauldron of Blood*, *Invasion of the Blood Farmers* and *Blood Legacy*, but not at a rate which kept up with the changing needs of the market place. More and more, a saturation release by TV advertising was becoming mandatory and gradually marketing costs loomed larger than ever for independent movie companies, already squeezed by rising production costs and variable revenues. The last straw came when the federal government moved to change tax laws in 1976 that closed the loopholes on the prime sources of Cannon funding. Their shares declined to 20–30 cents, and their annual revenue to only $1.9m. Tired of their constant rejection by the Hollywood system, and mindful of the frustrating 1964 trip when Sam Arkoff had bailed them out, Golan and Globus had looked at ways to break into the American market and produce films with the crucial 'American look' which would sell internationally. They had in mind a production company, but preferably one with a distribution facility. Allied Artists had been judged to be 'too much trouble, too much in debt', then their eyes alighted on the Cannon Group.

Cannon had a library of some sixty pictures either produced or picked up since their formation – almost all of them irredeemable junk that had had its day – or had it? With 3,000,000 shares issued, Golan and Globus needed $500,000 to buy the company, but that represented a major problem – they didn't have the cash. Not an insuperable problem, however, as it turned out. The cousins were convinced that the films in Cannon's vaults had been undersold in the international market, so they went to Friedland and Dewey with a typically outrageous proposal. Cannon should give them the rights to their catalogue in the foreign and ancillary markets for a 25% commission, this to cover the cost of buying Cannon. The proposal was accepted and as Golan puts it, 'In two weeks we sold more than they had in ten years. We had credibility abroad and a relationship over the years with distributors. We learned ways to sell their movies because, before that, we sold black-and-white Hebrew-speaking movies to China, Tibet, Tanganyika, Finland and Sweden. You sell Hebrew black-and-white pictures and you can sell anything! So that's what we did – we bought the company with our commission from their own movies – and inherited a $3m debt – and fifty-seven lawsuits!' It's a great story – but in fact they also required a loan of $350,000 to clinch the deal – provided by Frans Afman of Credit Lyonnais (of whom more later) enabling them to acquire a majority holding in Cannon.

This would have been enough to sink two lesser men, but not Golan and Globus. 'We wanted to make a fast buck to clear the debts so we moved the company to Hollywood and started from scratch to make the same kind of small picture Cannon had before us. We knew perfectly well that we had to elevate to make the Hollywood scene, and not just depend on exploitation pictures. Hollywood did not swallow us. The telephone did not ring. Everyone tried to frighten us about getting involved in the US. They said it was dangerous. But it simply couldn't be worse than in Israel, a country with galloping inflation and locked-in borders. The only thing about the US is that it's bigger and needs more money. To begin with we lost millions taking the advice of so-called experts and in sleepless nights wondered whether it was too tough here, whether we should go back to Israel, but we stuck by our decision. The US market is simply too important to have to go shopping around for a picture-by-picture distribution deal. We only had two possibilities ever – to start up our own distribution set-up from nothing or to find our own Mecca, an existing structure like Cannon. To have started a company from nothing would have required a tremendous capital investment and we didn't have the money. The acquisition of Cannon presented the best – maybe the only, alternative.'

Things didn't go their way to begin with, mainly because of the entrenched attitudes in Hollywood, according to Golan: 'You understand, Hollywood is full of bullshit. Only 10% of the people are really doing the movies and we said, "We must do what we say we will do." We discovered a beautiful way. We told everybody, but nobody believed it. We said, "If you shoot an *American* film" – and I kept saying, "American! American!" because that is the product that everyone in the world is looking for – "If you make an American film with a beginning, a middle and an end and with a budget of less than $5m, you must be an idiot to lose money, a complete unprofessional idiot in today's market. American films have a meaning to the world. They mean professionalism, a professional product. It must have a normal little story, with actors; that's all."'

Chapter Two
THE GOLAN DEPTHS

Since the acquisition of Cannon by the team was consummated prior to the 1979 Cannes festival this was the platform they chose to launch their new Cannon International Inc. Golan laid out his 'Ten Principles', quickly dubbed by industry wags as 'The Ten Commandments', mainly pertaining to the abolition of waste in movie production methods. 'If it doesn't appear on the screen, don't spend money on it,' summed up the golden rules. Golan spelled out that Cannon would be a conduit of product to distributors all over the world and that they would pay close attention to their needs. He asserted that they would soon begin the production of popular quality American pictures – pictures loaded with Menahem's 'American' look. A line of credit that would eventually reach $45m had been established with Frans Afman of Credit Lyonnais, a $4 billion bank, formerly known as the Dutch Slavenburg, before being taken over, amid some controversy, by its largest shareholder, Credit Lyonnais. Afman had survived the scandal at Slavenburg and seen heads roll all around him after the rescue operation by Credit Lyonnais. Their investment in other film companies and their association with Dino De Laurentiis dated back to 1972, Afman rationalising the bank's exposure in the often difficult waters of film financing as he explained, 'We thought of it as project financing – the sort we do for shipbuilding and aircraft.'

Golan's method of 'preselling' movies which Dino de Laurentiis had first introduced Frans Afman to, and which had subsequently been passed on ('He's my professor,' Afman would say, 'a genius'), went into top gear at Cannes. Often with no more than a catchy title and a star name, together with the now familiar, hurriedly-prepared and lurid Cannon poster, he would describe the film to foreign independent distributors. If they liked the sound of it, they would open a letter of credit with Cannon, the agreed sum payable only on delivery of the finished film to their territory. Cannon then took these letters of credit to Credit Lyonnais who advanced 75% of the letter of credit's paper value, accepting the letter as collateral provided it came from an accredited source. Golan would often boast that these presales put projects into profit before they even commenced production.

Presales not only gave them production finance, therefore, but also extra finance for acquisitions of all kinds. Golan claimed that foreign distributors would soon come to know that they could rely on the delivery of a Golan/Globus production and that if they happened to lose money on one film, then another down the line would make up for it. Golan saw the distributors as 'kind of service men serving the producers – so we don't allow him to lose money'.

Golan later claimed that his first task at Cannon was to immediately begin to turn their old tired image round from a maker of low-budget exploitation movies to a producer of quality motion pictures, but as Golan himself would occasionally admit – perhaps in an unguarded moment – *schlock* would still continue to be a large part of the Cannon inventory. The flogging of the old Cannon product which had enabled them to buy the company continued unabated. Puzzled customers at Cannes were advised that a Robert De Niro picture was 'ready for release'. Already tagged 'a Golan/Globus Production' – it had in fact been filmed in 1969 as *The Swap* and remained unreleased theatrically – as it still does to this day. Another little item – this time from the new Cannon, was to be

17

titled *Seed of Innocence*, which Golan tastefully described with the synopsis: 'They met – they loved – they brought a child into this world – they were only 14'.

Golan had the nerve to show his own title *The Magician of Lublin* at the festival, to what could be most kindly described as a mixed reaction. Unabashed, he informed one and all 'Listen, we are the beginning of the seventh major. We seriously mean it. We will fill the gap being left by Allied Artists!'

A year later at Cannes the duo revealed that things were now very much on the move as they unveiled the delights they had in store for the future. First up would be – *The Apple*. A mistake? No, with unfailing *chutzpah* and faith in their own product they would attempt once more to breathe life into this cold turkey. Now it was billed as a '$8m musical' (likely cost: closer to $1m), shot in Berlin and throughout Europe, with a cast of 'hundreds of young American and British actors and dancers'. Next up – *Seeds of Innocence*. Again? Yes, again – now it was a $2m Boaz Davidson production. Next – *Dr Heckyl and Mr Hype*, a $3m production – in fact a cheapie left over from the old Cannon, as was *Last Rites*, described as 'having impressed Golan and Globus as one of the most terrifying and scary movies they had seen lately'.

Murder by Mail was 'A chiller of a potentially demented murderer with a twist'. Soft porn was there also, represented by the old Cannon's *The Happy Hooker Goes Hollywood* and another horror subject, *Godsend*.

And for the future? *New Year's Evil* on a $2m budget (the calculation seems to be: divide each claimed budget by at least 4, often much more). Then – *Lemon Popsicle III – Growing Up* also at $2m, *Body and Soul* starring Leon Isaac Kennedy and Jayne Kennedy, budget $6m. *Bon Appetit* was to follow, although the planned Israeli-Canadian co-production to star Anthony Quinn on a $4m budget never did. The $8m *Death Sentence* and the $12m *Space Vampires* were next, then the $6m *The Ambassador* and the $8m *The Dorothy Dandridge Story*. 'Openings' soon in the US for Cannon pictures were trumpeted for *Teen Mothers* and *American Raspberry*, with Golan at his most lyrical as he described what he personally was trying to put over: 'I'm a storyteller,' he declared. 'I like to transfer good stories to the screen.

'I look at myself as a child enjoying a good story being told by my mother. I don't think I'm looking for styles in film-making, but instead simply a good story.'

There were in fact two additional productions announced at Cannes which would have an impact on the fledgling company. As usual with Cannon, the significant items tended to get lost in the plethora of claims, but these two stood out. One was *Enter the Ninja*, to be directed by Boaz Davidson, which in the end was helmed by Menahem Golan himself – it would go on to become a hit in almost every market in the world. The other was *Lady Chatterley's Lover*, for which Sylvie Kristel had been signed as well as her *Emmanuelle* director, Just Jaeckin. *Ninja* was claimed as a $4m production (more like $1–$1.5m) and *Lover* as $6m (more like $1.5–$2m). Golan elatedly claimed that the last teaming of Kristel and Jaeckin in *Emmanuelle* had yielded $100m at the box-office.

In all their wheeling and dealing, Golan and Globus had turned Cannon around from $1.9m in revenues before they took over to $6.14m a year later. Although profits were a wafer-thin $58,000, their shares went up to $1.20 – back from the brink. The shares they had acquired for $500,000 were already multiplying.

Lemon Popsicle III when it appeared was no longer *Growing Up*, but was changed to *Hot Bubblegum*. It followed in the successful path of the first two. *Death Sentence* became *Death Wish II*, with Charles Bronson reprising his vigilante role, and Michael Winner as director, after Paramount decided to pass on the project. Star power seemed to be the name of the game for Cannon by this time, and although they constantly claimed presales all over the world for their projects, they were still able to say 'Yes' to Columbia Pictures International when that company offered them a deal to release four of their efforts abroad – *Enter the Ninja*, *Death Wish II*, *Lady Chatterley's Lover* and *Body and Soul*, and the deal was seen as a tremendous financial boost for Cannon as well as being a nicely prestigious arrangement. It was also their first contact with a major studio – but not their last.

Enter the Ninja was important in that its success paved the way, like the first *Lemon Popsicle*, for a series of sequels. *Lady Chatterley's Lover* served its purpose, although it was a package that failed to deliver on any level, *Body and Soul* was a decent success relative to its true budget, casting aside the claimed $6m, and *Death Wish*

II racked up the best figures of all. Paramount's laid-back approach to the sequel had certainly turned a profit for Cannon and would continue to do so over the years. Capturing Charles Bronson had done them a power of good as well as providing a career boost for Bronson, since he only seemed now to be able to bring customers in to a *Death Wish* movie. However, this seemed to fire Golan with the need to enhance Cannon's star power further. Unfortunately they had not learned their lesson properly with *Death Wish II* and Bronson, even though they themselves spelled it out: 'Bronson with this subject matter and the right director and the fact that there is such violence in the world. It's timing as well as chemistry!' Golan had declared.

If Michael Winner made them money on *Death Wish II* he would blow a lot of it with his next project and its star, where the timing and chemistry could not have been more misguided. But that was in the future; for the moment Golan and Globus had another surprise up their sleeve – the formation of two subsidiaries in the UK, London-Cannon Films Ltd, a production company, and Cannon Distributors UK.

Not for the last time would the duo see the effect of this kind of announcement on their competitors. Although it was true that the formation of these companies hardly strained Cannon's overall budget, it seemed to be a timely indicator of what they intended to achieve, since before forming a distribution company one has to have a reasonable expectation of keeping it supplied with product. Those who had poured scorn on the fledgling company's chances had been made to pause, if only for a moment. Golan and Globus had left behind them in Israel a production and distribution company in Noah Films, together with cinema ownership, and it looked like Britain was now to be the first country to be the subject of their 'master game plan', a repeat of their Israeli performance. They had absorbed their lesson in Israel's relatively small, but typical and representative industry. If Israel was like a microcosm of each country's film production, distribution and exhibition set-ups, then they had learned what had to be done. They had seen that it was no good making popular films from which some remote distributor would cream the profits, and ultimately it was pointless to make pictures at all if you were unable to get them shown. The answer, therefore, was to tie the whole thing up.

20

Golan and Globus's blueprint was established right there and then, but industry onlookers failed to recognise it and in the years that followed, even their most ambitious film production plans would be punctuated by world-wide acquisitions of the means of showing these productions. They would build up a lot of celluloid over the period, but banks prefer bricks and mortar – the team never forgot that, and since it fitted in beautifully with their game plan, why should they? Besides, surely this was how the majors themselves had started?

In Cannes during 1981 Golan would underline the continuing importance to them of their Israeli operation where their interests were registered as G & G (Golan & Globus) – *not* Cannon: 'Although it has been two years since we acquired Cannon, you can say we have been operating in Hollywood for four years, but we have never neglected our base in Israel. Noah Films is our company and is still the number one independent production and distribution company in Israel.' With tongue in cheek he added, 'Yoram and I are no longer involved in Noah, but it is run by Amnom Globus, Yoram's brother, and produces one or two pictures a year. Cannon of course has the world distribution rights for those, while Noah is also a distributor and owns the largest chain of cinemas in Tel Aviv.'

He was asked how Cannon arrived at a decision on which projects to go forward with and replied, 'I make the final decisions but I have consultants such as our in-house director Boaz Davidson and Yoram. Usually when one of us has an idea we sit down together and I make the choice.

'*Enter the Ninja* became a hit because it created curiosity; it looked like a new kind of film in the field of commercial action – adventure films. It appeared to the buyer to be a step beyond a martial arts picture. *Lady Chatterley's Lover* was a combination of a classical book, considered erotic at the time it was published, with a sex symbol like Sylvie Kristel and a top director like Just Jaeckin: three elements that made another movie much in demand for us. I have been going to Cannes every year since 1964 and that is a lot of years. We have established a meeting place with our buyers on the beautiful Croisette. It's a busy time, but it is also a good time. We are having a martial arts show never before staged in Cannes, with *Enter the Ninja* and Sho Kosugi and his six-year-old son. We will be selling *Ninja* and *Hot Bubblegum* and Boaz Davidson's new film, *X-ray*.' (*X-ray* in fact turned out to be a total flop.) 'Then we will be showing some films from last year –' (wait for it!) '*The Apple* among them. Other new products will include *Death House*, *Schizoid*, *Maid in Sweden* and *Little Girl, Big Tease*. We'll show excerpts only from our new version of *Lady Chatterley's Lover* – it's a very special and unique film, then we will be announcing our new pictures for 1981–2 production.'

First up was to be *My Pal Clyde*, starring – it says here – the orang-utan from Clint Eastwood's *Every Which Way but Loose*. 'This will be his first starring role,' Golan enthused. 'It's a story about a monkey which has developed vocal chords and is taught to talk.'

After that would come *Revenge of the Ninja*, then *Gunga Din* in India in early 1982. Boaz Davidson would then ready his next *Lemon Popsicle – IV* tentatively titled *Screwing Around*. Davidson would follow this with *Crazy Times*, subsequently unheard of, and *Space Intruders* starring George Peppard, which never actually appeared either. Next came Golan's annual speech in which he again confidently stated, 'Cannon is the major among the independents. It's a new category. It's a major production company which is what we call independent and by the way, is the only public company of this size in America *[sic]*. It's a production company with a dressy look trying to create American motion pictures of major quality for the independent world distribution market.' Now well into his stride, he continued: 'The most demanded film in the world is the American film. The better or bigger or most qualified are produced by the five or six major companies, but now we have the money and can afford the big stars. Every country has between twenty and fifty independent distributors who cannot buy from the majors in order to get play dates in their theatres. If it is not an American product, he has to have the best French film or Italian film or Japanese film. Until five years ago, independent companies used to make B or C or D category motion pictures. Since we acquired Cannon, you can see by the way we are climbing, we have upgraded our product to become A category. We are looking to create major motion pictures for the independent distributor to be able to acquire and then compete with the major companies in this country. That's our philosophy and that's what Cannon is.

But it doesn't mean that we don't also sell to the majors – we do.'

Golan's own aspirations came to the fore as he commented modestly, 'Myself, I came to motion pictures from the theatre. I've been a director since I was born and I love to direct. Now that we have Cannon, I have less time to direct and I do one picture a year. Subject matter is important to me. I am like a child: I like entertainment. I like to bring entertainment to people and I am not carrying a message. I don't want to change the world, I just want to bring good entertainment to the world and its people. I'm a professional director so my personal ambitions are limited to directing films and to creating Cannon as a company that supplies this kind of entertainment. The more we develop, the happier I'll be. The best reward is when you overhear somebody saying to somebody else, "I had a wonderful evening last night, I saw a wonderful picture last night," and I stay anonymous, but know that what I have created has brought happiness.'

Now it was off into the stratosphere. 'A film director has a godly power. He has an idea, he puts it together and creates life – a story. I feel that God has given me something unique. A film director today in the 80s is the storyteller of the medieval times. I feel I am able to tell stories that people like to hear. The more they like to hear the stories, the happier I am. Basically, I'm a modern storyteller using the medium of our century.'

Now it was exit stage left lightheartedly: 'Yoram and I are two crazy men who would sell their trousers to make films! Besides our investors, we personally put our own money where our mouths are.'

His bemused audience was then treated to a handout list of other Cannon projects. They had acquired the US distribution rights of an Italian picture entitled *Alien Contamination*. They were contemplating participation in the first Western production in the People's Republic of China, for in conjunction with Bohemia Films of Munich there was an agreement with the China Film Corporation of Beijing to co-produce a feature entitled *Towards the Sun*, written and to be directed by William Janovsky, a Czech director living and working in West Germany. Although principle photography was stated to be scheduled for the following spring in the Tibetan mountains, nothing more was ever heard of this particular work. Other big projects which never made it to the starting line included *Superboy*, which appeared to be based on a wish-fulfilment story originated by Golan himself, who described it as a 'fantasy about a boy dreaming to become superman.'

By the end of 1981 Golan and Globus had increased revenues from $6,140,000 the previous year to $22,942,000 and had posted profits up from $58,000 to $2,340,000. The total value of the company had zoomed from $500,000 to a new worth of $3m.

Incredibly, Cannon soon discovered that they had managed to botch the supposedly sure-fire *Lady Chatterley's Lover*, for when it was finally released it fell flat on its derrière, having served its purpose in keeping Cannon's credibility afloat on a raft of expectation. Not for the last time would Golan discover that all that glittered was not gold. There was worse to come, for it seemed he had left his negotiating brains behind him when he gave the European co-producers a percentage of the gross receipts – before even the production costs were recouped. He had obviously anticipated the absolute gold-mine he thought the film was destined to be and probably felt since it was sure to take close to the $100m he claimed *Emanuelle* had grossed, it was still a bargain. He had to pay out $1,599,000 in one year alone, although the film was a loss maker, and it was a lesson he was never to forget. In the future he would never consider surrendering a share of the gross.

Now Michael Winner set about his next Cannon project. The company had made a considerable amount of money from *Death Wish II* – $22m US box office, $10m net, but only $2m to Cannon after Filmways, the releasing company, had deducted their share – together with a claimed $28m in foreign sales. Winner had in mind a bawdier remake of the 1945 camp Gainsborough picture *The Wicked Lady* and wanted no less a personality than Faye Dunaway to star. Golan was hugely enthusiastic – Dunaway would be a tremendous prize if she would agree. After months of trying to contact her at studios or through her agent, Golan was able to speak to her at her home, having been given her personal number. She was at a low point in her career, with *Mommie Dearest* having just been shredded by the critics. Although it would become a cult favourite with audiences who liked to hiss along with the movie, and Miss Dunaway, this was not the reaction she had had in mind.

There was just one thing – she was also keen to star in the movie version of Tom Kempinski's play, *Duet for One*. Okay, agreed Golan, we'll do that too! Just one more thing – she wanted her husband Terry O'Neill to direct *Duet for One*. Agreed also. Golan was elated by the signing – the 'major independent' had signed its first major star.

Dunaway's lawyer had another client which led Cannon to an attempt at prestige with *That Championship Season*. Jason Hiller's Pulitzer prize-winning play had been up for grabs for almost ten years without a taker – until Cannon was sold on the idea. Star power came into it, but again the subject and the timing were wrong, unlike on their coalescence in *Death Wish II*. Prestige galore came along as they signed up Robert Mitchum, Martin Sheen, Bruce Dern and Stacy Keach for the project, with Miller himself directing. In praise of Cannon, Miller went on record as saying, 'No-one else would have made the movie, no-one else had the courage. But these two picked up the script in New York on a Friday evening and called Saturday morning from Los Angeles with a deal. We were shooting six months later and they were on the money, and ethical, all the time. All the bad-mouthing you hear is the reverse of my experience with them. They took a big risk with me, and then left me alone except for when I asked for help.'

Golan mused: 'Our policy for better acceptance meant we had to keep concentrating on star names. You can break down the closed doors if you reach the talent personally. Give them the right material or let them do projects they are interested in. Stars want to work. We were not sure it would work at the box office, but on *That Championship Season* we organised a sharing deal whereby the stars and the director got $250,000 each and points. As a result we started getting calls from everyone.'

'They weren't taken seriously,' top agent Martin Baum maintains, 'until they made *That Championship Season* and signed Faye Dunaway for *The Wicked Lady* and *Duet for One*.'

After *That Championship Season* had lost millions Golan rationalised: 'We believed in its commerciality when we decided to do it. We probably made mistakes. We should have opened it up more. I miscalculated that a middle-aged story would attract the youth. They didn't come and that made the difference. It's a lesson. I'd be careful in picking up theatrical pieces in the future because critics make a very big difference to artistic movies.'

Contrarily this did not halt plans for *Duet for One* which had been a hit in London with Frances De la Tour, but a flop on

Broadway for Anne Bancroft. By the time it was eventually started in 1986, Faye Dunaway and Terry O'Neill had in fact both dropped out.

Another big star came their way with the signing of Katharine Hepburn, who would be teamed with Nick Nolte in *The Ultimate Solution of Grace Quigley* with Anthony Harvey directing. This was a project Miss Hepburn had wanted made for years and that every major studio, wisely as it turned out, had refused to back. The plot had Miss Hepburn teamed up with a Mafia hitman, intent on putting away all the superfluous senior citizens in New York City. Even Golan – can you believe it – had doubts about the subject matter, but decided to proceed anyway. The rationale seemed to be: How do you follow Faye Dunaway? Answer: with Katharine Hepburn.

Bryan Forbes would direct Roger Moore in *The Naked Face* for London-Cannon. Rock Hudson would film *The Ambassador* in Israel under J. Lee Thompson's direction and John Cassavettes was set to star in and direct *Love Streams*, co-starring his wife Gena Rowlands. On the face of it, it certainly looked as if their break-through into prestigious and star-laden productions had been thoroughly achieved, and certainly some of the ingredients looked good. *The Ambassador* was allegedly an adaptation of Elmore Leonard's *52 Pick-up*. *The Naked Face* was based on a novel by Sidney Sheldon, the best-selling author of *The Other Side of Midnight*. However, all the disparate ingredients needed to be perfectly blended to make a successful project and every single one of these star-studded items bit the dust, even though there was no denying the enthusiasm with which they were undertaken. When Cassavettes was producing *Love Streams* he offered his house as the set and worked for Union scale. Nick Nolte on *Grace Quigley* also worked for a fraction of his normal salary. When Katharine Hepburn informed Golan she had to have her English hairdresser flown in from London Golan balked and pointed out that it would add $80,000 to the cost of the film. Miss Hepburn promptly wrote a cheque for the amount, Golan gleefully recalling, 'I gave her an extra point in the picture, though.' He hilariously reasoned, but with some truth, 'What's wrong with a guy making $1m instead of $2m in eight weeks? I give credit to most of the stars. They want to work in their profession. They want to do movies. Every star does maybe a movie a year. What does he do the rest of the year? I always say he is going nuts. He is going to psychiatrists. He gets divorced. He is on the tennis courts. He has nothing to do. Just bring him something, or ask him what does he want to do! Do you know that there are scripts lying around Hollywood that everyone raves about but no-one will do? *Grace Quigley* was lying around for ten years and nobody dared touch it. That's the kind of challenging material that actors want to do. Everyone says that all they want is money but that is not true – stars already have money. What they want is to prove that they have talent, to show what they can do. Their lawyers advise against it – they are afraid of flops – but the actors are keen. And they will do challenging parts for less money.'

Globus the figure-man meantime spelled out his philosophy as he asked, 'What's an artistic movie? To me it's an art to get audiences into a theatre. For me, *Star Wars* is the most artistic movie ever made. Bringing people to see it for half a billion dollars – that's something. Yes, I want applause for our films – applause from the *bank*. After all, that's who we are grateful to.' When asked if he ever worried about the huge commitments Cannon were taking on he replied, 'You know, in our difficult days we had debts, we were late with cheques. In the end, we never left anybody owing a dollar. We never bankrupted our companies like so many others did!' By this time Globus was a family man too, also with three daughters.

He presented a more sober image than his older partner, straight down the middle and decidedly uninspired – except when it came to figures and their interpretation.

In 1982, with London-Cannon Films Ltd and Cannon Distributors UK in operation, Cannon snapped up the 130-screen Classic circuit from Lew Grade's on-the-ropes Associated Communications Ltd (ACC). Two of the pictures that hastened ACC's demise were Michael Winner's dreadful version of *The Big Sleep* (Robert Mitchum, Sarah Miles, Joan Collins) and another all-time Winner stinker *Firepower* (Sophia Loren and James Coburn). Now as well as a production and distribution company Cannon had an exhibition circuit of their own, fully vertical in fact, just like – why, just like their set-up in Israel! 'We bought it mainly to break the monopoly off English distribution,' Golan declared, an ironic statement in the light of events that were to follow much later. 'And we did it with a bank loan. One hundred and thirty screens in sixty-seven properties for £7m – and the valuation of the properties alone was £9.2m! This bargain gave us a place to show our films big; nobody in the business could believe that we cleaned the toilets and turned losses into profits in a year.'

What Golan failed to mention was that the purchase was largely financed by bank loans, secured on the assets of the cinemas, most of it repayable in 1987, until which time it would bear interest of 4.5% above the London Inter Bank interest rate, with $153,000 due in 1984, $383,000 in 1985, $537,000 in 1986, then a whopping $6,650,000 due in 1987. On top of this Cannon had to find over a million dollars a year to pay off the interest alone on their investment. There had been talk of the loan being financed through a stock offering in London involving a long-term secured debt, with warrants attached to purchase common stock, but the plans for this were shelved pending the return of 'more favourable market conditions'. Coincidentally, their original loans from Credit Lyonnais were all due to be repaid by 1988.

Golan/Globus and Cannon bore more than a passing resemblance to the set-up at ACC during Lord Lew Grade's heyday there and his determined effort to break into interantional films.

Grade's boast was always that he could raise the funding for his productions by a mere telephone call to his bank, even without pre-sales. Despite his undeniable drive, enthusiasm and superb salesmanship, his choice of movie subjects, together with the talent he chose to bring them to the screen, was more often than not sadly out of tune with the tastes of the movie-going public. His decisions moreover appeared to have all the hallmarks of a one-man band and he stoutly maintained that even his biggest flops would make money in the end because of the upsurge in the ancillary markets. He appeared to come largely to instant decisions and invariably produced constantly upwards-rising profit figures until the crunch came with *Raise the Titanic*.

Many saw Grade's ACC as a haven for second-rate talent and it is necessary to go back to Commonwealth United's activities as one of the first of the then new-styled conglomerates in the late 60s, to find a previous comparison with Grade, and later Cannon, in this respect. Commonwealth United swung into production with a vengeance, churning out 'B' films that were heavily disguised as 'A' films, and employing a welter of 'talent' that could not find a safe harbour elsewhere. They made films in every part of the globe where a tax shelter could be found – until suddenly it all went wrong and the great roll-over turned and started running backwards – the domino effect, terrifying in reverse.

Another foreign production subsidiary, Cannon Italia SRL, was established in 1982 and the productions were announced of *Hercules* to star Lou Ferrigno, *Mata Hari* to star Sylvie Kristel, *Nana* and *Treasure of the Four Crowns* to be shot in the 'Magic of Supervision 3-D'.

Old Cannon fans must have felt a decided twinge of *déjà vu* as they perused some of these titles. Golan singularly failed to see the humour in references by rivals to his catalogue as 'The Golan Depths' and he hit back with, 'Delivery is the name of the game. Not talking big or being funny but getting movies on the screen. When we announce one, people trust us so much, our associates are so certain we will deliver, that our bank no longer asks for a completion bond. In our business that is amazing. And it is still the two of us making all the decisions. Just us. Yoram and me.' (Boaz Davidson having exited.)

Meanwhile the old Hollywood guard was up in arms at the nerve of these two 'Go-Go Boys' or 'The Nosh Brothers', as they were dubbed, for along the way the Cannon team had began to break a lot of rules. They hired non-union labour to cut costs and would often work their crews eighteen hours per day, sending them to any location where the films could be made more cheaply and away from prying eyes. Every avenue of savings was explored, with all negatives being printed in the UK or Italy at often less than half the US costs which the majors bore. They were in constant conflict with the Directors' Guild of America (DGA) for paying below union minimums. Golan made the arguable point that if they met what he termed the 'ridiculously high minimums', then his low-budget films would cease to be low-budget and would simply stop being produced.

By the end of 1982 revenue was only marginally up, from 1981's $22,942,000 to $23,208,000. Their posted profit, however, was up from $2,340,000 to $4,387,000 and this time the financial world began to properly sit up and take notice. Their shares began to rocket and reached $5 each from their original 20 cents.

Now another epic was in the works. John and Bo Derek, having dazzled the world with their electrifying *Tarzan* – which the once-mighty MGM had released – now turned to Cannon with their new offering, *Bolero*, which they tagged, 'An adventure in ecstasy'. (Much more later.) Charles Bronson was to stay with Cannon for *Ten to Midnight*. A quaint project was their intended remake of an earlier film called *Gawain and the Green Knight*, now to be known as *Sword of the Valiant*, to star Miles O'Keefe and featuring Sean Connery; this one had industry wags noting that whereas for years it had been normal practice to remake hits, only Cannon would dream of remaking what had been a flop. Did they know something no-one else did? The answer was 'No'. Faye Dunaway in *The Wicked Lady*, now being touted as a '$15m project', would have help from Alan Bates and Sir John Gielgud (not enough to emerge victorious over Michael Winner's direction, however), and Vincent Price would star in a British horror opus, *House of the Long Shadows*, ignoring the fact that this genre had long since fizzled out.

One other film was in preparation, and it was to be Golan's new personal effort. He describes how he read it first during a turbulent jet flight: 'All of a sudden the plane starts dropping like a stone. Everybody is panicky but I don't notice! The oxygen mask drops from the ceiling, but I don't take it! I've got to finish the script. Just when I'm done, the plane comes out of its fall. Everybody is relieved, but all I can think of is one thing: If I could read a script through all that I've got to make a movie!' The subject was a Jewish boy-meets-Christian girl story called *My Darling Shiksa*. Golan shot it as *Alby's Place* and it would be finally released as *Over the Brooklyn Bridge* with Elliott Gould and Margaux Hemingway. Other tantalising titles on their slate included *The Graduates of Malibu High*, *Mute Love*, shot completely on location in Israel, and *The Last American Virgin*.

The previous year's *My Pal Clyde*, the one about the talking orang-utan, Clint Eastwood's ex co-star, was now the supposedly $6m *Monkey Business*. *Gunga Din* was now off indefinitely and a sequel to the old Cannon Company's *Joe* was planned with Peter Boyle as *Citizen Joe*. One more picture would be touted, and it was one that would have a pivotal effect on Cannon in the future. Again $15m was the claimed budget of *Sahara*, to star Brooke Shields and to be directed by Guy Hamilton. The genesis of this little number was – believe it or not – Mark Thatcher's lost-in-the-desert adventure. When he heard of this Golan recalled, 'I said to myself, that's a romantic story. The world is going back to romantic films.' Although he had someone else in mind for the female lead originally, he discovered that Robert Levine represented Brooke Shields as well as Faye Dunaway and Jason Miller – and that was it.

Next he saw Teri Shields, Brooke's mother, and won her over to the project. Of course she then had to be appointed executive producer on the project and gained strict approval over even the release of still photos of her daughter taken on the set. The script was rewritten no less than seven times before it was approved by all parties, including Mrs Shields. A new director, Andrew V. McLaglan, son of the late Victor, was set before filming proceeded in Israel.

While all this apparently expensive activity was going on there were Cannon-knockers everywhere and tales abounded of their legendary tightness with money. One of their directors said, 'They go through petty cash cheques to find one for two cokes by a person they saw drinking only one. They still think like small men, survivors – which may well be their undoing as they take on bigger things.'

A special effects man noted, 'They will save 50p on a flashlight battery if they can make you buy it for them. In all my previous film work, I got fair treatment with a hand-shake – not from them. With Cannon you get to where you walk away to save your self-respect, then they make a deal. And your contract had better be airtight because they are not finished looking for every conceivable loophole, trying to push you on every imaginable and unimaginable way.' Another of their earlier veterans confirmed, 'They take care of the stars, but by God that's it. For the rest they cut every conceivable corner.'

One Beverly Hills story which had a wide circulation, told of a rich Arab who asked his children what they wanted for their birthday. The boy who asked for an aeroplane got British Airways. The boy who asked for a boat was given Cunard. For the tiny tot who asked for a cowboy outfit, his father bought him Cannon! Not a community normally known for its indulgence towards outsiders, Hollywood found it hard to stomach the Israeli invasion, as it was dubbed. At the same time some of the more open-minded members of the Hollywood community found the dashing twosome something of a tonic. Here were two guys prepared to put their money where their mouths were and back their judgments – no crummy, cautious hierarchy to tiptoe through only to find yourself turned down by the top man, an employee like the rest and just as worried about his job security. Still the snide remarks abounded as the Cannon-ites seemed to be making continual inroads into signing up the stars.

Golan hit back with, 'Look, we're movie-makers, not heads of studios who come to their plush offices from law firms or talent agencies or business schools. Our school was the school of smacks in the face and getting up to make more films. When we first came to Hollywood, we found a closed society in which deal-making is more important than movie-making. For them, it's 10% making movies and 90% talk – on the tennis courts, in the Polo Lounge and at parties where a certain kind of cigarette is smoked. We have nothing to do with that, and we are buying no tennis rackets. What we are doing is going to the top – because we started at the bottom. You start at the top and expenses mean little. So a picture costs another $1m – so what. The hard way is to do it our way like by selling a black-and-white Hebrew-speaking picture to Japan. We appreciate every dime. The majors spend most of their money on ego-nourishing luxuries, frills never seen on the screen. We have only a hundred salaries to pay, which keeps our overheads extremely low. If I told you the majors employ thousands of people to make fewer films, I'd be exaggerating on the conservative side. Yes, we save money where we can by using non-union labour. A job is a job!'

And a debt is a debt. In 1982 they were hit by a law suit from a Chicago Financial Services Company, Walter E. Heller & Company, who charged that Golan and Globus had not repaid a loan of $450,000 used to finance a film they had backed eight years earlier. The suit was settled out of court for the full amount.

Stalwart Michael Winner continued to support them, this time in their fight to eliminate fat from budgets. 'There is so much waste in films,' he observed, 'but Cannon runs a careful operation. They are not like David Lean, with individual costumes for everyone or waiting ten days for the sun to shine just right.' This was one of

Winner's rare statements with which most would agree – for Cannon appeared to be the diametric opposite of everything that Lean stood for, namely quality and craftsmanship in motion pictures. In *Over the Brooklyn Bridge* the schedule was six weeks and a budget of $4m; Golan took pride in completing it a week early and $500,000 below budget by shooting twelve hours a day and six days a week. Shelley Winters at one point encountered a problem with her part, but Golan trampled over the problem, saying, 'This is a method actress. In order to say a simple line like "How do you do" she has to tell you about her grandmother. I said, "Say how do you do". She said, "But I don't *feel* it". I replied, "Then say it without feeling!"' Never mind that in the finished picture the location work jumped all over the place and in one scene two of the cast would go up to a restaurant on the seventy-fifth floor of a building, only to be seen dining no higher than fifteen floors up! Elsewhere people walked out of an eastside restaurant on to a westside street.

Occasionally rival producers would question even the basic validity of the Cannon system of presales, arguing that whereas it was perhaps possible to cover 50–75% of a film's budget in this way, the balance of the risk must lie with Cannon. 'Not so,' Golan would roar as he continually assured everyone, 'You can't lose. There is no risk.' Wall Street analyst Lee Isgur at this point offered, 'It sounds good on paper and they've got a lot going for them, but it's not a lead-pipe cinch.' 'Look,' argued Golan, 'we don't know *how* to lose money. There is nearly $1m profit on every film before we even open it in America.'

One fact that was certainly on Cannon's side was the rapidly developing market in TV, cable TV and video sales. From $3m in 1982 Cannon's sales to video distributors in 1983 soared to almost $12m. Cable TV sales increased from $2m in 1982 to almost $8m in 1983, with Charles Bronson's *10 to Midnight* garnering $2.5m on its own. A deal with Esselte in Sweden for the showing of twenty Cannon movies on television in Scandinavia over three years was reckoned to yield Cannon $2m over the period.

Although he would continue to be stung by complaints about the ill-treatment of staff, Golan would stoutly maintain that they had never alienated anyone who had worked for them – or at least anyone they did not wish to alienate. 'If you look at the list of the people who worked with us in the last two years, and who at this moment is working with Cannon, some of these people are working the second and third movie. I have no fight with them. They are all lovely and I love them because they are real artists.'

Hollywood was shaken to its foundations in 1983 when Cannon triumphantly signed Sylvester Stallone to star in *Over the Top* for a record fee of $12m. Where on earth was the money coming from? Well, actually, it wasn't – not for quite a while, as it would be three years later in 1986 before the film would finally be made. Golan loved the favourable publicity engendered by the signing and even before the actual announcement was made, as the rumours of it swept Hollywood, he was asked to confirm or deny the scoop.

Savouring the moment, he rose from behind his desk until his bulk dwarfed the neat figure of Globus at his side. Beaming broadly, he jubilantly replied, 'Look, I gave you no comment, but after I say no comment, I say there is no smoke without fire, all right?'

On the respectability front Soviet director Andrei Konchalovsky was signed to direct *Maria's Lovers*, to star Nastassia Kinski, Robert Mitchum and John Savage. Golan had first met Konchalovsky at the 1979 Cannes film festival when the Russian had won the Golden Palm for *Siberiade*. He had been allowed out of Russia on a leave of absence and was anxious to direct American pictures, primarily a script by Japanese maestro Akira Kurosawa which would end up later as *Runaway Train*. Golan saw the signing of Konchalovsky as another scoop for Cannon – commerce was tied up with the signing of Stallone, now a nod to art with Konchalovsky! Also, so far as Golan was concerned, the Golden Palm award at Cannes was the ultimate accolade, at least of equal ranking with the American Oscar, and now he was employing a director who had won it, someone Golan therefore had tremendous admiration for. (Being a director himself, of course, he probably saw it as an association of artists, a meeting of minds!) No major studio showed any interest in the forty-two-year-old Konchalovsky, so it was to Cannon's credit that they saw fit to sign him – for whatever reason – and it was the start of an association that would endure for several years.

In the spring Golan had been invited to sit on the jury at Cannes, only to have the invitation mysteriously withdrawn a week later.

Rumour had it that one Hollywood major had threatened to withdraw all his productions from the festival rather than have Golan sit in judgment upon them. An infuriated Golan threatened to sue the festival organisers, but withdrew the threat when he received an apology from Robert Favre Le Brett and Gilles Jacob. The organisers also agreed to a late-night screening of *The Wicked Lady* to compensate for the slight. Hollywood had a field day, many believing that the snub was only too appropriate and had put Golan firmly in his place. No such luck – for Golan retorted, 'All I care is to do good movies and sell them well. My mother used to say, "If you throw Menahem out the door he will come back in through the window!"'

To strengthen their foreign distribution and exhibition strength in line with their policy of controlling their own destiny – the model according to Israel and more evidence of their 'master game plan' in action – Cannon acquired the Rank-Tuschinsky outfit in Holland, one of the leading distributors in that country, who handled United International Pictures' product and owned thirty-two cinemas. Now their strength abroad in Britain on the production, distribution and exhibition side, in Italy through Cannon Italia SRL and in their native Israel, was further augmented. Still they needed one more thing to apparently set their seal on their success – a secure outlet for their product in the US market, considered all-important.

Their 1983 revenues totalled $62,600,000, up from $23,208,000 in 1982. They posted profits of $9.7m, more than double 1982's $4.387m. They needed to bow to no-one. Levitation had taken place with no visible means of support. The moment was ripe.

Chapter Three
THE LION ROARS

Hollywood Reporter noted that meetings were rumoured between Golan/Globus and MGM executives, notably Frank Yablans. Was there a deal in the offing? There surely was. Still reeling from Cannon's Stallone scoop, the Hollywood film community was stunned again when it was announced by a magisterial Golan, accompanied by the beaming, dapper Globus that all future Cannon productions would be released in the US and Canada exclusively by Metro-Goldwyn-Mayer. This was a dizzy peak, for on the face of it they had been accepted by a major to add to their own schedule of pictures – and one of the greatest names in film history. Not only that, but as details of the agreement emerged, it became clear that Cannon had negotiated an outstandingly sweet deal by any standards. Even as they were able to bask in the prestige the association lent them, Cannon could not be accused of giving in easily to MGM – quite the contrary!

They were to keep a portion of each rental dollar generated by their movies whether or not MGM made its basic distribution costs back. 'Unprecedented' was the word most used to describe this, for normally a supplier could only expect to participate in *net* rental proceeds after the distributor had deducted costs of advertising, publicity and the making of prints. Cannon was set to receive at least 30% of the gross rentals, rising to a maximum of 65%, given a large enough rental inflow to MGM. The 30% figure was to be paid after the point where gross rentals doubled advertising and print outlays, then rise by 1% for each additional $1m of gross rentals up to the maximum 65% figure. There was only one tiny snag with the deal: MGM would pay out no up front money and Cannon and Frans Afman were said to be in a huddle at Cannes over the possibility of a common stock issue of 1,000,000 shares to raise cash. In a research report published by E. F. Hutton, one of Cannon's investment bankers in 1984, the benefit of the MGM deal was spelled out. A film that grossed $16m in box office receipts would yield about $8m in gross rentals, Cannon receiving 30% of the first $6m, 31% of the seventh million and 32% of the eighth million for a total of $2.4m.

With help from Furman Selz, Hutton duly prepared a prospectus for the money-raising share flotation, proclaiming that the MGM distribution arrangement would ease Cannon's need for substantial expenditures on domestic release costs of their motion pictures. In a significant note amortisation of film cost (44% of distribution revenue in 1983 and 42% in 1982) was acknowledged to have increased in proportion to the increase in distribution revenue and a statement clarified that the company amortised film costs under the income forecast method, which provided that film costs are amortised for any motion picture in the ratio that the revenue earned in the current period bore to management estimate of the total net revnue to be realised. In other words, when a film is in production all costs are capitalised in the balance sheet as assets. When a film is set to open theatrically, all marketing and print costs are capitalised as well. Then as the film is set to open, management makes a forecast of the total future amount of revenues the film can generate. A ratio is then set up between costs and forecasted revenues. This ratio is the amortisation rate. Management can from time to time revise these income forecasts, which might result in an increase or decrease in the rate of amortisation of any motion picture. The significance of these amortised film costs is that they represented the principal assets of Cannon.

As of March 31st 1984, Cannon had $103.9m of unamortised film costs for released or unreleased films and the company estimated that it would amortise 95% of these films' costs by March 31st 1986. Cannon made a great play of the 'fact' that most of their pictures were amortised (ie: expenses paid off) over a two–three year period compared with the industry's average three–five year term, claiming that taking this 'conservative approach and estimating gross revenues from any given picture would enable the company to then speed up its cost recognition if revenues came in faster than expected.' They would maintain that in this respect they were more aggressive in amortising their film costs compared to their competitors. The truth of this was that the rest of the industry average which Cannon quoted, seldom in fact took place, as in reality the major studios changed their bosses frequently. Each time a new studio head arrived a stock write-down would be ordered to enable the new arrival to start off with a clean slate. So while the majors in theory spun their revenue estimates and cost recognition out over a longer period than Cannon, in practice this seldom happened except when there were long-term contracts in place for the product.

Cannon differed from the majors in one main respect. Since 1979 there had been only two bosses at the top with never a change, just 'Yoram and me'. When Cannon stated three years, therefore, chances are that that is precisely what they meant.

Naturally, when someone has spent $15m or so to make a picture, a view must be taken as to its worth in terms of revenue potential. The subjectivity involved here nonetheless has always been seen as potentially leading to chances for dubious practices, since these estimates, tied as they are to the rate of costs write-off, are crucial to a company's year-on-year profitability.

Let's suppose that a company, having spent $6m on a project, estimate the revenues from that project to be $24m – over one of Cannon's three-year periods, for example.

Obviously it would be unreasonable to expect the company to absorb the full cost of the film in year one, hence the linking of the amortisation rate to the rate at which the revenue actually comes in.

Now the film goes into US release and in the first year brings in $8m in revenue – one third of its full $24m estimate. Fine – that means that the same one third of its full cost ($6m) can now be written off, ie, $2m. The company therefore ends up with a paper profit at year one of the difference between the $8m revenue and the $2m cost write-off, ie $6m. There is only one problem – if the picture has only taken $8m in its first year, surely it will never make the company's estimate of $24m – will it?

Now the film enters its second year of release, probably foreign and ancillary distribution, and turns in a further $4m. Since $4m is only one sixth of the original $24m gross revenue estimate, only a further one sixth of its full costs of $6m is now due to be written off, ie $1m. So in year two with the difference in revenue ($4m) and cost write-down ($1m) there is *still* a net paper profit of $3m.

Now we enter crunch year – year three. Let's suppose that the film has in fact run its full course in years one and two and that *no* further revenue is forthcoming in year three. $3m costs still remain to be written off – representing a $3m *loss*, since there is no revenue to set against it.

In the three-year lifetime of the movie, therefore, the following has been achieved for the production company by over-estimating revenues – whether inadvertently or not:

1) In Year One – a $6m profit
2) In Year Two – a $3m profit
3) In Year Three – a $3m loss.

As can be seen, the high forecast has edged the profit into the early years and reserved any loss for the final year; revenues of $12m have been received, against the original estimate of $24m. The picture in this example comes out with a total profit of $6m. Let's now see how this would work out on a wildly over-estimated loss-maker.

This turkey-to-be has cost $12m to make and revenue estimates are set at $36m. In year one the film takes only $6m – that's one sixth of the full three-year estimate. So only one sixth of the costs of $12m, ie $2m are written off. Year one shows a net paper profit of the difference between the $6m revenue and the $2m worth of cost recognition, ie $4m.

In the second year the turkey struggles to do a last-gasp $3m. Okay, that's one twelfth of the three-year revenue estimate – so let's write off just one twelfth of the total $12m cost – namely $1m. Paper profit on this outing: the difference between $3m and $1m–$2m.

Now, in crunch year three the turkey is buried – there is *nil* revenue – but no less than a whopping $9m of costs to write off! The three years' figures look like this, therefore:

1) In Year One – a $4m profit
2) In Year Two – a $2m profit
3) In Year Three – a $9m loss.

An *overall* loss, therefore, of $3m, but only emerging in year three – where the delayed cost-recognition bill comes in for *$9m* after the paper profits in years one – of $4m – and two, of $2m. So a film that is stillborn in the market-place can *still* by this method be shown to make a profit in years one and even two. The only absolutely foolproof way of getting over troublesome crunch years would be *always* to have more first-year product entering distribution every single year that passed.

Suppose that a company made just one single film in year one, on which it overestimated revenues. They would thereby show a paper profit in year one, but possibly be in trouble by year two – certainly by year three. Okay, in year two, that company had better make sure they have at least two new films ready for release – and overestimate their revenues in the same way.

On this basis, of course, the company have put themselves on a dreadful treadmill. Every single year they are in a position where they must always have more films available for year-one release than they had the previous year. Always their new openings must exceed those of the films entering crunch year three – when their overestimates come home to roost.

Only one thing could save them – the miracle, just one single miracle – in the shape of a *Star Wars*. This would wash away all their sins, clean their whole operation up and render over-optimistic accounting on other films irrelevant. There is, for sure, nothing dishonest about income forecast accounting – it is in fact the prescribed method for the film industry. Cannon would later maintain that they overcome any 'day of reckoning' scenario by revising their estimates 'from time to time', as their prospectus indicated. Nevertheless, unless clearly spelled out this could obviously lead to uncertainty whether a group is depreciating its film costs at a fast enough pace.

Cannon's films generate most of their revenue in their first year of release when they pass through their theatrical, video and cable 'windows'. Some of their films are never shown on more than a handful of screens, beating a quick path to the video market. This leaves very little behind for future revenues.

If a company enjoyed no hits whatever, the going would fairly soon get difficult, for it would not be easy to live on illusory profits. Cash-flow difficulties would constantly present themselves, despite even a partial presales policy. More money would have to be raised from the banks or from public securities offerings and since this could only be achieved by an outwardly successful company, it would be essential for any company operating in this way to continuously report increased profits unfailingly. They must *never* be seen to flag – or the cash-flow from bank overdraft facilities and from public offerings would cease overnight. They could never afford to pay dividends and surely it would be the ultimate salt in the wound to be forced to pay tax on illusory profits? There were even ways for certain companies around that problem, though not indefinitely: Cannon, for example, paid no dividends and were to find a tax haven in the Netherlands Antilles.

Although this permitted method of film-industry accounting may seem incredibly flexible, there is one caveat – companies are *obligated* to take an *immediate* write-down as soon as they realise that revenues have been over-estimated, to reflect the shortfall.

Another item that would please the banks and the public would be for a company to shore up its asset base, or property portfolio, by taking over companies rich in these assets. 'Property portfolio' in the film world means – in the main – cinemas, so how, apart from being bricks and mortar, would these prove an attractive proposition?

1) To keep the banks happy.
2) To keep any foreign money earned working in the country where the profits were made – for future tax purposes and to take advantage of any foreign tax shelters available.
   – but mainly –
3) To assure them of the one thing vital to them to guarantee playdates for their pictures, ie cinema ownership.

'I grew up on MGM and I love this lion,' Golan declared. Although the MGM arrangement was seen as being the seal on Cannon's success, by now the MGM company itself was but a shadow of what it had been, and needed other peoples' pictures to supplement its own sagging release roster. Even so, on behalf of his clients Faye Dunaway and Brooke Shields, attorney Robert Levine was cockahoop over their success, as he had every reason to be, confirming as it did his 'good judgment' in advising his clients to go with Cannon. 'What is amazing about these men,' he enthused, 'is that they are absolutely fearless. Obstacles that would dissuade lesser men are simply things to overcome. They are not intimidated, and they put their own money on the line for everything they believe in. They make the decisions – the buck stops. When I met them in London I was taken with their enthusiasm, their energy, and what seemed to me their trenchant knowledge of the way the movie business worked. In the M G M deal they may have the final piece of the puzzle they needed.'

Cannon dismissed claims of conflict of interest when dealing with G & G in Israel, including Golan–Globus Productions Limited, Noah Films Limited, G & G Israel Studios Ltd and the theatrical arm. G & G had 'granted' to Cannon rights for the world (excluding Israel, West Germany and Austria) to all motion pictures they produced, under terms Cannon maintained were at least as favourable to them as they could have obtained from third parties. Payments of $633,000 were said to have accrued to G & G by 1983. In turn Cannon granted to G & G the exclusive right to distribute all past, present and future Cannon pictures in Israel on the same 'as favourable as third party' terms.

Cannon would maintain that of course they would not simply locate films at G & G studios in Israel to keep these studios busy, but because Israel provided the ideal location for these pictures and that the rental charged to Cannon would be 'no more than the same fees and charges made to other, unrelated parties for comparable use'. They covered the fact that Cannon had bought the stock of 'certain companies' controlled by relatives of Mr Globus and a director of the company 'for a net book value ($600) and assumption of loans ($3,988,000)' made by Cannon in connection with the production of 'certain motion pictures in which Cannon had distribution rights', by maintaining that after these purchases Cannon were in the same position as if they themselves had produced the motion pictures.

Menahem Golan took another opportunity to lash out at his

tormentors and amplify on the way he and Globus continued to operate in contrast to the establishment, despite the MGM tie-up: 'Hollywood is a closed society, very ruthless. Money talks. The people who run the majors are paid very well to protect themselves. One reason why they resent us is because we have lowered the statistic for what was considered Hollywood's average budget. We are not limousine people. If Yoram's daughter needs an apartment, we buy it if we have the money. If I need something for my daughter, I buy it. We take only what we need. Money has never been important to us. We don't account to each other. There is perfect trust. We respect each other, defend each other's mistakes and live with each other's decisions.'

Industry onlookers pondered on the rationale behind MGM's decision to go for the Cannon deal. Had they been dazzled by their product in the past? Was the prospect of distributing Michael Winner's *The Wicked Lady* and Golan's own *Over the Brooklyn Bridge* so irresistible? When one columist wryly commented on Cannon's *schlock* output, MGM's then chairman (albeit briefly) Frank Yablans joked, 'Sounds like all the other studios!' Referring to Cannon's 'Supervision 3-D' epic, he added, 'You have to start somewhere – obviously we do not expect twenty-two films of the calibre of *Treasure of the Four Crowns*, but every studio has a mixture of exploitative and quality films and I don't look for Cannon to be any different.'

Among the first pictures lined up for MGM release were the claimed $15m *Sahara* (try $7–8m) and the alleged $15m *The Wicked Lady* (about the same). The Mark Thatcher-inspired *Sahara* was supposed to kick off the release schedule in the Christmas season of 1983, but MGM took a look at the finished film and quickly changed their minds. Golan had enthusiastically endorsed the December release date. He and Globus no doubt had anticipated the takings, and the resultant cash gusher, to Cannon before MGM pricked their collective bubbles. All the fuming and cursing from Cannon had no effect on MGM's decision, and indeed they would not even agree to a full release in the spring of 1984, deeming that all *Sahara* was good for was a few test engagements on the West Coast.

When these took place, the result was a disaster. But surely,

Golan must have rationalised, Brooke Shields had taken $40m in *The Blue Lagoon*? Sure Menahem, just like Sylvie Kristel took $100m in *Emmanuelle* before Cannon got its hands on her in *Lady Chatterley's Lover*! MGM was adamant – *Sahara* was totally withdrawn for ever from the main market-place in the world with only a few hundred thousand dollars in box office gross – the MGM deal could not have had a more ominous start. Was the movie as bad as all that? One reviewer emerged ashen and hollow-eyed, describing the picture as 'One of the worst films I have ever seen. It has to be seen to be believed!'

In truth *Sahara* was not the worst picture ever produced – there must be at least one or two others that were marginally worse. The problem with *Sahara*, mainly resulting from the vacuous story line, was terminal dullness. Brooke Shields was supposed to be playing a frisky filly, but did she really need to play the part so literally? Apparently her mother would not allow her eyebrows to be trimmed a little – pity, for it was often hard to see her features under them, and it eventually became all too clear why John Rhys-Davies had been cast opposite her as the villainous Sheik – he was the only actor they could find who could match her inch for inch in the eyebrows stakes. The attempted tone of the movie was tongue in cheek, but under Andrew McLaglan's direction the effect was more foot in mouth. James Silke had worked hard to write something playable from Golan's own story line, but was not equal to the task.

The only moment in the film where it sprang to life was when a member of the cast was attempting to take advantage of Miss Shields. As Brooke's molars chewed him up, the villain yells, 'Yes, bite me, bite me! I love it!' at which Brooke looked decidedly nonplussed. Here she was giving her all and someone was actually enjoying it!

Eventually the whole hapless enterprise simply collapsed under the dead weight of sand – and those eyebrows.

Enter Micky Hyman in March 1984, hired as Cannon's chief operating officer. He was seen by outsiders as having the ability to add depth to the Cannon team and fill the void invariably left when Golan and Globus were absent. An ex-attorney, Hyman had previously helped to found the CBS video division and the MGM/UA Home Entertainment Company. His tenure at Cannon was to be brief – and stormy – with 'Yoram and me', for although they needed help they were manifestly unwilling to allow an outsider much of a glimpse of their inner sanctum.

Michael Winner's *Death Wish II* benefit immediately struck hard rock as *The Wicked Lady* took only an abysmal $700,000 in its release; next up was Golan's own cherished project, *Over the Brooklyn Bridge*. Down it went also, slain by some dreadful reviews and audiences who stayed away in their millions. Victor Canby in the *New York Times* called it, 'a crudely humourless romantic comedy that has more failed ethnic jokes than might be heard in a decade of Miami Beach nightclubbing. There isn't, however, any real screen play; Mr Golan's comic touch is not great. The movie is not a complete loss, though. It uses so many Manhattan and Brooklyn locations that it might easily be recycled as a promotional film.' '*Over the Brooklyn Bridge* is my private baby,' Menahem Golan had confided at a reception held at Sammy's Kosher Rumanian restaurant on New York's lower East Side – maybe he should have kept it that way.

After these debacles, even MGM demanded a renegotiation of their deal with Cannon, and confronted with the possibility of the whole arrangement blowing up in their faces, Golan and Globus were for once powerless and agreed to new terms. Print and advertising costs were now to be deducted up front before Cannon received its share of the rentals, although that share would now rise. E. F. Hutton was quick to emphasise the positive side of the new deal and pointed out that for a film that grossed $16m at the box office and therefore yielded about $8m in gross rentals, Cannon would receive 80% of the remaining $5m after a deduction of print and advertising costs of $3m, for a net realisation of $4m. Still a good deal for Cannon, but this time with one major difference in that the films actually had to *perform*. Even this new arrangement looked delicate however, as insiders at MGM were soon reported as being unhappy at the quality of Cannon's overall product and the effect it was increasingly seen as having on their own precarious image. Future Cannon pictures which might be regarded as potentially successful on a critical level, like Cassavettes' *Love Streams*, Konchalovsky's *Maria's Lovers* and *Grace Quigley* (abbreviated from *The Ultimate Solution of*), also worried

MGM because of what they termed the special marketing problems they would present. In lay terms this meant they saw them as totally uncommercial.

On top of this a major storm was brewing over *Bolero*, following MGM executives laughing the film to scorn during a showing which Cannon had laid on for them. Menahem Golan was mortified and personally signed a critical telex to the Dereks informing them of MGM's reaction. It read, 'After about 15 minutes the audience could contain itself no longer and broke into uncontrollable fits of laughter punctuated by sarcastic remarks which were literally shouted across the screening room. The film was totally insufferable, a total embarrassment. It is certainly not a motion picture by film industry definition.' Golan, the great showman, never one to call 'stinking fish', was even more mortified when someone released the contents of his telex to the press. Now the war with the Dereks – for such it turned out to be – was public. The Dereks stoutly defended the picture, John Derek with, 'Bo may well shock audiences, but at least the sexuality is honest and beautiful', while Bo declared, after Golan demanded a new cut, 'He wants more sex and less dialogue. That would turn it into a porno film. He is a monster!'

Eventually a truce of a kind was called and Golan stated, 'The Dereks are going to Rome to score the film and with the final dub the cut will be only Derek's. And then we'll see how it tests. Only after the sneaks will we make a determination whether to go and do some more work on the film. We will check with the audience cards and come to a conclusion.'

With the new cut submitted and softened down in an attempt to get an 'R' rating instead of an 'X', the Dereks continued to attack everyone in sight. Bo maintained that Cannon and MGM executives had 'flipped over the idea of the film being sexy while we were in production. They were drooling.' They declared that apart from 50% profit participation in the picture, their contract with Cannon made no reference to rating, only artistic control. Golan was asked about this and snapped, 'It was a mistake to give it to them, but that's a fact.' However, after the leaked telex, he realised he had to divert attention from MGM's dissatisfaction with the picture. He declared wistfully, 'It's that love-making that gave the censor the problem. Those scenes are superb – the most beautiful love scenes ever shot. Two people making love in a way you have never seen before. It's simply poetic.'

He described the dispute with the Dereks as 'A war on the way to a truce – we are negotiating a peace treaty. Derek is a very stubborn man. I like Bo very much but you've got to understand that she is connected to a man who calls his company Svengali. He's very creative. He shot his wife in detail making love to another man. He's a writer, director, cameraman – when one carries so many crowns there must be some kind of heavy ego.' Asked if he would make another picture with Bo Derek he replied with a sad smile, 'If she were free I would.' Would he do it if John Derek were involved? The mood darkened. 'I doubt it!' he snarled.

One industry spokesman was asked at this point what the likely outcome would be if MGM did the unthinkable and refused to release the picture. He replied, 'The movie would revert back to Cannon, and if the Dereks are planning to sue Cannon, the film could be on the shelf for years.' The word back from MGM was not good. The film was still an 'X', but irrespective of that they still thought it was a piece of junk and they were adamant – under no circumstances would they release the picture. Golan raged, but to no avail, for relations between Cannon and MGM were now at a new low.

As Cannon tried to decide what their next move with *Bolero* would be, MGM released the Cannon Italia production of *Hercules*, with Lou Ferrigno – incredible to think of the once-mighty MGM releasing such trash, but it did take $9m at the box office. A further break in the clouds which helped to lift the increasingly poisonous atmosphere between MGM and Cannon came with the inauspicious teen-dance movie which Cannon had rushed through production in a matter of weeks to cash in on the current craze, entitled *Breakin'*. No work of art, the film nevertheless had many plus points in its favour. It was topical – beating Orion's much bigger–budgeted *Beat Street* to the market place. It had an excellent sound track – and the energy of the young and talented cast powered the whole thing along superbly. On a budget of $1.2m the film grossed $38m and for once there were big smiles all round, although Cannon would still hit back later at MGM over their obstructive attitude even to this winner.

Golan promptly urged MGM to put out a 1,000-print release of their next movie, *Making the Grade*, which had been shot as *The Last American Preppie*. MGM reluctantly agreed and the release was to prove their swan song for Cannon as *Making the Grade* failed miserably in the expensive release which Cannon had urged. To Golan and Globus' mortification the film had to be withdrawn from cinemas all over America. Then the unthinkable followed as MGM indicated that enough was enough – they would release *no* further Cannon product. 'Is there life after MGM?' the headlines screamed, as the move precipitated the biggest crisis the Israeli duo had ever faced. The whole benefit had gone up in smoke and they were stuck with a list of unreleased pictures on which they, not MGM, would now have to find the release costs – unless they could interest another distributor, which looked highly unlikely. Their cash-flow was wrecked as far as the US market was concerned and they were thrown right back on their own resources.

There was only one answer – a public securities offering to raise cash, on which E. F. Hutton, together with their co-banker Furman Selz, would work night and day. They had to – for either Cannon got new cash somewhere or they were finished.

At first Golan tried to put a brave face on it, implying that it had been Cannon who had made the move to end the deal. 'We didn't depart in a fight,' he maintained. 'The relationship between the two companies is still good.' He stated that he was now looking into two possibilities, the first of which involved setting up Cannon's own distribution arm so that they might truly control their own destiny in the US market, and the other to negotiate with majors like 20th Century Fox and Universal for a film-by-film release deal. He claimed, 'We have sixteen pictures in the can and no major has so many.' Although this was possibly true, it was the quality of the sixteen pictures which MGM had questioned and there was no rush to buy from 20th Century Fox, Universal – or anyone else for that matter, and in the end Cannon had to face the fact that they would have to release the pictures on their own – or they never would be released. Cannon had fallen into the blackest of black holes, to the undisguised glee of their enemies in the Hollywood community. Their fall from grace, courtesy of MGM, was seen as a just reward for their gall and *chutzpah* in daring to set themselves up as a rival to the majors. Another worry emerged as during the Cannes Film Festival a CBS '60 Minutes' crew compiled a report on the group. Replying to a question on whether he was at all concerned about what might be the investigatory nature of the programme, Golan retorted angrily, 'We have nothing to fear from the investigation and we are answering their questions right away. One never knows how these things turn out, but we don't mind fair criticism.' He maintained that Cannon had $150m committed to production for eighteen films in eighteen months and that Cannon was 'in profit overall. If we stopped operations today we would have made money.'

In view of Golan's previous utterances on presales and how they were always totally covered by them, Golan now astonishingly admitted for the first time that 'Not all our productions are in profit before we make them.' He hastily added however, in case anyone got the wrong impression: 'But we come out okay overall.'

A negative report in the *Wall Street Journal* referring to the problems Cannon would have in getting a US release for their rejected pictures caused an overnight loss of two stock points. Micky Hyman protested that the collapse of the MGM deal would not spoil Cannon's immediate prospects, but the *Journal* pointed out that their reliance on presales from Pay-tv, video and foreign distribution rights, of which they had $105m in commitments 'heavily borrowed against', meant that a large amount of that total 'could not be collected until the films MGM rejected are released in the US'.

The cousins' backs were to the wall, but they had to exude confidence in Cannon and the future, and in many ways it was their finest hour. The two stock points loss, a considerable worry, was corrected after a series of ambitious plans for the future were announced, together with reassuring estimates of forward revenue and income were released. These made it look, despite their vicissitudes at MGM, that anyone who failed to buy Cannon stock had to be crazy.

'Cannon will be the next major!' Golan thundered. 'We're still friendly with MGM, but they needed us more than we needed them. From now on nothing can stop us. Stallone was only the beginning – soon we'll be signing multi-picture contracts with all the top names in Hollywood and right now' (again) 'we've more movies on stream than any of the majors.'

For several weeks more, although it must have choked him,

Golan managed to keep some measure of cool over the aborted agreement. He had to, since the new public offering was being prepared and he could not afford to rock the boat. As soon as it was sold out, Golan let fire. The world was to know in no uncertain terms that he and Globus were infuriated with MGM. They even went to the astronomical length for them, of expressing personal concern over Cannon's financial future in the face of its mounting debt. Golan raged as he recounted that during the *Bolero* fiasco, Frank Yablans had told different things to different parties: 'Yablans told me the movie was unreleasable. Then when he saw Bo Derek he went over kissed her, saying what a good movie *Bolero* was.' Golan's voice rose to a crescendo of fury as he added, 'He just wanted to kiss Bo Derek!'

He continued to insist that it was Cannon who had withdrawn from the arrangement on June 19th 1984, albeit after MGM had made continuation untenable. He stated that the subsequent delays in getting their own pictures out had cost Cannon at least 15–20 cents per share. Globus wandered into the debate, complaining that MGM had had no idea how to handle *Breakin'*. 'They thought it was only for black audiences,' he asserted.

He claimed that during 1983 and the first half of 1984 Cannon's domestic rentals totalled $15,845,000. Of that $9,727,000 was revenue from MGM and of that total, $5,160,000 was attributable to *Breakin'*. He maintained that it had been the disagreement over the potential of *Breakin'* which had been the straw that broke the camel's back. He further claimed – to the astonishment of everyone who saw the movie, or read any of the roasting reviews – that MGM had bungled *Sahara*'s chances in deeming it of limited marketability. He stated that had the picture been released as Cannon had originally suggested, at Christmas 1983, then it would have done much better in the market-place. He claimed that since it would now cost Cannon at least $16m to finance the release of the rejected MGM pictures, this had been the reason Cannon were obliged to return to the finance market for the second time in a year. Globus summed up his feelings by asserting 'MGM hurt our pictures and hurt our company.'

So there it was – out in the open, but only with the latest $50m offering safely sold and yielding $70m in total through being oversubscribed. To have griped about their treatment at the hands of MGM earlier, and admitted hurt, might have prejudiced the offering's successful outcome and the duo were far too canny to let that happen. Now they had a further $70m to play with. There had been no hiding the seriousness of the cash-flow problem brought about by the blocking of revenue from the unreleased MGM pictures. 'It really solves their cash crunch,' declared Misia Celichowska (Dudley), E. F. Hutton's research analyst. Well, at least for the moment it did.

Cannon duly went ahead with an unrated release for *Bolero* through their own newly-formed distribution company. With their securities offering money now in place, they took a decision to go for an expensive saturation 1,000-print release.

Despite being what Golan lip-smackingly described as 'the hottest of the hot versions', box-office results were dismal and the film lost money for Cannon before finding a market on video release less than three months later.

The battle was not yet over with the Dereks, John Derek stating of his dealings with Golan and Globus, 'It's the most horrific experience I ever had. I'd like to pull out the goddam plug and drain them. I think they are totally disrespectful people. They have no concern for the law, they have no concern for this country, they have no concern for anything except themselves.'

Golan was stung to reply, 'Listen, he is the jerk of all jerks! The man sat in front of me very arrogant – he sat on the floor, he and Bo, and I said, "Listen, if we are going to work together – and I know how difficult you are from all the rumours – but if you are going to hurt me or my company, I'm going to fight back. And I'm not the kind of a man who will stab you in the back. I'll stab you in the front!"' At least Derek was left with the story to dine out on for years to come.

Another complaint came from Bo Derek as she declares that she had not been paid her full $1.5m fee for *Bolero*. Golan was furious. 'That's all wrong,' he railed, 'I'm being maligned.' He maintained that Bo had already been paid $1.2m in cash and the remaining $300,000 would be paid when she and her director-husband handed over a toned-down TV version of the film. 'I'm not going to have my name smeared any longer!' he threatened.

Globus had set the scene on '60 Minutes' by saying, 'We are not the kind of people of Ma Maison or Jimmie's in Hollywood, the restaurant, you know, the fancy, expensive restaurants, that we will go and take a cavalcade of people to spend thousands of dollars and charge it to the budgets. We are not this kind. We are eating sandwiches here – that's true, believe it or not. We are eating sandwiches in our offices every lunch. Coca-Cola is our wine.'

Elmer Bernstein, composer of the *Bolero* theme music, described how he was supposed to have been put up in a first class hotel by Cannon and had to move to a more suitable hotel of his own choosing. 'We found that no arrangements had been made by the company to pick up our hotel bills. They said, we'll reimburse you. Days would go by, we'd say, "when?" And they'd say, "Oh, they're coming" and nobody would say you're not going to get them. And it got to be a kind of comedy.'

Had Bernstein ever seen an operation like Cannon before? 'No' he replied.

Bo Derek declared, 'I was telling somebody the other day that if we could never work again – or if the only way we could ever work again was to work with these people, we would never work again. We would give up our ranch, and we'd give everything up, we'd go back and make moccasins on the beach someplace, or do something. It was *that* bad.'

As far as Golan stabbing them in the front was concerned, Bo's final comment was 'They've stabbed us every place *but* the front, every single place and they're constantly stabbing, constantly.'

Golan's reply was, 'Making motion pictures is constantly being in a war because you have to face so many problems and so many challenges and so many difficulties that you are in the middle of a war and there is in a war, wounded people.'

At the end of the day Golan and Globus got what they deserved out of *Bolero*, the final straw that brought the whole MGM deal crashing down around their ears.

Chapter Four
THE RAZOR'S EDGE

On November 6th 1984, in the wake of the MGM fiasco, Misia Dudley of E. F. Hutton went on record to lower her estimate for Cannon's earnings for the year from $2.30 per share to $2.10 per share, stating that her downward revision was the result of Cannon's decision to hold broad release of four 1984 films until 1985, thus putting their revenues into a new fiscal-year term. She stressed however, that her downward estimate had nothing to do with what she termed 'perceived weaknesses in Cannon's current operations'.

The four films whose broad release was delayed, and were apparently the sole reason for the down-grading, were *The Naked Face*, *Grace Quigley*, *The Ambassador* and *Maria's Lovers*. One wonders how much Menahem Golan had these items valued at on Cannon's books as 1985 entries, for when they were released they all quietly died the death in the market place, as did *Love Streams*, this time courtesy of Cannon. No MGM to blame this time for a bungled release – if Misia Dudley had known that these films were about to bite the dust, would she then have perceived Cannon's operations as having no weakness? In true Cannon fashion, of course, by the time these four opened and closed they were already banging the drum, not for four new films, but eight. Later instead of the eight it would be sixteen – for the only way to lose these unfortunate non-performing films was in announcing list after list of future box-office 'smash hits'.

'The Middle East is a powder keg ready to explode. Israel with a population of 4m is surrounded by eight Arab countries with an 80m population,' the pre-credit titles tell us, and we know which side *The Ambassador* is on immediately. Condemned for its shameless Israeli bias that does no service whatever to the Israeli cause, the film starts like some kind of poorly cut, second-rate travelogue as Rock Hudson, speeding along in a jeep with Robert Mitchum, asks him, 'What's that?' and receives the reply, 'That is Moses's tomb.' Next a preposterous plot begins to unravel with Mitchum sleep-walking through his part while Ellen Burstyn acts like a victim of librium deprivation. This time Rock Hudson doesn't get to play the lead, and one is reminded of the Ronald Reagan casting joke before he was elected president – Reagan for president? No, Reagan for president's best friend! The bones of Elmore Leonard's *52 Pick Up* had been dug up, laid bare and shipped to Israel. J. Lee Thompson's lumpen non-direction and Max Jack's dreadful script provide the *coup de grâce* as they concoct a hideous slaughter-of-the-innocents finale that sits uneasily with the tacky B-film preceding it. The whole cheap enterprise, all the worse for having a real-life tragic backdrop to which there are no glib solutions, collapses into parody, soiling all the participants – and the viewer as well. Propaganda like this undermines the very cause it alleges to support and reduced the Cannes audience, to whom it was first shown, to hysterical laughter at the ludicrous dialogue, then to howls of derision. It was none-the-less reported to E. F. Hutton that the Cannes reception had been favourable, and this was incorporated into their report when compiling Cannon's securities offering prospectus.

One interviewer dared to raise the subject with Golan of their growing reputation of not paying people on time, and the tone of the smooth-flowing interview changed immediately as he snarled, 'Everybody gets paid on time. Show me one man that we owe a cent.' He was asked about Shelley Winters, who claimed that her payments were six to eight weeks late on three movies she had made for Cannon and that she had once taken an expensive diamond and emerald ring from a movie set as hostage for her pay cheque. Golan exploded. 'This is the biggest lie in history!' he snarled. 'I'll put her on the 'phone, let her tell it to you.' He then yelled to his assistant, 'Get me Shelley Winters!' Unfortunately he was unable to reach her but Winters later stuck to her guns, insisting her story was true and elaborating, 'They pay you, but they are late. Golan let me keep the ring in lieu of my pay cheque.' She stressed that this had not put her off working for the company: 'This (business) is a crap shoot. It's an artistic crap shoot and you've got to believe in your artistic decision. And they love to make films and they love the business and I wish some of those bastards were around again. We hate them, you know – Louis B Mayer and Harry Cohn, but they loved the film business and they created great stars and they created great films.' Of Golan and Globus she declared, 'I would still work for them anytime. I like them – they are funny.'

David Wheeler would not agree with Miss Winters' comments. He had been hired by Golan to direct *Breakin'* for the magnificent honorarium of just $10,000, including a complete script rewrite. Wheeler accepted this, grateful for the opportunity to direct his first movie. The deal included the promise that he could hire his own production crew, an agreement which, he says, was immediately reneged upon when Cannon refused to hire the cameraman he wanted and forced him to accept instead someone of Cannon's own choosing.

Wheeler also maintained that Cannon tore up his editor's and make-up people's deal memos, adding that on the second day of shooting Cannon gave control of the movie to the cameraman. Of his experience with Cannon Wheeler reflected, 'It was worse than film school. All these people who didn't know what they were doing running around, and everything was so cheap. It was like a madhouse and the working conditions were ridiculous; the discussions were incredibly amateurish.' He was fired on the fifth day of shooting after being told that he didn't make enough noise to sound like a real director. 'He said, "Yell, scream, make me believe you are a director." They didn't know what film-making was about. They think directors are generals. They should stick to making under $2m exploitation films and nothing else.' Perhaps, although he was not to know it at the time, Wheeler was lucky to get out. The producers and screen writers of *Breakin'* subsequently sued Cannon for $14m for what they claimed were unrecorded profits and personal damages.

Another battle took place at Cannes as Festival selector Gilles Jacob refused to accept *Maria's Lovers* in competition. Golan and Globus promptly set up their own event, running concurrently with the main festival. They dubbed it the 'Cannon Film Festival' and headquartered themselves on the Rue D'Antibes. After his personal snub in 1983 Golan was standing for no more nonsense. He took out full-page advertisements in the trade press challenging Jacob and his jury to come and see *Maria's Lovers*. 'Why do they bother to have a film selection committee in Paris when Jacob chooses all the movies himself?' he complained. 'He's like a mini-Napoleon. That's why I've started my own festival this year – next year I will have my own jury too!' It was left to Paris journalist Gilbert Gautier to say what everyone else was thinking, 'Knowing that man, he'll have his own judges too!'

Film critics Roger Ebert and Gene Siskel of TV's *At the Movies* criticised Cannon's selling methods and denied that they were true film makers at all. 'When I was in Menahem Golan's hotel room at the Cannes film festival,' Ebert recalled, 'he had one entire wall covered with this giant chart and shown down the left-hand side were names of 27 would-be movies, or possible movies, and across the right of the chart were 60 different territories like Italy, France, but then also Angola, Zambia, and then they had gold stars. It's like bingo. When a movie has enough gold stars, it's been sold in enough markets with advance payments or guarantees, then they've got the money to make it, then they make it and ship it out.'

Siskel added, 'They're deal makers. To date, they have not made what I would say is a really fine film. They're not film makers. Their interest seems to be the deal. I think they think they're smart if they make money. That's their goal. They're businessmen. They could be selling cars. They could be selling T-shirts.'

Golan retorted, 'Maybe it gives an impression that you sell a T-shirt. Just be a good T-shirt seller, good and honest.' Was that enough? 'That's very important. All due respect to Mr Siskel and Mr Ebert, very nice young gentlemen who are selling criticism for money on television.'

There was no doubt that Hollywood wanted rid of Cannon, and Golan astonishingly seemed about to oblige them as he stated that they were considering a move to the East Coast, for 'reasons of cost and convenience'. Many saw the touted move as a piece of bluff, as the lease on their premises at that time on Sunset Boulevard had expired. One industry insider stated, 'They're like poor men grabbing ketchup sacks in McDonalds when they should be eating at the Ritz. They may go bust before making the truly big pictures they dream of.'

As usual Golan proved no slouch at hitting back at his detractors and he contrasted their style of decision-making with the hidebound rigidity of the majors as he declared, 'They usually fail, for they are wedded to the old system of distribution through studio affiliates, which is as outdated as empires. It is hard for them to give up their empire mentality. They still get their money from the ticket buyer, when and if he buys, instead of getting it in advance to make their product. They still rely on their hierarchy of salaried officials in various countries while our partners are local independents who know their market much better and put their money on their choices. We dream as much as them that our next picture will make a magic $100m, but meanwhile we cut our costs.'

Golan was submitted a project by Chuck Norris, who had by this time scored at the box office with some small-budget action-man-type hits. Golan read the screenplay for Norris's proposed *Battlerage* over the weekend in Sam Arkoff style, while trying to lose some fat at a health farm. He called Norris early on the following Monday morning, full of enthusiasm. The deal was on – but only if two films could be squeezed out of the subject by filming them back-to-back in the Philippines – two for the price of one, that is. Two days later the poster work was prepared and Cannon began presales.

'It will be the first picture about this subject that is so hot,' Golan announced, rubbing his hands with glee – and ignoring the fact that this was not quite the case, Gene Hackman's *Uncommon Valor* having predated the Cannon project. None-the-less, the decision to proceed was to prove one of Golan's better judgments. When filming was completed Golan looked at the two pictures. They had been shot so that number two could be held as the 'sequel' to number one. The trouble was that the second picture seemed so much better. Again Golan made the correct commercial decision and released the 'sequel' first – retitled *Missing in Action*.

The simple-minded adventure struck a responsive chord with its target audience, and to the delight of Cannon's bosses the gross box-office for *Missing in Action* climbed to $28m. Since it had only cost $1.5m to make, this box-office figure translated into big money for Cannon. The gross netted down to rentals of over $11m and with deduction of $3m for marketing costs, this still left them with a juicy net of $8m alone from the US market, or $6.5m after the film's negative cost was recovered – and the rest of the world still to go. Whoever suggested that Cannon's forward revenue estimates were over-optimistic? Here was one proof positive that they most certainly were not. At least – not in this swallow's case, but a long hot summer was about to settle in.

Missing in Action II, already in the can, was announced immediately – but surely this predated the action of the first film? No problem, decided Cannon, as they proceeded to dub it *Missing in Action II – The Beginning*. Golan predicted, 'It'll be even hotter.' He had made the correct commercial decision on this occasion in deciding to release the 'sequel' first – but he was unable to boast about it, as that would have been poor publicity for the passed-over *Missing in Action II – The Beginning*.

'Hotter than hot' was their expectation also for the *Breakin'* sequel, *Breakdance II – Electric Boogaloo*. With an increased budget the film was being rushed through to cash in on the dance-craze and success of the original. It was expected that Cannon's own releasing arm would handle this, as there was no downside involved, due to the still relatively-peanut budget.

Although a potentially big hit was anticipated with *Boogaloo*, the one they were concentrating on and had prepared for years finally went into production in England under Tobe Hooper's direction, Golan being convinced he was the director to bring Colin Wilson's *Space Vampires* to the screen. Dan O'Bannon and Dan Jacobi had hammered out the script and John Dykstra was in charge of special effects. Hooper had been the subject of some controversy after what many felt was the revolting spectacle of his *Texas Chainsaw Massacre* hit. He had been the director on the Spielberg production of *Poltergeist* although it was rumoured that Spielberg had taken over the reins himself on more than one occasion. His other credit was on a further dubious-taste item in *Chainsaw* vein, Universal's *Funhouse*. Steve Railsback (ex-*Helter Skelter* and *The Stuntman*), Frank Finlay and Peter Firth were cast in what was reported to be Cannon's most ambitious production to date, claimed to be budgeted at $22.5m. This time they were aiming for the $100m mega-buck jackpot – one to silence once and for all the doubting Thomases who called their future revenue estimates over optimistic.

If *Missing in Action* had given them something to think about – this one would blow them away! They had been forced to flog *Space Vampires* around the majors, looking for finance in return for US rights, but the only one to bite was Tri-Star, who were trying to get big in a hurry and saw this as their chance. They put $12.5m into the kitty. The trade could see why, but eyebrows were raised when it was further announced Tri-Star would also be releasing *Breakdance II – Electric Boogaloo* in the US.

The reasoning behind going to Tri-Star to chip in to the budget made sense in the case of *Space Vampires* – the budget was too big, whether $15m or the claimed $22.5m, for Cannon to finance on their own and protect their 'downside' at the same time. There was puzzlement, however, as to why *Breakdance II – Electric Boogaloo* had been added to the deal. Surely, it was felt, Cannon would have been better to release the low-budget *Breakin'* sequel themselves and cash in on what looked to be a sure-fire smash hit – with no downside to protect as on *Space Vampires*? The truth is that the option was taken out of their hands, as Tri-Star insisted on getting the *Breakin'* sequel's rights, otherwise there was no $12.5m advance – and no deal – on *Space Vampires*. They thus insured themselves against what would be an expensive mistake if for any reason *Vampires* failed to click. Since Tri-Star was their last stop on *Vampires*, Cannon were forced to reluctantly agree to the two-picture deal, thus forgoing the cream of any profits that might accrue from either picture. To rub salt into the wound, Cannon were also forced to surrender to Tri-Star the potentially valuable cable-TV rights to both movies.

Their other production plans began to sound more ambitious. Richard Chamberlain would star in their remake of Rider Haggard's *King Solomon's Mines*, to be filmed back-to-back in Africa with the sequel, *Allan Quatermain*. Chuck Norris would follow *Missing in Action II* with *Invasion USA*. Bronson was set for *Death Wish III* with the ubiquitous Michael Winner at the helm (the two of them tied together as if in unholy wedlock). *Rappin'* was to be their new teen-fad film as they now followed in producer Sam Katzman's tradition of cheapo music exploitationers like *Rock Around the Clock*.

Another new *Ninja* adventure would follow, this time *American Ninja*, to be directed by their in-house Sam Firstenberg (here they were trailing behind Run Run Shaw and his martial arts epics – a long way behind). The new moguls were therefore hardly following in the tradition of Jack Warner, Harry Cohen or Louis B. Mayer. No, it was more Sam Katzman and Run Run Shaw. Not MGM, Columbia or Warner Bros – more Republic or Monogram. Come to that, their efforts at shooting for some kind of tenuous respectability with the likes of Cassavettes and Jason Miller, also had their precedents in movie history, for it had been only Republic who were prepared to back Orson Welles towards the end. *Schlock* producer Albert (*High School Confidential*) Zugsmith had actually turned over a new leaf at the end of his career and produced Orson Welles's *Touch of Evil* for Universal, while the original master of the 'thin thrill', William Castle, had also turned his back on his earlier epics like *The Tingler* and *The House on Haunted Hill* to join forces with Paramount and produce the Roman Polanski classic, *Rosemary's Baby*. At least Castle made it all the way to the box-office with his prestige picture, unlike Zugsmith or Golan/Globus.

There was nothing unique by this time in their relationship with Credit Lyonnais. The original founder of 'pre-selling', Dino De Laurentis had been joined by Carolco, David Begelman, the Salkinds and several others. What did continue to set Golan and Globus apart (or 'The Globs' as they became known at this time) was their absolute single-mindedness and flair for self-serving publicity. Lee Isgur, the Wall Street analyst, put it this way: 'They hustle a little better.' An example of Cannon's corporate hustling was the $500,000 they laid out in Cannes in the spring of 1984 on a gigantic sales and promotion campaign, culminating in a lavish gala ball at the Casino. What *Variety* had dubbed, 'Doing the Cannes-Cannes' was given a new twist by the energetic Cannon team and their wheeling and dealing. Asked to comment on Cannon's success Syd Silverman, *Variety*'s editor, replies, 'They got where they are by busting their ass.'

Slowly but surely the Hollywood community was forced to swallow the hard fact that Cannon seemed to be here to stay – MGM or no MGM. How they actually made money – despite Golan's no-risk claims based on their presales policy – on films that barely achieved any release at all in the US, and often the same elsewhere – was still beyond most people's comprehension.

However, some of the prestige of their uncommercial offerings began to rub off. John Cassavettes' *Love Streams* won the Berlin Festival's Golden Bear Award while Jason Miller's *That Championship Season* had been regarded by some as a worthwhile enterprise, though in the long run both films were judged overall not to be good enough – either as art or commerce. They were seen to fall into the uncomfortable middle ground between the art houses and the circuits, 'foreign' pictures except for the absence of sub-titles – in the end, surely not a good thing, either in terms of kudos or cash.

For some time Cannon had held out against the minimum compensation scheme of the Directors Guild of America (DGA). In the end the DGA backed down and thrashed out two separate agreements, one for the rest of the industry and one specifically for Cannon. Under the new agreement, on films budgeted at below \$2.5m, they could pay directors, first and second assistant directors and unit production managers 50% of the normal DGA minimums, with recoupment of the balance-deferred contingent upon break-even points being reached. That point would be deemed to be reached when 75% of gross receipts received by Cannon from the exploitation of any given picture exceeded 233% of the budget. The repercussion for other independent producers was immediately apparent – if Cannon could get this agreement, then they were free to apply for it also. Next – what was to stop the majors wanting to follow suit? The DGA stated that the pact should trigger an increase in low-budget films and would lead the way in bringing non-union productions into a contract, for until this juncture Cannon had constantly been featured on the Guild's unfair labour list.

The DGA's comment on other independents applying whole-sale for the same terms as Cannon was terse: 'There is a caveat. Deferment is tied to recoupment and we would have great concern making the same deal with companies that might not be around when the time came for recoupment. Cannon is a major independent and we know they will be here.' Golan hailed the pact as a cool new wind which had been long overdue and a victory for commonsense, while the DGA declared that Cannon would now be promptly removed from the Guild's unfair labour list. On its being placed there in the first instance Golan grinned and commented, 'We are rebels by nature.' Asked if the DGA would be able to track whether recoupment was or was not being accurately recorded – vital to their members' compensation – the Guild replied, 'Cannon furnish us with the budget. It would be difficult for them to hide anything.'

Golan seized the occasion to sum up where Cannon now stood: 'The agreement follows our way of working, the kibbutz way of everybody pulling together for a common goal, a complete revolution in Hollywood. Just because we are so well protected commercially we can afford to take on creative challenges.

'We are no gutless executives safeguarding our jobs by saying no. We are no lawyers or financiers. As film-makers we take risks for serious projects and give artists a freedom to work they never had in Hollywood. Why do you think we were the first to present "a film by John Cassavettes" in the European way, not just "directed by" as Guild rules require? Because we know films are the creation of artists and that is how we work. We are still in the process of changing from exploitation movies. We are determined to keep our overheads low, to work in Hollywood without falling into its trap. With all respect, with the unpredictability of this business, we believe we can make some movies that will pack theatres and others that may win Oscars. The truth is that movie-makers cannot survive without the applause Yoram likes from the banks, but we now also want to do better films – more challenging, higher quality, better scripts.' Now Golan would relish his role of the anguished, torn artist as he declared: 'I walk the razor's edge between artistic value and commercial flops, not to mention the question of being true to myself and the matter of our ruining our family life for our hobby. We have sometimes been ruthless to others, always been ruthless to ourselves and like everybody who rushed forward so fast, we left some good things behind – but can't go back.'

Cannon expanded further into Europe in 1985 by acquiring the Gaumont Italian theatre circuit for around $15m. Fifty-three cinemas were in the deal, spread from Rome to Palermo, with a total capacity of 49,396 seats. The breakdown of properties was listed as eight fully owned, plus nineteen leased properties and twenty-six theatres which booked through the chain. Menahem Golan declared, 'Cannon now has exhibition circuits in four European countries; we have set up a new company, Nuovo Cannon Italia, and an investment programme of $10m.' He challenged the Italian custom of no business during the summer season as he declared, 'I simply cannot believe that exhibition ends in May to resume late in August, so unlike the Italians; we intend to keep our cinemas open twelve months a year. To do this we will start immediately to air condition and renovate for in-season as well as summer comfort. We intend to open refreshment counters in every house and bring in pop-corn machines. Can you imagine a theatre situation without pop-corn? It is an important part of our revenue in England and Holland, for refreshments play an important role to increase audiences. We will not eliminate excess theatre personnel but move some over to the refreshment counter. We will be proposing this to the unions in a meeting right after the holidays.' He added that Cannon would also multiplex the biggest houses in the circuit.

Cannon's take-over coincided with amendments to the Italian law restricting the number of cinemas by zone, giving them a free hand to multiply theatre space as they chose. 'The new Cannon Italy circuit will welcome products from American companies,' Golan continued. 'We already have a friendly working relationship with UIP in Israel and Holland and we want them for our circuit here.' The deal had been actually agreed as of 31st December 1984, thus enabling the Italian company to claim that the circuit was no part of their operations in 1985.

Golan enthused, 'The move makes our set-up in Italy fully vertical, as we are already involved with Fulvio Lucisano's Italian Intl on the production and distribution side. We plan to increase production from three a year to six features in 1985 – half international and half domestic – through our other continuing company,

Cannon Italia SRL and this is only the beginning! We firmly believe that movie theatres in Europe will again come into their own as they have in America. We found a difficult market in England and Holland when we acquired circuits there and the Italian film crisis brought on by TV is a challenge. But if you give and not just take from people who pay admissions, you are in a good position to achieve planned goals. The first thing we will do on an Italian circuit is to clean up every washroom in every theatre. Italy was one of the five top world markets and we can help recover such status. We would like to acquire a circuit in Germany, but so far bids are too high for houses in terrible shape. Eventually we will become circuit owners there however, also in Spain – then we will go shopping in America.'

Later in the week it was announced that the Cannon group had gained direct access to the West German theatrical film market through its acquisition of United Artists Intl, a European holding company which owned 50% of the shares in German film distributor Scotia Intl-Filmverleih. Scotia chairman Sam Waynberg would head the new company and become a member of Cannon's board of directors.

The Cannon/Gaumont Italy deal had meanwhile run into trouble. Employees of the circuit had staged a series of one-day walk-outs in protest against the acquisition, with a union leader declaring, 'The main problem is jobs.' Within days of the first walk-out, a number of management-level employees were dismissed, triggering the second wave of strikes. In April when Menahem Golan and Yoram Globus confirmed physical possession of the circuit, having arrived from London with a cheque for the final payment, Golan declared that all union problems were now solved with the exception of Rome, which remained the hold-out centre of union agitation. He roared, 'It's the moment of truth for them! We are ready to meet them. I will tell them we are the biggest producers in Italy at this time. We started one of our productions yesterday and we have three more ready to start within a month for a total investment of $20m. If that's not creating employment, I don't know what is.' Yoram Globus declared himself elated with circuit results from Britain: 'For the first quarter of 1985, we are starting to reap the fruit of expensive theatre remodelling and renovation in the past two years. Our quarterly report will show a profit of almost a half million pounds.' (Many would ask if this figure was before or after the interest charges.)

'In 1982, the same circuit lost $1,700,800. When our Italian theatre face-lift and the multiplex programme is completed, our contribution in bringing back the lost audience will be better appreciated.'

Strikes in Rome continued none-the-less and Cannon's nine cinemas there were shut. Golan bellowed, 'Our entire operation is in alert for a possible total withdrawal from the Italian market! We are prepared to relocate four productions, close and sell the circuit, rescind a lab order for 1,000 prints and terminate Cannon presence in Italy completely.' The duo left for Israel to spend Passover there, but returned to Rome the following week when they declared that the conflict between Cannon Italia and the entertainment unions was now developing into a war of erosion. Regarding the strike in the nine theatres in Rome, Golan declared, 'We made a generous offer a month ago to take on all fifteen of the excess Gaumont distribution personnel, conditional on a guarantee from the unions of no more strikes. When they went ahead and struck our theatres several days later, we withdrew our offer and are sitting tight. At this point in the season, the strikes will cause more hardship for the theatre personnel than for Cannon. We are not giving up.'

The dispute now boiled down to excess Gaumont help. Cannon had taken over 200 circuit personnel with the buy and confirmed from day one that there would be no redundancies, but with Gaumont committed to vacating Italy totally, their fifteen distribution personnel from that division – which had been Gaumont's big loss-maker – were out of a job. This group conducted its battle with the unions to be taken on by Cannon. Globus at this point agreed to take on six of the excess fifteen personnel, provided Cannon could choose which six.

The Cannon circuit in Italy drastically shrank with the formation of a new chain by two top Italian exhibitors, Marco Valsenia and Ernesto De Sarro, of thirty cinemas. When Cannon had taken over the fifty-three-theatre circuit from Gaumont, they had actually bought only eight sites together with the leasehold properties. The balance of the circuit had booked through Gaumont and was supposedly to continue to do so after the takeover, but now, with

65

the formation of the new independent circuit, Valsenia and De Sarro had practically reduced Cannon's exhibition strength to the actual cinemas bought from Gaumont Italia, and the leasehold sites.

In a further development in West Germany Cannon acquired the nine-screen Ewert theatre group, now to be renamed the Cannon Theatre Group with effect from July 1st, the day the buy-out became effective, thus adding to their West German involvement which included the recently acquired 50% ownership of Scotia-Cannon. Manfred Ewert was to be involved in the eventual creation of a 150-screen chain concentrated in cities having populations over 200,000.

Meanwhile a compromise was reached on the Cannon-Italia front with Cannon guaranteeing to keep all of Gaumont's in-theatre workers and agreeing further to take on an unspecified number of exhibition management personnel and some distribution personnel. In the wake of losing half the circuit to the breakaway group, a shaken spokesman declared, 'The major task is now reorganisation of what we have left. The situation is chaotic and we have to start all over again to restructure the circuit and make it solid. It will be another year before things are as they should be, but by the end of 1986 we forecast a smooth-running, profit-making operation.'

Chapter Five
TAX HEAVEN

The next appointment for the company was in court, trying to stop production of a Charles Bronson film, *Murphy's Law*, from going ahead without Cannon's participation. They claimed that they had obtained agreement from talent agent Paul Kohner and producer Pancho Kohner to finance and produce the film before going ahead and promoting the film at Cannes. Meantime the defendants allegedly had made a deal with Hemdale Leisure Corporation which in turn sold certain video rights to Vestron Video. Cannon then alleged that they had been told that they had no deal in the film, while Kohner claimed that the deal had been with Hemdale all along. Cannon claimed more than $30,000 in expenses, together with $50m in lost business and $5m in punitive damages with the defendants named as the Kohners, Vestron, Hemdale, Charles Bronson himself, screenwriter Gail Morgan Hishman and Jill Ireland (Bronson's wife), who was to have served as co-producer. Cannon produced what they declared to be a key document, a letter from Paul Kohner which they argued was evidence of the agreement they had to make the movie. Kohner vehemently denied this and stated, 'We were in negotiations with Cannon and hopeful to conclude them, but Cannon's terms were unacceptable to us. They had no right to announce or sell the movie at Cannes – but Golan, in his customary way, went about and started selling the film!' Hemdale announced quick as a flash that it was counter-suing Cannon for conspiring to take away their right to produce *Murphy's Law*. They wanted to have distribution of the film enjoined, together with $65m damages. At the end of the day the picture would come out as a Cannon release, with the entire matter having been settled out of court and away from the glare of publicity.

Exit Micky Hyman as the news of his sudden resignation filtered through from the embattled Cannon fortress. No explanation was given, other than Hyman's desire to pursue other opportunities and neither Hyman nor the Golan/Globus team could be reached for comment. Henry T. Weinstein, who had recently been appointed head of production, denied that his coming to Cannon had anything to do with Hyman's departure and he further denied any knowledge of the internal operation problems which had been rumoured in the press. Hyman had been widely liked and had been expected to operate with some degree of autonomy – if anyone could – in the Cannon set-up. Industry sources now speculated that it was Golan and Globus's inability to allow anyone else to take an active role in running their company which had hastened Hyman's exit, noting also that Cannon had begun to acquire a history of sudden departures. Billy Fein, a producer with a distribution record, had left them after a short tenure, as had Robert L. Fieldman, a former Columbia Pictures distribution president, after a brief stay as a consultant hired to set up Cannon's distribution organisation. The week after Hyman's departure Cannon announced that Christopher Pearce, who had joined them five years earlier, had been named executive vice-president and chief operating officer of the Cannon Group Inc, moving up from his position as production vice-president. Producer Henry Weinstein would take over Pearce's production chief post as an executive vice-president, and Pearce, now a director of Cannon, would report directly to Yoram Globus.

In the UK a Royal Charity Premiere was arranged for London-Cannon's *Ordeal by Innocence*. As released by Cannon distributors, the premiere was held at Cannon's flagship West End theatre in London's Haymarket. Golan, for once not in an open-neck shirt or a safari jacket, but a tuxedo, was presented to the Queen of England. Later he was asked for his impression of the auspicious event and replied, 'It was boring. It was a tense two hours. I'm a fat guy you know. The seats are narrow. I had to worry all the time where my elbow is.' He should also have been somewhat concerned about the film they had come to see, although its frustrating failure was a mystery in itself. A reasonable script by Alexander Stuart was well put over by an interesting cast headed by Donald Sutherland, Sarah Miles, Christopher Plummer, Ian McShane, Diana Quick – plus Faye Dunaway in black-and-white flashback, while the direction by Desmond (*I Was Happy Here*, *The Uncle*) was deft and unobtrusive. Largely due to the less-than-riveting story however, one of Miss Christie's weakest, the movie stubbornly refused to work. One of the main problems was the tossing out of the 'whodunit' angle three-quarters of the way through the film. One reviewer was moved to declare, 'The director did it!' He was wrong – the culprit was in fact Miss Christie herself. It was a pity that a film with so many good elements in it failed to gel, but an odd pleasure to see a Cannon picture with a minimum of post-production over-dubs. It was also an effective idea to use black-and-white photography for the flash-back sequences. Just one loony touch was left in which Cannon probably thought enhanced the picture – instead, the Dave Brubeck quartet's score, which could hardly have been more jarring or less appropriate, was the final straw that broke it. Again Golan reported to E. F. Hutton and Furman Selz that there had been a good reaction at Cannes to the film, with the exception of the ending, which he stated would be changed. To all intents and purposes this did not appear to happen and the film went out on a decided fizzle.

In 1984 the major studios had started shooting 130 films, up 8% over 1983 and a decade-long record, and independents – as Cannon was still classed – started shooting 188 features, a significant 46% increase in 1983. In 1984, 411 films had been released and had earned $46 billion in box-office receipts. Average marketing expenses involved in a national saturation release were now routinely in the region of $5m to $6m.

Tri-Star's first outing in the two-picture deal with Cannon came with their release of *Breakdance II – Electric Boogaloo*. Featuring the same talented young cast as *Breakin'* – Adolpho Quinone, Michael Chambers and Lucinda Dickie, Cannon had poured considerably more money into it than they had for *Breakin'* – and it showed on the screen. Although still popular, the craze was no longer as hot as it had been, and director Sam Firstenberg had made the sequel much more stylised. Unarguably a far superior movie to its energetic but amateurish original, and positively bursting at the seams with neon-bright colour and vitality, the film none-the-less ended up as a bore, for *Breakin'* had said it all. Alienation among its target audience threatened constantly as cops and construction workers, kids and pensioners alike, joined in the breakdancing at every opportunity.

Admirably borrowing from the dance sequences in the classics *Easter Parade* and *Singin' in the Rain* for some surprisingly ambitious – and well-realised – sequences the threat of overkill in the kaleidoscopic, almost non-stop singin' and dancin', finally was a turn-off and the audience was lost. The take for Tri-Star's release came to less than a quarter of *Breakin'*'s, which added up to a major disappointment. Tri-Star took the first cash, with very little left for Cannon and what there was apparently held against the results of *Space Vampires*, in which somewhat bigger bucks were involved. For Cannon distributors abroad also the film was a failure. What of the talented cast? Lucinda Dickie had another shot in *Ninja III – The Domination* after *Breakin'*. As for Adolpho Quinone and Michael Chambers – no further casting news to date for this talented pair. Tri-Star's insurance against the failure of *Space Vampires* was well and truly blown.

With head held high despite the MGM debacle, Cannon revealed its 1985 line up of twenty-two titles, a company high – never mind that many of them were casualties from the aborted MGM deal. *Emmanuelle IV* was due to open in New York in January, *Maria's Lovers* was due to follow regionally in January, as were *The Naked Face*, *The Ambassador* and *Hot Resort*. *Grace Quigley* and *Hercules II* were due to open in 'undetermined regions' in February and a foreign pick up, *The Key*, was set for regional distribution in March. This made eight theatrical flops out of eight for the year so far.

Their first wide relase of the year would be their UK pick up from Palace Pictures *Company of Wolves*, in March, then *Missing in Action II* would follow. In the spring there were limited runs planned for *Thunder Alley*, *Mata Hari* and *Story of O – II*. *Rappin'* was due to debut on a wide release in May and be followed by Chuck Norris's *Invasion USA* in August. *Thunder Woman* and *American Ninja* were due out in September, followed by *Death Wish III* in October. Autumn was also due to see the release of *The Berlin Affair* and *Camorra*. Andrei Konchalovsky's *Runaway Train*, starring Jon Voight, was due to arrive in December, together with *King Solomon's Mines*. Cannon breezily reckoned that the number would be swollen by the time the year was out, overlooking the fact that the line up of twenty-two titles in the first place looked extremely unlikely, depending on one's definition of release. In the generally accepted sense many of the pictures lined up had scant chance of a proper, meaningful distribution. Items like *Hercules II*, *Hot Resort*, *The Naked Face*, *The Key*, *Thunder Alley*, *Mata Hari*, *Emmanuelle IV*, *The Story of O – II* and *Thunder Woman* were headed for nowhere. Others like *The Berlin Affair* and *Camorra* would simply not arrive, and like all Cannon announcements from the very beginning this list of releases required to be taken with a considerable pinch of salt, for the cost of launching a film was becoming a daunting prospect.

In *The Naked Face* we were treated to the spectacle of Roger Moore as a psychiatrist whom someone's out to murder, only they keep getting it wrong and wind up killing his patients and staff instead, while Roger wanders through the chaos, stepping myopically over the bodies, looking for all the world like Mr Magoo. Enter Dastardly and Muttley, alias Rod Steiger and Elliott Gould, as the two unlikely cops investigating the case. Steiger's theory is that Roger Moore must be the culprit, and in a performance of terrifying, positively operatic awfulness, Steiger's hairpiece proceeds to chew up not only the sets, but all the rest of the furniture in Chicago as well. This is bad enough, but Elliott Gould now thinks he's Droopy, as well as acting like Muttley, and Art Carney is taken on for about fifteen seconds as a private investigator by Moore, but gets rubbed out before he can even get his dentures in. Moore's doctor brother-in-law is seen removing a bloody pair of surgical gloves after an operation, all so he can then bounce into his office where Moore's waiting for him and exclaim, 'I'm sorry I took so long, but that last one was a real bitch!' With any luck at all this will remain writer/director Bryan Forbes's last one and boy, is it a bitch! The dialogue is so ripe it crawls along before your startled eyes. After five minutes Moore is questioned by the chief of police, who asks him what his theory is. He swallows before announcing, 'I think . . . eh . . .' 'Yes, yes?' 'I think someone's – trying – to – murder – me.'

At the end of this howler-of-howlers and farrago extraordinaire Moore resigns his practice, then just before she is shot, the third-last person in Chicago asks him how he plans to fill his time. 'I'm writing a book about the criminal mind,' he confides. Bang, she's dead too. His book should contain at least one chapter each on Sidney Sheldon, Bryan Forbes, Menahem Golan and Yoram Globus.

After Golan and Globus's threat to leave Hollywood and situate themselves in the East Coast, Gotham's Kaufman Astoria Studios had been seen as the most likely relocation site but now Cannon announced it had turned down the opportunity of going to the Astoria and settled instead for an eleven-year lease on four floors of a building on 10th Avenue and 36th Street in Manhattan, which made the move to the East Coast appear a bigger piece of bluff than ever. The building was due to be remodelled, with Cannon beginning the move within three months and completion scheduled for August. From their current headquarters in temporary accommodation on Madison Avenue, Menaham Golan noted: 'We declined to consummate the deal with Astoria because we are an independent and do not want to tie ourselves to one studio. We have been courted by Los Angeles and New Jersey Authorities to settle with them, but we have chosen New York for its convenience.' For the moment, anyway, but Menahem's observers felt they would soon be back on their own terms in Hollywood, where they still maintained their offices.

In case anyone thought they were turning stale, the duo announced their plans for a cherished long-term project, the entering of the theme park business, in Jerusalem, to be named 'Bible Land'. This had one observer noting that no doubt the parting of the Red Sea would be one of the attractions, a mere trifle for the Golan/Globus team.

Cannon and Jack Eisner reached a deal for world-distribution rights in the believe-it-if-you-like '$6m picture' *The Children's*

War, but this could not be finalised until Eisner's legal right to the title was resolved. That was being hotly disputed in a court-room breach-of-contract suit that would finally prevail, and the title would be changed to *War and Love* as part of the settlement. The film would turn out in its pathetically limited release not to have been worth the bother of the court case, edging into the top fifty film chart in the US for one solitary week at number fifty before disappearing for ever.

US distributor's share of the box office gross of a movie was now down to 39% and eight out of ten features failing to recoup their investment from the US domestic market, with six out of ten not even recouping with revenue from world-wide distribution and ancillary marketing thrown in. Naturally, Cannon could never be included in this grim reckoning.

Using the figure of 39% of the gross as a guide, a $12m picture required to take almost $31m to break even in the domestic theatrical market alone. If saturation release was decided upon, adding $5m to the film's budget to arrive at a total cost of $17m, then the picture would require to take over $43m. Thankfully there were foreign sales, which were reckoned to average a further 30% of domestic gross, with ancillary sales to cable TV and video worth about 40% of the eventual total. From all of that an average distribution fee of 30% had to be deducted – except for Cannon, who chose not to charge their films anything.

With guaranteed minimum sums upon delivery available from foreign distributors, Cannon were in fact still due additional revenue at the point where the local distributor's expenses had been fully covered and he had earned his own minimum acceptable margin, this having been settled in advance by mutual agreement. So, in theory, if the film did well, then extra revenue would find its way back to Cannon over and above the minimum guarantee sum. This begged the question – if the system worked so well, why would Cannon now decide more and more to set up their own distributorships in foreign territories, so far in Italy, Holland, Germany and the UK, with Israel under G and G? Perhaps they had felt there was an element of withholding true box-office results by foreign distributors only anxious to part with the agreed minimums. Menahem and Yoram certainly must have seen some advantage in forfeiting third-party collateral for the territories in which Cannon would increasingly pursue the setting up of their own distribution organisations – apart from having a guaranteed outlet for their movies. This was no small consideration, nor was being able to nail down bricks and mortar assets in each country. However, they were leaving themselves open to having to finance larger and larger chunks of each of their pictures themselves, getting further and further away from their original concept of having a movie 100% financed before production commenced.

Cannon announced that an upgrading of their inventory was envisaged by the establishment of an international buying operation under the helm of Kenneth Rive, the British art film distributor who merged his Gala films and other quality productions for territories in which Cannon was either distributor or an exhibitor. He would co-ordinate buys from his London base, where he would also continue to programme a section of the Cannon Classic theatre circuit with art films. Menahem Golan noted that 'The acquisition activity of Cannon has no limits! The Company will make fifteen to twenty features a year and pick up any number for the various territories in which Cannon is trading. We can immediately evaluate the worth of a picture and our company is growing all the time. We are looking for theatres in France and Spain – and Greece too, since we have a lot of money stuck there.'

There *was* life after MGM – the proof was that Cannon still managed to post record profits for 1984, up from 1983's $9.7m to $12.4m on revenues increased from $62,600,000 to $108,700,000. The gains were attributed by Cannon to their domestic distribution organisation and their success with two pictures in the US market, *Breakin'*, albeit through MGM, and *Missing in Action*. It now seemed that the set-backs only fuelled their progress even more and that they would survive the toughest going. While other film companies were buffeted by variable revenue and lack of hit pictures, nothing, it seemed, could stop the Cannon steamroller. More projects were brought on stream – perhaps because they had to be. It's much harder to hit a moving target! It seemed that Misia Dudley of E. F. Hutton had been unduly pessimistic in the downgrading of her per-share earnings estimate for the year from $2.35 to $2.10, for this in fact worked out at $2.55 – clearly she had reckoned without the resourcefulness of the dynamic duo.

A glimmering in the wake of these results of how Cannon classified revenue and profits was revealed. Of the $78.8m advances and guarantees eventually due to the company, $22.8m had already been included as revenue and profits, even though the actual cash was due to be received only in the following twelve months. Financial observers – not for the first or for the last time – would mutter the phrase, 'mismatched revenues'.

Gradually it emerged that Cannon had found the answer to their prayers – a solution to the high taxes they were having to pay on the profit figures they trotted out with uncanny regularity. The answer lay in an area related to their financial mecca at Credit Lyonnais in Holland, but several thousand miles away in a part of the Caribbean known as the Netherland Antilles. Because of complex tax treaties with the USA and forty countries round the world, the Netherlands Antilles afforded both US and foreign producers an extraordinary legal tax haven for their foreign income. In 1983 Cannon had established 'Cannon films NV' to produce and distribute films outside the US, having been advised by a tax expert that US producers could avoid US taxes by causing a production to be undertaken by a foreign subsidiary. Providing that subsidiary carried out its operations in a certain way and met certain requirements, then US taxes could be deferred until the subsidiary's profits were repatriated to the US – only in Cannon's case they didn't believe in repatriation! In 1984 they stated in their annual report: 'The company's current intention is that all undistributed earnings of Cannon NV and Cannon NV's foreign subsidiaries would be reinvested indefinitely outside the US, because of its foreign investment plans and that accordingly domestic income taxes would not be accrued on these undistributed earnings.' Before discovering the benefits of a Netherlands Antilles base, Cannon had made provisions in 1982 to pay 43.4% ($1.9m) of its $4.3m in pre-tax income in Federal, City, State and foreign taxes. In 1983 Cannon had made provisions to make 41.2% ($4m) of its $9.7m in pre-tax income – although they had established their Antilles subsidiary in the same year, they could only claim $1m in operating profits out of it in that period, indicating that the flow of foreign income to its Antilles subsidiary had not yet fully begun in earnest. Now came the pay-off that made the whole exercise a tax-saving gold mine. By 1984, with its Antilles company in full swing, Cannon was able to make provision to pay only a tiny 2% ($254,000) of its $12.4m in pre-tax income on taxes, by claiming that nearly $12m in operating profits was coming from its Antilles subsidiary. Despite an increase on its pre-tax income in 1984 over 1983, Cannon had therefore managed to reduce its provision for taxes by a whopping 94%, claiming that most of its profits were now flowing from the Antilles subsidiary, where the effective rate of tax on foreign royalties was a mere 1–3%. Attempts at interviewing other companies involved in the Netherlands Antilles drew a blank, as most were reluctant to discuss their involvement on the grounds that it might lead to the US government snooping around and the possible end to what constituted a legal tax-avoidance scheme. Here was the compelling reason, quite apart from their master-game plan, why Cannon were positively obliged to invest abroad. If the money is not returned to the US it is virtually tax free and can be used willy-nilly in buying up theatre circuits and investing in local productions wherever a local facility exists.

Cannon's own distribution organisation, perfectly geared and motivated to handle exploitation pictures of the type their masters churned out, were unable to position the quality British picture, *Company of Wolves*, in the US market-place. The fantasy picture was heavily sold as a sex-laden horror movie and the campaign badly misfired. The picture had been excellently presented in other countries, including Britain, for what it was – and it had scored impressively before being flattened by Cannon's distribution arm. Their awful mishandling alienated the audience the picture might have enjoyed in the US, and further turned off those who came expecting typical Cannon *schlock* horror. Despite a large and expensive print release, net rentals to Cannon struggled to reach $2.35m.

Andrei Konchalovsky's *Maria's Lovers* failed even more dismally and never achieved a wide release. Some of the reviews were politely favourable, some were not – the film overall being judged too 'Russian' and too mixed in style. Nigel Andrews in the *Financial Times* wrote, 'The characters seem to have been born not in real life, but in previous movies. The settings hover uncertainly over the Atlantic somewhere between Baltimore and the Baltic.' He criticised the 'freeform ineptitudes of tone that rampage through this movie' and summed it up as a 'piecemeal portrait of America in which too many paintbrushes have clearly spoiled the wash'. Another case of no kudos, no cash. Konchalosky later told an interviewer, 'Cannon wanted me to make it very sexy, but I know I'm not able to do something like that.'

He said of Golan, 'He is the last tycoon. Here at last is a producer who can take a decision, creatively, and follow it through.'

To Golan's credit, Konchalovsky was still given the cash to do his original project, *Runaway Train*. Some script revision was required, for although the action was set in America, Kurosawa had written it for the Japanese mind. Were we about to get another hybrid from Konchalovsky? Paul Zindel had been one of the cooks on *Maria's Lovers* and it was decided to ask him to help out on *Runaway Train* as well. Yugoslavian Djordje Milcevic also found himself called in, but no-one cried 'too many cooks', although the dialogue was still judged to lack a certain *je ne sais quoi*, especially in the prison scenes. Robert Duvall, originally suggested for the Jon Voight role, put them right: 'Get Eddie Bunker' (author of *Straight Time* – filmed with Dustin Hoffman – and an ex-prisoner himself, having spent seventeen years of his life inside). When Bunker's contribution was completed, Golan cast his eye over the patchwork script. After two hours' perusal, he excitedly called Konchalovsky on the phone, yelling, 'We do that *immediately*! *Right* away! *Right* away!'

The end of New York shooting on Cannon's *Death Wish III*, directed by Michael Winner, was reached at the beginning of May before the unit moved to London to finish the picture. Golan had insisted that the film had to be rushed through to meet a release date of October 25th: 'This is not unreasonable,' declared the ever-compliant Winner. The film's total shooting schedule turned out to be fifty-one days, compared with the original for Paramount in 1974 of thirty-nine days, Winner attributing this to more special effects in the new picture. The budget for the film had been variously reported as $9m (by Cannon) and 'well over $10m' (by Winner) – a case of Cannon's parsimoniousness versus Winner's ego.

Cannon released their *Missing in Action* 'prequel', *Missing in Action II – The Beginning*, with high hopes of a repeat performance of the first picture's $28m box-office performance, but lightning did not strike twice and *Missing in Action II – The Beginning* took less than a third of the takings the first release had enjoyed. Although the budget was minuscule, marketing costs were not on the wide release Cannon organised, and they were extremely disappointed with the US domestic theatrical performance of the feature, although with ancillary and foreign theatrical rights the picture still ended up solidly in profit. Chuck Norris as the star in *Invasion USA*, however, was not quite the crock of gold Cannon had hoped for.

The Lance Hool-directed picture was a simple tale of Asians torturing and tormenting long-suffering American troops, until Chuck Norris just cain't take it no more. The movie was little more than a violent cartoon and was so hamfisted in execution as to be laughable. Not funny for Cannon, though, to see their Chuck-wagon broken down, and the annoyance was compounded when Norris's next film, Orion's *Code of Silence*, went on to gross $20m.

Franco Zeffirelli reached agreement in London with Menahem Golan and Yoram Globus to direct the Verdi opera *Otello* on film for the Cannon Group. Golan confirmed this and noted, 'Placido Domingo will star in the title role and Zeffirelli will supervise recording of the opera in July at La Scala with the cast, the La Scala symphony and choir.' With a single bound they were into opera.

Cannon stated it was negotiating with Tarak Ben Ammar for below-the-line participation and filming of *Otello*, which thus became the fifth Cannon production from its base in Rome, adding that negotiations were also underway to have Cannon produce Francesco Rosi's *Saturday, Sunday and Monday* in an adaptation of the Eduardo De Filippo play with a cast headed by Sophia Loren and Marcello Mastroianni. Others in production were Liliana Cavani's *The Berlin Affair* on location in Vienna, Lina Wertmuller's *Camorra* in and around Naples, Filippo Ottoni's *Private Defectives* and the first Cannon co-production with France, *Salome*, to be directed by Claude D'Anna. Cannon had also joined their partners Fulvio Lucisano and Vittorio Annibaldi in what they politely termed 'taking away' the projected Bud Spencer picture, *The Genie*, from public companies Sacis and Istituto Luce. Lucisano's Italia Intl would release in Italy and Cannon would have it for the rest of the world, the two companies cross-collateralising profits, if any. The deal had seemed set for Luce and Sacis to release the picture until the last-minute distributor change. *The Genie*, to be directed by Sergio Corbucci, was set for New York and Florida filming during May.

Cannon reported further rising profits and revenues for the quarter ended March 30th 1985. Their profit was up to $2.1m, a leap of 19.4% over the $1.7m profit posted in the same period a year ago. Of the revenue, motion-picture distribution had accounted for $19.8m compared with $13m for the same period in 1984. Cinema operations had accounted for $6m in the quarter, compared to $4.1m a year earlier.

It was noted that Cannon's push into the world of art movies in their on-going attempt to upgrade their image had failed to dampen Golan and Globus's appetite for stunting. Jean Luc Godard had been signed up for *King Lear* for Cannon at Cannes – on the back of a napkin. Cannon stated that its promotional clout and family of offshore distributors would give noted film-makers like Godard *et al.* a better-than-ever shot at making it at the box office, adding that most of the pictures would be low-budgeters in any case, in the $1–1.5m range. The way Golan told it, Godard had sought him out with the *Lear* project, adding loquaciously, 'It gives us the most modern and controversial director in the world dealing with Shakespeare's far-sighted view of the generation gap.' He went on to say that their arty inventory was aimed at what he perceived to be a maturing international theatrical audience. There was no question, however, of Cannon figuring to lose money while gaining prestige, although they expected to look after any of their customers who got burned with these offerings.

Golan also let drop that a one-hour documentary dedicated to his career and Cannon's meteoric rise was in the works. In charge of the project was journalist and film critic Gideon Bachmann, with Cannon financing half the project and Bachmann putting up the remainder. If you can believe it, Golan stated that already there were presales in the project which Bachmann hoped to have finished by the end of 1985. There were many who would ask incredulously to whom these presales had been made.

When Katharine Hepburn's *The Ultimate Solution of Grace Quigley* had been misguidedly touted for a Cannes entry in 1984, Golan and Globus had been beside themselves with excitement. Globus enthused, 'That it should happen that I should actually live to talk to the African Queen who I saw in Israel in the movies when I was a child, this I can't believe.'

Would Kate Hepburn appear with her movie at Cannes? 'Definitely you can say this is absolutely a 99% possibility for sure,' Golan declared. 'If our movie is accepted I'll take Kate by the hand and put her on the Concorde. I already asked her in person. Not on the phone even. And she didn't say no. So right now it's a 100%, almost.'

Unfortunately the movie was not invited and it was only after many months of desperate procrastination that *Grace Quigley* was finally released, opening to eleven unfavourable reviews. It fully justified MGM's lack of confidence in it by doing terrible business in its limited locations. With the title shortened from the original mouthful, *The Ultimate Solution of Grace Quigley*, the version the New York critics saw was a truncated one, thirty minutes having been hacked from its running time by Cannon. Katharine Hepburn disassociated herself from the movie when she heard what had been done to make it more 'commercial'. Panic-stricken, Cannon re-inserted the cut footage for its West Coast premiere. The reviews were better, but business was not. London, therefore, got the shortened New York version, which lost several supporting players and one entire sub-plot. Alexander Walker in the *Evening Standard* wrote: 'Let's just say *Grace Quigley* is a terrible mistake on everyone's part, one of the most distasteful pseudo-black comedies I have ever had the misfortune to endure.' The MME agreed, adding that 'The mind responsible for *Grace Quigley* is undoubtedly a sick mind – but even that can't save the picture. Not so much a black comedy as a black hole.' Cannon would have done better leaving it on the shelf, or better still passing on it originally, as everyone else had done.

Menahem Golan claimed that he had tried to buy MGM/UA from Kirk Kerkorian, the 51% stockholder. Although he was reluctant to go into detail about the terms, he stated that 'Kerkorian didn't want to sell'. Although many in the trade were now reconciled to the fact, with Cannon anything was possible, as in pigs might fly, this one still seemed to take the biscuit. It was becoming obvious to close Cannon observers that life with Cannon would for ever be a series of big-deal announcements. Cannon-watching was becoming a full time occupation. Their latest attempt – and their last for a long time, to do a Sam Katzman impersonation – came to grief with the wide and expensive release of *Rappin'*. This one struggled to return rentals of $1,247,495 against an estimated $3m in release costs and wrote 'finis' to any idea they might have had of more quickie music-exploitationers. They had been lucky with *Breakin'*, pushed their luck with *Breakdance II – Electric Boogalo*, now they were totally out of luck – and money – with *Rappin'*.

Unabashed Golan now stated that the company was considering an offer for a West German cinema chain and negotiating for an unnamed American 400-cinema circuit. He maintained: 'Cannon's credit lines are all open and we don't owe any bank any money. The company is financing itself purely out of cash-flow.' (Credit Lyonnais – were you listening?) In the next breath Golan stated that Cannon might be seeking to raise as much as $200m from investors by offering them a 50% interest in a current package of pictures. He elaborated, 'We will take no distribution fee off the top and investors will get 50% of the first dollar. The investment is protected by Cannon's pre-licensing of the films to the foreign market.' The $200m offering would in fact be revised sharply downwards after meetings with Cannon's underwriters, but Golan's initial utterance served to prime Wall Street critics that Cannon would once again be on the prowl for more money in the near future. Why – with everything they made presold?

In Cannes, Cannon declared they had sold a package of thirty-one features to Viacom for Global TV Syndication, while Menahem Golan claimed that Cannon had moved $60m worth of library and new product at the event in various media, following an alleged $75m haul at the American film market in February. A new concept was aired by the trade at Cannes for deals with foreign territories. The product-output deal called for no minimum guarantee from the buying distributor and cross-collateralisation of gains and losses within product packages. At the end of the day the supplier had to absorb more of the risk in passing up minimums and unsurprisingly Menahem Golan came firmly down against the concept, stating hilariously that 'Since nine out of ten pictures don't make money anyway, the supplier that doesn't get something in advance is headed for the boneyard!' If some of his faithful band of foreign distributors had been listening, they might have formed the impression that they were already paying too much for Cannon's product – if their box-office takings hadn't already indicated that.

Golan reported a postponement on his earlier decision to re-locate Cannon's headquarters from Hollywood to New York City, adding mysteriously, 'There are things happening in our company over the next six months which may involve a development which would keep us in Hollywood. We don't want to make a decision yet on what would be a major commitment regarding our permanent headquarters.' He noted that they would continue to occupy and enlarge the office space they rented in Madison Avenue on a one-year basis, while maintaining their main office and post-production activities in Hollywood.

Only a few weeks after this, it was announced that Cannon was moving back to Hollywood to brand new offices that were being custom built for them. How Hollywood must have collectively groaned – it really had been too good to be true!

Worrying news for all the industry, Cannon included, was that box office for 1985 had now slumped to a five-year low at $459m compared to 1984's $602m.

Cannon's answer was to purchase the rights to produce *Superman IV* and all future Superman films. Menahem Golan stated that negotiations had begun with Alexander Salkind, owner of all picture rights to the 'Superman' character, on the final day of the Cannes festival. 'It's the biggest deal in our company's history,' he trumpeted. 'We'll commence production of *Superman IV* in 1986 on a budget in the $30m range.'

Alexander Salkind had let it be known earlier that he had experienced considerable difficulties on the *Superman* series, maintaining that it had taken until the second in the series was released before he saw any returns, due to the high budget involved and the fact that with presales on the projects made to Warners, they received the first of the revenues. It was also a fact that with each successive *Superman*, the market appeared to shrink. Although the first in the series recorded US domestic rentals of $82.8m, the second sank to $65.8m, still a creditable total, but then the third in the series took in a less-impressive $37.2m, before Salkind's *Supergirl* sank without trace. This begged the question of how much Cannon's *Superman IV* was worth, bearing in mind the projected $30m budget. What there was no doubt about was the alacrity with which Cannon would immediately proceed to presell

Superman IV, while the amount Salkind was paid for the *Superman* rights remained undisclosed. Tri-Star had misguidedly picked up the *Supergirl* rights for the US market and planned their first attempt at a public securities offering to coincide with its anticipated success at the box office. When the picture bombed, the public securities proposal was promptly scrapped.

Sure enough, only a few weeks later, *Variety*'s headline ran, 'Deal with Warner Bros for *Superman IV* seen bolstering Cannon finances'. Warners were to get domestic distribution of the film, together with the long-delayed Sylvester Stallone feature, *Over the Top*, the addition of which to the Warners' release schedule was not deemed to be surprising since Cannon traditionally had sought involvement from a major for their more expensive productions – as in the case of *Space Vampires*, with Tri-Star putting up $12.5m of the $22.5m budget – to 'protect our downside', as Golan put it, overlooking the fact that it also denied them the cream from even the biggest hit, as this would go to the participating distributor. It seemed also that Warners were to get video and cable rights on both pictures, leaving Cannon only with free domestic TV rights to sell.

By the fall of 1985 *Over the Top* was now reported as budgeted at $25m, with Stallone still to receive $12m as per the original 1983 deal. Shooting was scheduled for January 1986 with direction in the hands of Menahem Golan himself, who stated that the pact with Warners involved a 'normal advance guarantee' and a 'standard distribution fee', understood by the trade to be in the 30% range. With the Warners' deal Golan claimed that the company had totally covered production costs for *Over the Top*, which had been presold world wide, and that presales would begin for *Superman IV* at the Italian film market, Mifed. Did Cannon's finances need bolstering by Warner Bros? It had taken Golan less than a month after acquiring the *Superman* rights to trade them off in a deal, and the stark fact of Warners' 30% distribution fee means that Cannon themselves will be the last to see any returns. What Cannon had got instead is what they needed most – upfront money.

More money still was required, despite claimed presales on every picture and bank loans and securities offerings for the rest, and Cannon announced in September 1985 that a new line of credit for $65m had been negotiated with a consortium of bankers headed by the First National Bank of Boston. This was to be in addition to the previously arranged $45m from Credit Lyonnais in the Netherlands. Their joint credit line would now total $110m, although worryingly they could not get their hands on the Boston Bank money for the time being. As their Wall Street critics looked on open-mouthed, it was stated that on the financial horizon for Cannon loomed a $50m public offering for which a prospectus was being prepared, covering ten films budgeted at under $10m each. This had been reduced from the $200m offering Golan had announced in May, his financial team having advised him that this was going too far. Golan again described the proposed offering as a partnership in production and added that the investment would cover 50% of each film's budget for production and advertising. As structured, Cannon would not take a distribution fee, but a 10% overhead charge subtracted upfront, with all revenue world wide being split fifty-fifty. He explained that the push for production finance would not only help to cover the expected $150m slate of approximately twenty-three films in the current year but also free up cash for Cannon's continuing acquisition of theatres world wide. Golan acknowledged that Cannon were still heavily dependent on success in the foreign market but claimed that he was not that discouraged by recent problems and that other ways and means could be found to solve any currency problems and decline of income. Many would keep returning to the salient question – if their entire production slate of films was financed by presales, why did they have to resort to another public offering in the first place? Golan's claim to be financing Cannon through cash-flow generated questions as to his definition of cash-flow. Generally this was acknowledged to be a company's internally-generated cash, but in Golan's definition additional bank borrowings and public securities money seemed to be included.

Golan highlighted one of his answers to current problems as being to focus on foreign production which would contribute films to the individual local markets, instancing the three films Cannon were producing in Holland which he claimed could turn a profit in the Netherlands and Germany alone. In addition, currency frozen in Greece and South America could be turned into local production, taking full advantage of local subsidies when available. He gave *River of Death* as an example, planned for production in

Colombia. He acknowledged that the company's bread and butter remained in the foreign market, but stated that he was intent on a bigger piece of the domestic pie not only for financial reasons, but for the sake of the company's image. In view of the size of the US domestic market, this seemed eminently sensible to anyone in the business, for Cannon had been missing decent returns on any US release since *Missing in Action* had grossed $28m in 1984. Golan stated, 'It is important the way the public looks at us. We don't only want to be involved in *schlock*.' He was intent on winning some Oscar nominations and awards at Cannes as symbols of the company's growing respectability and he expected to do this with the likes of Robert Altman's *Fool for Love*. This did nothing so much as put cynics in mind of their previous attempts to elevate their image with Cassavettes's ill-fated *Love Streams* and Andrei Konchalovsky's *Maria's Lovers*, not to mention Jason Miller's earlier *That Championship Season*.

He stressed again that art films remained but a modest investment with Cannon, with even a project like *Otello* deemed to be commercially viable through lower salaries and a percentage of the gross to the principals. Golan stated that the company was now in a position for the first time to attract major talent, but he was adamant that he had no plans to abandon the commercial projects on which the company had built its reputation. 'Theatrical is not the only mouth to feed,' he averred. 'If Hollywood produced five times as many films as it does now, it would still not meet the demand. There is space for the mediocre!'

Cannon released operating results for the half year ended June 30th, showing a 22% earnings increase over the comparable previous year. Net profit was $5.2m on revenues of $61.8m against net profit of $4.2m on revenues of $35.8 for the same period in 1984. Once again the pessimists were silenced!

Cannon acquired the ninety-one screen Star circuit, the fourth largest in Britain, for a reported £4.4m, so together with its previously acquired Classic chain, Cannon now controlled the second largest circuit in the UK with a total of 216 screens at ninety-five sites, behind ABC with their 286 screens at 106 sites. 'We have to be in exhibition big to help the distribution of our product,' Golan declared. 'Given the way the majors dominate distribution it is very difficult to make healthy profits, so our idea is to become the UIP of Europe. Eventually we would like to create our own Europe-wide exhibition management headquartered in London.' Cannon were now clearly seen to be pursuing the policy that originally led to the creation of the majors, controlling the exhibition and production interests that fuel each other directly and controlling the chain of supply.

Now came the release of Cannon's claimed $22.5m *Space Vampires*. That they had poured their own – and Tri-Star's – money down the drain seemed to be indicated by *Variety*'s opening review, describing the picture as an 'unintentional laugh-fest' when it appeared under its new title of *Lifeforce* (Tri-Star, for $12.5m, having insisted on the change). It had been produced in Britain and was reminiscent of several old Hammer movies, especially *Quatermass and the Pit*. The only difference – apart from not being nearly as good – was that it had cost fifty times the price of *Quatermass*. Frank Finlay's tendency to ham was totally unrestrained by the hapless Tobe Hooper, and Steve Railsback – so good in Richard Rush's *The Stuntman* – seemed totally lost, but in a way it was unfair to single out any individual actor in such a project, since the dialogue by Dan O'Bannon and Dan Jacobi was virtually unspeakable. It was almost as if they had aimed for a stilted British 'B' film style straight out of the 50s and it was the sort of bungled effort one of the old-style Hollywood moguls would never have put into production, for one glance at the truly awful script would have called for the project to have been aborted. Did Golan and Globus really want to be the descendants of Hammer films? If so – they should have made it better. Alexander Walker in the London *Evening Standard* wrote: 'The year's worst film. There cannot be another as bad on the way.' After only two releases the Tri-Star deal was off, as MGM's had been before it, so now it was all down to Cannon's own releasing arm once again – until Warners did the honours next, that is.

Tri-Star's release of Cannon's *Lifeforce* grossed $12m, which boils down to domestic rentals of approximately $5m. This would have brought the film out after US theatrical release with the following results, had it been a major studio release, using latest industry figures which related US performance as a guide to total world-wide all-media results:

1) Total negative cost:	$22,500,000
Split: Cannon:	$10,000,000
Tri-Star:	$12,500,000
2) Total domestic rentals:	
(39% of domestic gross box-office receipts)	$ 5,000,000
3) Add 30% of the eventual total to arrive at foreign rental:	$ 2,150,000
4) Add 40% of the eventual total domestic + foreign + ancillary to arrive at ancillary:	$ 4,933,500
Total =	$12,083,500
5) Now deduct 30% average distribution fee, all media and markets:	$ 3,625,050
Total revenue =	$ 8,458,450
Total shortfall =	$14,041,550

As it was the actual result was more difficult to pin-point because of Cannon's presales arrangements abroad. However, foreign theatrical distributors should only have paid $2.1m for the picture – all the movie was worth as a US flop. By Golan's normal account, combined with their ancillary partners, they would have coughed up at least the balance of Cannon's budget.

In a surprising announcement, Warner Bros stated that Sylvester Stallone would be making his next picture, *Cobra*, for them, although it would be a Golan/Globus/Cannon production. Why were Cannon apparently prepared to let Warners get the *Rambo* follow-up that could have been theirs with their long-touted *Over the Top*? Trade rumours had it that *Cobra* was to be completely a Warners' production despite the token Cannon billing, and that Cannon would collect $1m in cash from Warners in return for releasing Stallone for *Cobra*. This would also suit Cannon inasmuch as it would push the heavy cash outlay on *Over the Top* – already pledged by foreign distributors in advance – into a new fiscal period. Warners agreed to present *Cobra* as a Golan/Globus/Cannon production as a face-saver, with the additional sweetener that should *Cobra* prove to be successful and spawn sequels, then Cannon could have a 50% participation in these. This was the deal that Golan and Globus are said to have agreed to, although they would also claim to have a net profit position, of an undefined size, in *Cobra* itself. It was not typical of Cannon's usual bombastic style that they would fail to divulge the size of the net profit position and there followed an equally untypical low-profile approach on *Cobra* as Warners confirmed they would be handling the picture in all territories world wide.

Over the Top's production was now put on ice until June 1986, and the agreement to give Warners Stallone for *Cobra* first was widely seen as a mistake – apparently for the sake of a mere $1m in cash they had thrown away the services of Sylvester Stallone at the hottest time in his career.

Cannon's next wide release was for in-house director Sam Firstenberg's *American Ninja*, starring Michael Dudikoff – there was no question about the star's agility, only his total lack of screen presence. However, the net US rental of the latest *Ninja* totalled $3,875,675, enough to cover marketing costs and even contribute to negative costs. Foreign and ancillary rights would contribute to make this particular outing a modestly profitable one, despite being made with about one-tenth of the skill behind an average TV movie. The entry would doubtless go down a treat at video level.

Things seemed to be getting tighter all over as it turned out that the general box office for September 1985 had been the worst in five years, with the cumulative totals for 1985 now 15% behind the previous year. The figures were actually much worse if computed on ticket sales, without inflation factors such as increase of admission prices being taken into account, for these had plummeted to a seventeen-year low.

Enter Barry Lublin as Cannon's new Chief Financial Officer (CFO) in July 1985. He came to Cannon directly from Cannon's auditing firm of Mann Judd Landau, where he had been the officer in charge of auditing Cannon's accounts since 1980 as well as a full partner in the firm. It was thought surprising that Cannon still retained the services of Mann Judd Landau, considered to be a small firm of auditors, for whom Cannon must have represented their biggest single account by far. With Lublin moving to take over the CFO position at Cannon, Lublin's previous assistant was now moved to the position Lublin had previously occupied – in charge of Cannon's auditing.

Variety previewed *Invasion USA*, describing it as a 'nasty actioner aimed at the *Rambo* market, with a brainless plot' where star Chuck Norris, who co-wrote the script, 'hits the nadir with this vicious-minded commodity from the Cannon group', but added, 'Yes, it will make some money.' It went on to open at 1,735 cinemas across the US and received one favourable and nine unfavourable reviews, which hardly concerned the picture's target audience. Box office totalled $6,891,609 in the first three days, but by the following weekend takings had plunged by a huge 49%, then a further 50% seven days later. It bowed out with $16,479,122 and could hardly claim to have conquered America. This time even the Nosh Brothers could not disguise their disappointment. If Chuck Norris could get Orion more than $20m with *Code of Silence*, what was wrong with them?

For the first time in fifteen years Menahem Golan would not be present at the Italian film market, Mifed, with Yoram Globus, owing to his commitment to direct the new Chuck Norris/Lee Marvin opus, *The Delta Force*, in Israel. The philosophy here seemed to be that if Chuck Norris was no longer sure-fire on his own, as in *Invasion USA*, he should be bolstered by Lee Marvin. Sceptics would question the validity of this, since Marvin had failed to perform meaningfully at the box office for many years. Menahem Golan's decision to undertake the direction was seen as his attempt to ensure that Norris again basked in a box-office winner. Cannon were keen to protect their investment and who better to handle it than Golan himself?

Thus unaccustomedly thrust into the spotlight, Globus stated that he would finalise deals on his own in his partner's absence following the pattern of the technique they had originally established. He maintained that their continuing success lay in the development of relationships with overseas distributors and emphasised that he wanted to stick to the same ones wherever possible. To counter criticisms of flops such as *Lifeforce*, Globus anxiously stressed that Cannon was still able to turn out the likes of the *Ninja* offerings for only $2m, resulting in an average budget for Cannon entries still held at $5m, despite the excursions into $10m-plus projects.

He stated that presales on *Superman IV*, which he now claimed had a budget of $40m, would be a priority, as well as lining up a director for the project. As a realistic goal Globus stated that 'next year Cannon expects to take a significant share of the box office in every part of the world'. He acknowledged the wide release of *Invasion USA* with 1,735 prints but added, 'We don't have to open every film with 1,000 prints. The region-by-region release utilising 75–200 prints can still be a profitable route, as witness our successful recent handling of *Ordeal by Innocence*.' It was in fact many years since a net of less than $1m had been considered a success in the US market.

Globus stated that the group had lined up some $240m worth of firm contracts from third-party buyers even before beginning the Mifed market and in a lengthy interview while in Milan, he ticked off the company's assets to counter worrying arguments from some of the Wall Street community that Cannon had far too much debt and was over-leveraged. Although actual company debt stood at $216m at the beginning of December, Globus stated at this interview only weeks earlier that the total company debt was 'in the area of $150m'.

The $240m sales figure quoted covered hard sales of Cannon product both past and future according to Globus, who declined to update figures relating to the company's 1985 roster of twenty-three pictures which he claimed had a negative cost of $97.6m as of June 20th. By the same date, advances and guarantees for the entire package came in at a claimed $91m. He pointed to three buy signals from stock analysts, including Paine Webber's veteran motion picture overseer Lee Isgur, which had helped to counter the now downbeat analysis from E. F. Hutton, and he argued that Cannon's 2.5–1 debt to equity ratio was not out of line for a film business company. He strongly maintained that the company's shares were undervalued at $22 each with earnings for the year pegged at $3.

Although he declined to comment on 1985 earnings projections, he maintained that the $3 per share figure was near enough the mark, give or take 10%. If $3 per share were to be achieved, he pointed out that Cannon's stock would be selling at about seven times earnings, which he considered to be a low price-earnings multiple.

He further revealed that the line of up to $65m in revolving credit with the First National Bank of Boston would be signed and sealed within the next few weeks, for although the deal had been closed by Cannon some months ago, a definitive loan agreement had never been executed. Instead Cannon had negotiated an interim credit agreement with the Boston Bank in late August, permitting them to borrow up to $25m. This deal was due to lapse on November 29th. As of late August, Cannon had also been indebted to its other major bank creditor, Credit Lyonnais, on the tune of $41.4m out of the total facility of $45m.

Globus stated that as of June 29th Cannon had more than $172m worth of 'receivables' which would qualify as acceptable collateral, far more in fact than was required. He hinted that once the revolving credit arrangement with the Boston Bank was finalised then Cannon would accelerate the search for a suitable US theatre chain to buy. In reply to one question which referred to the stake that he and Golan had in Cannon, Globus revelaed that he and his partner owned 30.1% of the company's stock or a total of 1,411,667 shares. Shares controlled by their respective spouses brought the total to 1,953,667 shares or 41% of the total of 4.8m shares on the market, or 6.5m shares fully diluted. He further stated that he and Golan had years ago bought an unspecified number of their company's common stock at 20–30 cents per share. 'And we haven't sold one share,' he declared. 'That's how much faith we have in our company!' The total value of their holding at late 1985 was $69m.

He conceded that he was disappointed at the box-office reaction in the US for *Invasion USA*, the picture Cannon had hoped would be the company's long sought-after box-office breakaway. Despite their fatuous printed handout at Mifed declaring the picture a 'resounding success', Globus conceded that he had anticipated more. Although the picture had cost $13m to produce and another $4–$5m to launch, Globus stated that there was $7m expected in foreign sales.

On top of the big budget the true likely launch costs would have been nearer $6m than their claimed figure, and even allowing for Cannon's thriftiness, this is how the figures would have emerged had *Invasion USA* been a major studio item:

1) Take the negative costs:	$13,000,000
2) Add marketing cost most likely:	$ 6,000,000
Total Cost =	$19,000,000

3) Take domestic *rentals* (ie the approx. 39% of the domestic *gross* box-office receipts that actually accrue to the distributor) $ 6,900,000

4) Add 30% or slightly over, of the eventual total domestic and foreign take, for foreign rentals (or add 43% to domestic) $ 2,967,000

5) Add 40% of the eventual total domestic + foreign and all ancillary rights (video, TV, cable etc.) to arrive at ancillary (or add 69% to combined domestic and foreign gross) $16,667,000

Total = $16,667,000

6) Now deduct 30% average distribution fee, all media and markets $ 5,000,000

Net Revenues = $11,667,000

NET DEFICIT = $7,333,000

Cannon could now only avoid a proper reckoning by either understating budget and marketing costs or overstating foreign and media sales and the preceding table is how *Invasion USA* would have ended up in the books as a Columbia picture or a Universal picture, because of their more conventional marketing methods, where a film's worth is greater or lesser depending on its performance in the US domestic market. Obviously, with Cannon's method of presales, the importance of domestic box office in determining the foreign worth of a movie is not so great, but equally Cannon have little opportunity to cash in on a domestic box-office smash hit, because they have already sold the film ahead for a fixed cost, where a Universal or a Columbia on the other hand are in a position to demand higher payment for a proven smash. Cannon have therefore protected downside by presales, but are unable to take advantage of a film that is unexpectedly successful. Certain fixed costs remain the same for all companies – prints cost money, even if Cannon pay less than the going rate. Distribution in the US is expensive and costs Cannon the same as anyone else, except that they don't charge themselves anything! All the trumpeting Cannon does obviously costs money also and Columbia and Universal have never been known to take a fifty-odd page advertisement in *Variety* or to spend $500,000 at Cannes. The most glaring difference is that a film like *Invasion USA*, having netted only $6.9m of domestic rentals, would normally be considered worth only $2.96m in the foreign market. If, as Globus claimed, Cannon had received $7m in foreign guarantees for the picture, there was going to be a lot of distributors, who would be increasingly wary of carrying on down the same road with Cannon, having paid double the going rate for a loss-maker. When *Invasion USA* hit the UK, for example, it was only able to achieve the most marginal release, even through Cannon's own exhibition division.

On *Death Wish III*, due in November, 1985 at 1,500 cinemas in the US, Globus maintained that Cannon was already in profit although the budget for the movie was $9m and the launch costs would be similar to *Invasion USA*. He later claimed that the final Mifed sales came to $56m in third-party contracts, which was a new record for the annual event.

Chapter Six
PREJUDICE, JEALOUSY & MISINFORMATION

While on location for *The Delta Force* Menahem Golan was found at a lunch break urging the cast, 'The soup is good and hot – eat, eat, eat!' He boasted that he would soon feature Lee Marvin and Woody Allen in Jean Luc Godard's *King Lear* and added, 'I gave Jean Luc all of Switzerland and half of France,' meaning the profits from those countries, not the actual countries themselves presumably. The cast would also get 50% of the profits by taking next to nothing in advance and in the end it sounded like no less than 150% of the movie had already been committed upfront! 'Do you ever get frightened it will all go wrong?' he was asked in between mouthfuls of soup. 'I say money goes, money comes,' he replied. 'I am not frightened I will go bankrupt. There can, however, be jealousy and rumours. I heard people say we use Mafia money. I never met people from the Mafia in my life. I don't know the phone number of the Mafia. Sometimes I am hurt by all this nonsense – but you develop the skin of an elephant. If you are true to yourself you have nothing to fear. We are not tempted by our success to be foolish in Hollywood. I am there because it has the best creative talent and the best potential.' (The interviewer did not point out that he was actually in Israel at that particular moment in time, the main purpose apparently being to keep the G & G studios busy). 'I am an Israeli! I won't fall for Hollywood!' he declared.

He was indignant when he was questioned on the element of wish-fulfilment in his changing the TWA hi-jacking story into a triumph for the mythical *Delta Force*. 'I am giving people the satisfaction of seeing what they wanted to happen, happen. I am changing history a little. We are going to bring this out while the story of the hi-jack problem is still hot.' He then added thought-fully, 'And it will also save us interest charges!' Menahem became animated as he talked about *Death Wish III*, which as he spoke was briefly lodged at number one in the American film parade, in a soft period between the majors' pictures. 'It has a rape in it like you've never seen!' he enthused. 'It's very strong – like Michael Winner said, "It's World War III!" It's the most violent movie I've ever seen, but don't misunderstand me, it's an anti-violence film! It may get good reviews – I don't know. My wife was holding her stomach, but she sat through it! Fantastic movie!' If only a few more people had agreed with Golan's opinion of this repulsive film. *Variety* for one properly cut it down to size by describing it in no uncertain terms as a 'monotonous shoot-out'. It opened at 1,460 theatres and grossed a total in its run of $16.1m at the box office, or a net to Cannon of $6.4m before distribution costs were deducted, (or not deducted, in the case of Cannon!) against a $9m budget and $5m print and advertising costs. After its opening box office it slipped by 41% in its second weekend, 30% in its third, 49% in its fourth, and a further 31% in its fifth – and mostly last – weekend.

Winner's latest was in fact a pedestrian vehicle chockful of gratuitous violence, pandering to the lowest common denominator in the audience. A perfunctory script made no attempt at character-isation and the film trundled from one scene of excess to the next, culminating in a particularly lurid and ludicrous finale where half of a New York suburb was blown away. One can only speculate on the state of the minds responsible for this claptrap, from sponsors all the way down to the director.

Variety previewed *King Solomon's Mines* next, judging it to be 'A second-rate imitation of *Indiana Jones*'. It opened at 1,122 theatres and grossed $14.4m total box office, netting Cannon $6m against a budget of $11m, and advertising and printing costs of $4m minimum. In the second week the takings had dropped by 24%, then by 60% in the third and 51% in the fourth week, following the well-worn Cannon formula, now firmly established and making three in a row with *Invasion USA*, of a quick widely-hyped opening followed by a fast fade. The pattern was now being noted by an increasingly wide number of industry analysts.

Jose Quintano and James Silkes's dumb script for *King Solomon's Mines* was outdone by J. Lee Thompson's rapid direction. Richard Chamberlain as the unlikely Harrison Ford replacement looked stunned throughout – as well he might – and the atrocious special effects and superficial attempts at fleshing-out cardboard characters killed off any chance the film might have had of even doing a mini *Indiana Jones* at the box office. Poor Sharon Stone. Poor Herbert Lom. Steven Spielberg had done it all before – but so very, very much better.

Ted Turner's bid for MGM/UA turned out to be for the sum of $1.56 billion – this is the company that the bold Golan/Globus team had claimed they had offered to buy earlier in the year.

The inglorious episode of buy and sell back, then split and sell back again, with Kerkorian and Turner playing God with thousands of people's lives, set a new low in Hollywood financial history that not even Cannon could compete with, for Turner never did have the money to buy MGM/UA. As commentators wondered what on earth the regulatory bodies at the SEC and the FCC were doing by apparently turning a blind eye to proceedings, 'junk bonds' became household words. It was a sordid spectacle, which proved in real terms to be the dying roar of Leo the Lion, eviscerated for all to see.

To add to the doom and gloom, October's box-office attendance figures turned out to have been the lowest for nine years, off 10% from 1984. The industry seemed to be settling into a severe slump, possibly video-induced, or was the cure simply the old perennial need for more good pictures? For Cannon it seemed that at last the quality picture, and the commercial success of which they had been dreaming, had finally arrived in the form of Andrei Konchalovsky's *Runaway Train*, described by *Variety* in a rave review as 'An outstanding action picture' and 'Sensational', but warning ominously, 'Cannon's distribution arm will be tested to the limit by the challenge of attracting both the college buff crowd and the mainline audience. The picture unquestionably delivers, but the word must be got out to both groups.' Cannon opened both *Runaway Train* and Robert Altman's version of Sam Shepard's *Fool for Love* on only a few screens in late December, 1985 to qualify for 1986 Oscar consideration and awaited the box office results of a wider release for *Runaway Train* in January. Jon Voight was subsequently nominated for an Oscar as 'Best Actor', although he did not win. The Foreign Press Association awarded him a 'Golden Globe', however.

With metronomic precision Cannon announced higher yields for the first nine months of 1985. Earnings had risen to $8.5m on revenues of $96.1m, up from $7.1m for the previous year on revenues of $62m. The news gave their shares an extra boost.

Despite the fact that Menahem Golan and Yoram Globus appeared on the surface to be relatively underpaid, considering that they were hard working entrepreneurs priming the activities of the major independent film company in the US, it transpired that initial appearances were deceiving. Golan and Globus were due $350,000 in direct compensation in 1985 – however, on top of that it seemed that in June 1985 Cannon's shareholders had approved an incentive compensation plan for Golan and Globus, giving each of them $1.6m cash forthwith. Globus explained that the payment was to make up for money both he and Golan had not extracted in salary over the last three or four years. According to company documents, each of them was due $750,000 up to December 31st 1984. However, even that was not the whole picture, as it emerged that Golan and Globus were also entitled to 3.5% of the amount that Cannon's pre-tax earnings in 1985 and in each of the next two years would exceed the average pre-tax earnings of 1982 and 1983 – an average of about $7m.

Their professed love of movies suddenly made sense – yes, they loved movies, but it seemed they liked money from movies too.

Thorn-EMI announced in November 1985, that TESE (Thorn-EMI Screen Entertainment) was up for sale, the deal to include the ABC cinema circuit, the largest in Britain. Rank and Cannon emerged as the two main bidders, Cannon having formed a liaison with Gerald Ronson of the Heron Corporation to co-finance their bid of £110m. This is what Golan and Globus had been praying for. It was a pity they had bothered about the Star circuit earlier in the year, but never mind – this was the big one. With ABC they would have almost 40% of the UK screens. The feeling in the Cannon camp was that they *had* to achieve this – almost regardless of the price. Yes, it meant further increasing their already colossal debts, but they reasoned that any bank would accept the TESE asset base, not only of bricks and mortar but also their 2,800-odd film library, as collateral. Both offers caused a storm of protest from industry bodies, individuals and unions. Rank already had seventy-nine cinemas of their own with 200 screens and Cannon's Classic/Star total was ninety-five cinemas and 216 screens, so both bids were deemed to pose problems with the Monopolies and Mergers Commission in terms of exhibition. The Rank bid was also felt to be tricky on the grounds that they already owned Pinewood Studios and the takeover of TESE involved the ownership of Elstree Studios which it was feared Rank would shut down. Cannon/Heron were depicted as outright opportunists who were not valuing the company as a going concern – but as an asset-stripping operation, and on this basis producer David Puttnam protested to the Prime Minister's office on the undesirability of either bid going ahead. A further bidder then emerged in the form of TESE chairman and chief executive Gary Dartnall, who together with his fellow executives had put together a management buyout package.

As speculation reached fever pitch, the team of Golan/Globus was taken by surprise at the virulence of the anti-Cannon lobby. The group was bitterly criticised for lack of support for the UK film industry in the past but Menahem Golan dismissed these claims, furiously condemning much of the opposition as thinly disguised racism, and stated, 'We have made an offer and I think we are the most serious contenders. In the first place we don't know of any other that is as high, and secondly after due investigation of what it is we are proposing to buy and if we find that the material warrants it, we are prepared to be flexible in price. We feel we are the best management for the operation as Cannon has proved itself to be the most exciting exhibitor, producer and distributor of movies in the UK.[?] Add to that Gerald Ronson's ownership of Heron's Media Home Entertainment and you can see that we will bring terrific management and people with financial resources.'

Menahem was just getting into his stride as he continued: 'All the suspicion and rumour in the press is based on prejudice, jealousy and misinformation. When people say there is a danger of stripping the studio or the cinema chain they could not be more wrong. We are the biggest investors in the industry in this country since we came here thirty months ago. We have made seven films here and we have used more equipment, more studio space, and employed more technicians than any other production company in England. We have renovated theatres more than any other chain and we have produced a bigger percentage rise in admissions to our cinemas – bringing people back to the movies – than anyone else. To claim that this is a threat to the industry in England is a joke. We have injected new blood into the industry in its most difficult days. The unions have raised concern about the future of Elstree Studios. If one of the bidders is already an owner of a studio then there would be a danger that Elstree Studio would be closed. But Cannon doesn't have a studio and it is no secret in the business that we need one. It might as well be in England, where we are well known, where we understand people and where we have our international headquarters. [Since when?] If we are successful in our bid for EMI we will start in January with a plan to bring *Superman IV*, *Spiderman*, *Duet for One* and *Captain America* to Elstree. That means jobs for thousands of technicians and work for part of the studio for a year. That is not asset stripping, that is investment.'

Now there was no stopping him as he continued: 'Look – the first reason for buying EMI is that we think the combination of the two circuits would be a good thing, as Cannon is strongly represented in the West End, but weak in the provinces. EMI is strong in the provinces, but not well represented in the West End, so the circuits are naturally complementary – put them together and you have a full chain. Secondly, the combination of Cannon and EMI gives us potential to compete with the US majors – on its own EMI couldn't do it. Cannon is not far from it, but together we definitely have the potential; we will be a major company. Thirdly, we need a studio. Fourthly, we are very keen on EMI's library – it is a terrific asset which Cannon can use in a way that nobody before ever has. We will take on all the commitments of EMI – the bad as well as the good. Of course we will try to make the bad ones better. We will not break any agreements and we will try to keep good faith. If we do have to extricate ourselves from some commitment, we would do so in a professional manner. A big plus is attracting Gerald Ronson to the film industry, since what we all suffer from is financial power. Here comes Gerald Ronson giving us *carte blanche* and cash. We are not just talking about £110m. We are talking about fulfilling the financial requirements of the day-to-day running, plus forward commitments. To do that you need a fortune and you need good management and between us we meet both requirements.' To anyone who knew of their Antilles deal, Golan's next statement would lose its altruism:

'Since we came to England we have invested over £50m in this country. The company is profitable but we have not taken one pound out of England because we are committed to grow here, and every bit of profit made goes back in here to make something we are proud of. We are already proud of what we have done. Ask anyone in our company – ask any usherette – and you will find a pride in our achievement that you will find nowhere else in this industry. As well as money we have what EMI needs. No-one else can offer that.' And EMI had what they needed – the ABC cinemas!

Peter Noble in *Screen International*, while not regarding the takeover as a *fait accompli*, went on record to state: 'Whatever the outcome of the Thorn EMI takeover saga, with Cannon and Heron in there with a chance, I am reminded that some three or so years ago I answered the carping critics of Menahem Golan and Yoram Globus, industry folk who seemed to do nothing but predict disaster for the two bustling Israelis. In my column I said "Given the incredible track record of Cannon, my prediction is that by 1986 Menahem and Yoram will confound their critics and rule the world." Gentlemen, I rest my case.'

Michael Winner went to Cannon's defence in a letter to the London *Evening Standard* which was headed, 'Cannon – just the shot our cinema needs' – well, the company had certainly proved a shot in the arm for him. His letter ran: '"The Israelis are coming!" scream David Puttnam and others (they're American, actually) at the spectre of alien hordes of Visigoths decimating the resplendent British film industry. What a joke! If ever we need a shot in the arm from people who have been substantial friends in the past, it is now. Our only two substantial sources of production, Goldcrest and EMI, have wobbled to a halt (a tribute to British Film Year?) and EMI have been spending most of its production money abroad anyway – throwing up *Morons from Outer Space* for its British fans. By contrast shares in Cannon which were going for $1 in 1981 have zoomed to $30 this year. Experienced Cannon watchers have seen them spend vast amounts on UK productions in recent years, probably more than EMI. In particular, they have understood that you need a base of popular films for an outgoing industry, topped by more daring artistic ventures.' Winner did not go on to name either the popular films which Cannon had produced in Britain, nor their more daring artistic ventures. He continued, 'I can think of few companies that would risk backing films by Jean Luc Godard, Robert Altman, Lina Wertmuller, Franco Zeffirelli and John Cassavettes. Cannon had eight films in the London Film Festival – vandals? I have worked for both companies and looking at the list of bidders for EMI one would have to be carrying patriotism to madness-extremes to believe that any group has the track-record of Golan/Globus/Ronson. Never mind the funny names, David Puttnam, they've got the drive and success in management we sorely need over here!' Cannon reprinted this letter in a full-page of *Screen International* and added a further six pages to trumpet their achievements in Britain to date.

A week later Gary Dartnall and his team emerged victorious in the bid battle. When informed that Cannon had been shut out, Golan defiantly retorted, 'I was worried about aspects of the deal anyway!' before adding prophetically, 'And I don't think this is the end of the story, either!'

Another of the criticisms levelled at Cannon was that it had not contributed to the National Film School nor the Film Financing Consortium set up following the demise of the National Film Finance Corporation. Despite Golan's blustering he obviously felt that there were fences to be mended and one of his first moves was to ask David Puttnam, who had described the potential Cannon deal as 'disastrous', to a working breakfast with him to try to mend fences, after which Golan stated, 'At least he now agrees that we are committed to cinemas in Britain and not here to rip off the industry.' Puttnam declined to comment. Coincidently, when British Film Year was wound up in February, the organisers stated that unlike the other chains, Cannon had contributed nothing to the cost of their road show, while taking full advantage of their facilities. A rip-off? 'We were *royally* ripped off by them,' they stated unequivocally.

Rip-offs seem to be the flavour of the month for Cannon at this time. They had asked Emir Kusturica, the young Yugoslav director of *When Father Was Away on Business* to come to the US as their guest to promote his Cannes Golden-Palm-winning movie, which they had picked up for domestic distribution. On his return to Yugoslavia he was asked what he thought of the company that had sponsored his trip and replied, 'It's a rubbish company capable of telling me, on the last day of my stay in New York as their guest, that I must pay for my meals!'

In January and February, prior to the announcement of a new securities offering, Golan stated that by his calculation Cannon had grabbed 20% of the total box-office gross in the US during the last quarter of 1985. In fact the figure was closer to 7% for this period, which represented a considerable increase nevertheless on the first nine months of the year, for Cannon's per month share of the market looked like this:

JANUARY	2.730%	JULY	3.022%
FEBRUARY	0.063%	AUGUST	0.000%
MARCH	3.818%	SEPTEMBER	4.476%
APRIL	0.026%	OCTOBER	7.427%
MAY	4.150%	NOVEMBER	8.585%
JUNE	0.020%	DECEMBER	6.855%

The market-place showing of each distribution company for 1985 would later reveal that the top nine companies took 92% of the total box-office gross, with the rest – including Cannon – sharing the last 8% between them:

1)	WARNER BROTHERS	18%	5)	COLUMBIA	10%
2)	UNIVERSAL	16%	6)	PARAMOUNT	10%
3)	FOX	11%	7)	MGM/UA	9%
4)	TRI-STAR	10%	8)	ORION	5%
			9)	DISNEY	3%

In a review of the 166 films released in the USA in 1985, which had produced a yield in rentals of $1m or over, Cannon had nine films listed, of which they themselves had released seven:

Film	Net Rentals	Chart Placing
Invasion USA	$6,923,802	(At No. 55)
Death Wish III	$6,446,675	(At No. 57)
King Solomon's Mines	$6,000,000	(At No. 63)
Lifeforce (through Tri-Star)	$5,000,000	(At No. 78)
Missing in Action II	$4,217,312	(At No. 93)
American Ninja	$3,875,675	(At No. 100)
Company of Wolves	$2,350,225	(At No. 128)
Electric Boogaloo (through Tri-Star) (continuing from 1984)	$2,200,000	(At No. 131)
Rappin'	$1,247,495	(At No. 156)

As a perspective, Universal's *Back to the Future* was champion at No. 1 with $94m, about three times as much as *all* of Cannon's entries put together. Even Cannon's most 'successful' film *Invasion USA* was lowly No. 55 on the list. The nagging question persisted – did their pictures make money for people or did they not? In fact – did they make money for Cannon? Apart from two hits in long-ago 1984 – *Breakin'* and *Missing in Action*, Golan had yet to add to his paydirt with any film in the biggest market in the world.

In January 1986, the *New York Times* turned its attention to the Cannon story. One Wall Street analyst, Dennis I. Forst of Seidler Arndec Securities in Los Angeles, was quoted as saying, 'As well as they're doing, they are getting a little cocky. Their cost of productions has gone up, the leverage of the balance sheets has gone up and their overhead has gone up – so it is a different company than it used to be.' Just when Cannon was reaching for respectability, the *Times* noted that Cannon stock was currently caught in a fierce controversy over accounting practices, clarifying that, 'Estimates of future revenues play a big role in accounting in the movie business and some critics charge that Cannon has been too optimistic. The controversy has led to harsh exchanges, questioning the motives of both those who praise and those who denigrate the stock. Many of the critics are short sellers of Cannon stock, who stand to benefit from alarm over the company's prospects.' Golan angrily began to blame a San Francisco investment house for every piece of adverse financial publicity that came their way.

One banker was quoted as saying, 'I know enough about them to know that I don't want to deal with them,' citing their reputation as negotiators. A major studio executive chipped in: 'They are impossible to do business with.' They still had their supporters, and Joseph De Lillo of Wake Capital Securities, a Los Angeles brokerage firm, rushed to their defence: 'They tell it like it is, and a lot of people feel insulted by that.' Expansion, the *Times* noted, had strained Cannon's balance sheet, and pointed out that long-term debt and obligations had soared, as had the overall ratio of debt to equity; per the *Times*, to 3.6–1 from 2.8–1, producing concern at Cannon and prompting them to offer inducements to convert debt into equities in an effort to shore up the balance sheet. According to Lee Isgur, the ever-optimistic Paine Webber analyst, Cannon would soon be generating enough cash to reduce their debt or make further acquisitions. Their estimate of eighteen releases in 1986 meant that there could be at least one big hit, the *Times* continued, quoting Isgur, 'They are going to come to bat eighteen times and if they just hit one double or triple, wow! With only 6.5m shares on the market that would have a big impact.' Some analysts still felt that a Cannon face-lift could come expensive, reckoning that as Cannon matured it would lose its 'financial magic touch', for already it was far too highly leveraged. The irony lay in the fact that Cannon's potentially better-quality films could turn out to be less profitable, or indeed big-budget losers.

Isgur seemed to have spent little time pondering either the likelihood of a smash-hit from Cannon's eighteen entries (his computer would be no help here) or the astronomical costs to Cannon of the total marketing expense to cover eighteen releases – and the consequences of failure. Even in movies there is such a thing as batting average.

In mid-February 1986 Cannon announced that they had filed registration statements with the Securities and Exchange Commission (SEC) for a $100m securities offering, up from the last-mooted $50m, still less than the original $200m Golan first suggested, broken down as $75m senior subordinated debentures and $25m in convertible subordinated debentures, both of them with a repayment date of March 15th, 2001. The announcement went on to state that the net proceeds from the proposed sale would be used for the repayment of bank indebtedness and for general corporate purposes including production, distribution and exhibition of Cannon motion pictures and cinemas.

While the *New York Times* article had indicated that *long-term debt* and obligations stood at $72.5m at the end of September 1985, an 8k filing on December 2nd, 1985 in fact revealed that *total debts* for the company stood at $216,713,000, up from $180,000,000 at September 30th, 1985; also that the company had already drawn $31m from the revolving line of credit with the First National Bank of Boston that totalled $65m. Cannon's last securities offering in October 1984 of $70m had been handled by Furman Selz Mager Dietz and Birnie Inc, together with E. F. Hutton. The new $100m offering was being handled by junk bond specialists Drexel Burnham Lambert, with only a commission paid to Roy Furman – but not this time by E. F. Hutton, who perhaps felt that they had gone as far down the line with Cannon as they cared to by this time. Hutton had also advised a 'sell' on Cannon's shares while Globus was at Mifed.

To coincide with the offering, a series of announcements on Cannon's future projects was made, combined with an aggressive summary of where they now stood in relation to the majors in the industry. Menahem Golan had claimed since 1982 that Cannon had been turning out more pictures than any other major and articles on Cannon had constantly picked this up and repeated it as if it were solid fact, which must have been gratifying indeed for Menaham and Yoram, and proved the old adage that if you repeat something often enough it will be believed. Year-on-year statistics, however, told a different story, as listings were now produced not only of the ranking of each studio, together with the number of releases, but with the actual box-office gross of each studio revealed:

Ranking	Studio	No. of Releases	Box-office Gross
1)	WARNER BROTHERS	22	$540,000,000
2)	UNIVERSAL	14	$479,100,000
3)	PARAMOUNT	13	$410,300,000
4)	20TH CENTURY FOX	17	$309,600,000
5)	COLUMBIA	16	$305,600,000
6)	TRI-STAR	11	$279,400,000
7)	MGM/UA	13	$240,400,000
8)	ORION	12	$198,600,000
9)	BUENA VISTA /TOUCHSTONE	9	$111,000,000
10)	CANNON	7	$ 76,600,000

If Cannon had been producing more films than any major, then they must have accumulated a vaultful of unreleased pictures. Certainly, on top of the seven pictures registered here, they had *Grace Quigley*, *The Naked Face*, *Ordeal by Innocence*, *War and Love*, and *When Father Was Away on Business*, but these obtained such a limited, regional release that they were almost impossible to track and in any case other studios listed also had these regional releases, so what we had on the chart was a comparison of like with like. For that matter, *When Father Was Away on Business* and *War and Love* were pick-ups that Cannon had not actually produced, but had merely acquired for domestic distribution. The question therefore was still begged – where were the missing Cannon films? Or were we down to the risible *Hot Resort* type of nonsense which only got a handful of bookings in total? With Golan's dynamic mixture of showmanship and bombast he had made Cannon *sound* like a major. Cannon appeared to have made all the running while the rest of the studios were just lying back, passing on deals, putting pictures into turnaround and delaying decisions. The reality was that at the same time Warner Bros had taken $540m at the box office to Cannon's $76m, while Universal were beating them hollow with $479m. Paramount were raking in $410m, while Cannon ended up making a poor showing at No. 10 on the list – indeed the minor 'major'.

The proposed new securities offering lodged with the SEC for approval, coincided with the opening of the American Film Market

(AFM) in Los Angeles, and for this event Cannon would once again boast of a bigger and more star-studded line-up of future productions for sale than ever before. The list of proposed films was loudly proclaimed in *Variety* in a fifty-five page advertisement, whereas *The Delta Force* headed their fairly scant list of actual completed films – as opposed to future projects – to be touted at AFM. With *The Delta Force* were a mere four others – *Dumb Dicks* (ex-*Defective Detectives*), *America 3,000* (ex-*Thunder Warriors*), Lina Wertmuller's *Camorra* and Liliana Cavani's *The Berlin Affair*. Contrast these with the list of Cannon forthcoming attractions:

Sylvester Stallone headed the list in *Over the Top*, first announced in 1983. The picture was described as being about the sport of arm-wrestling and 'filial love', with a script by Stallone himself, so clearly it was a project that was close to his heart. Wags in the Hollywood rumour mill had it that Stallone was signing for $9m for the picture originally, then asked for it to be upped to $12m when he heard that Menahem Golan was to direct. Christopher Reeve would star in *Superman IV*, with no director yet set. John Travolta would appear in a project 'being specially developed for him' that was as yet untitled. Roy Scheider and Ann-Margret would appear in John Frankenheimer's *52 Pick Up* from the Elmore Leonard novel – (this is the one that is supposed to have been the basis for the movie, *The Ambassador*). Charles Bronson would next appear in J. Lee Thompson's *Murphy's Law*. Chuck Norris's next would be *Kick and Kick Back*. Diane Keaton would appear in Bill Forsyth's *Housekeeping*. Julie Andrews, Alan Bates and Max Von Sydow would appear in the film version of the Kempinski play *Duet for One*, to be directed by Andrei Konchalovsky, Faye Dunaway having dropped out of the project, first announced years earlier. Placido Domingo would star in Franco Zeffirelli's version of Verdi's *Otello*; Joseph Zito would helm *Spiderman*; Dolph Lundgren would appear in *Masters of the Universe*; Amy Irving and Trevor Howard were set for *Rumplestiltskin*; Christopher Reeve would also appear in Jerry Schatzberg's *Street Smart*. Next came 'An untitled Roman Polanski film'; Jean Luc Godard's *King Lear*; Michael Winner's *Captain America*; George Segal in *Who's in the Closet?* to be directed by Menahem Golan; Norman Mailer's *Tough Guys Don't Dance* to be written for the screen and directed by Mailer himself; *North/South*, a Francis Ford Coppola and George Lucas film to be directed by Godfrey Reggio; Louis Gossett Jr in *The White Slave*, an adaptation of Marek Hlasko's novel *The Second Killing of the Dog*; J. Lee Thompson's directorial version of the Jules Verne novel, *Journey to the Centre of the Earth*; Robert Carradine in Jack Smight's *Number One with a Bullet*; *Second Life* to be directed by Maximilian Schell; *Too Much* to be written and directed by Eric Rochat; a Tobe Hooper film, *The Texas Chainsaw Massacre II*; John Stockwell in *Choice Kill*; Peter Boyle in *Citizen Joe*; Bud Spencer in *Aladdin*; *It Ate Cleveland* in Monstervision; *The Assault* to be directed by Fons Rademakers; Michael Bat-Adam in *The Lover*; Hans Scheepsmaker's *Field of Honour*; Luca Bercovici's *Rockula*; Richard Chamberlain and Sharon Stone in the *King Solomon's Mines* sequel, *Allan Quatermain and the Lost City of Gold*, directed by Gary Nelson; Sam Firstenberg's *American Ninja II*; Tobe Hooper's *Invaders from Mars* starring Karen Black and Timothy Bottoms; Raoul Ruiz's version of *Treasure Island*; Mickey Rooney and Susan George in *The White Stallion*; *The Barbarians* to be directed by Sijan; Shari Shattuck in *The Naked Cage*; David Carradine in *Behind Enemy Lines*; and Bud Spencer in *Ben Bonzo and Big Bad Joe*, to be written by Menahem Golan. The total number of productions listed came to a mind-numbing fifty-two – if all the projects came to fruition, even over a two-year period, it would mean a Cannon film unleashed on the world every two weeks – although a glance at some of the titles and prospects seems to indicate that the world can relax for a while longer.

Chapter Seven
FAIRY TALES ALREADY

The Delta Force, as directed by Menahem Golan personally, opened on February 14th, 1986 to almost universally bad reviews, *Variety* reckoning, however, that it would 'Hi-jack quick box office and rack up some hefty numbers for Cannon in quick, wide release' – before the rotten word-of-mouth got out. It was noted that Golan's direction was 'crudely efficient' as the film went into its blanket release at 1,720 cinemas across America. One reviewer described it as 'mindless junk' and condemned its blatantly racist (ie anti-Arab) slant. On TV, critic David Sheehan agreed with this comment and put the following on record on his own behalf: 'This is an exploitation movie in the very worse sense of the term. Brainlessly concocted to inspire vengeful hatred towards Arab and Palestinians with a very manipulative restaging of the TWA hi-jacking of last June, *The Delta Force* is such a flagrant attempt to celebrate irrational racial hostility, I think you are bound to be at least slightly sickened by it no matter what your political or ethnic sympathies may be. In fact one encouraging thing is that the paying audience I saw it with groaned and moaned a whole lot more than they cheered. I think that because it is so crude and cartoony maybe it won't have that much effect.' It was ironic indeed that Golan himself was now being indirectly accused of racism after applying the allegation, somewhat misguidedly, to his British Film Industry critics.

Still the duo had high hopes: could this be their first $100m blockbuster? In short order the answer was an unequivocal 'No'. People outside the business, including some very gauche reporters, seem to think that anything that grosses a few million dollars is minting money. Phrases like 'it took $6m in its first three days' sound sensational and naturally distributors push these figures for all their worth. The point is that many films are finished and taken off a few weeks later, having been hyped to obtain quotable opening figures by dint of mass openings, combined – as was the case with *The Delta Force* – with saturation TV and press ads. Spending $5–6m on a saturation launch to achieve opening weekend figures of $6m and an eventual $17.7m take (net return to distributor: $6.9m), can hardly constitute brilliant economics, but this in fact is what happened to *The Delta Force*. Never mind that those first three days represented more than one third of the eventual *total* US take! What happens after the big opening? TV ads are dropped, press ads shrink in size (they're both far too expensive to maintain after the opening) and it's all down to the public's word-of-mouth. If this is good, a film can develop legs, ie, it can stand on its own two feet without the need for further hype. If, however, the word is not good, the film quickly dies and can be taken off its theatrical run for ever in very short order. This in fact was becoming the typical Cannon pattern, as a glance of what happened to their product in the market-place in 1985 will substantiate – any money Cannon made was quick money, with 92–100% of total takings achieved within a maximum seven-week period:

Film	Box-office Gross	Number of Weeks in Release	% of Total Take achieved in first 5 weeks release
Invasion USA	$17.5m	6	92.3
Death Wish III	$16.1m	7	95.7
Missing in Action II	$10.8m	5	100.0
Company of Wolves	$ 4.4m	3	100.0
Rappin'	$ 2.9m	2	100.0

On the other hand, here are the same year's 'leggy' films from other studios:

Film	Box-office Gross	Number of Weeks in Release	% of Total Take achieved in first 5 weeks release
Beverly Hills Cop (PARAMOUNT)	$229.9m	33	43.1
Cocoon (20TH CENTURY FOX)	$ 75.9m	16	61.4
Witness (PARAMOUNT)	$ 65.6m	20	48.2
Desperately Seeking Susan (ORION)	$ 27.3m	19	51.6
Passage to India (COLUMBIA)	$ 27.2	15	48.9
The Emerald Forest (EMBASSY)	$ 24.5m	15	71.4

This was the kind of money achieved through good word-of-mouth and repeat business, and that naturally was the kind of result that Cannon aspired to along with everyone else. However, Cannon's films simply did not lend themselves to this kind of result, not since 1984 and *Breakin'* ($38m gross through MGM release) and the original *Missing in Action* ($38m gross through Cannon release), and these were still fast-buck pictures that had distinct upper limits. Since then no title released by Cannon had even broken the $20m barrier and perhaps, since the typical Cannon film had Menahem Golan's personal stamp all over it, this was hardly surprising. The pity of it continued to be that when something with quality, albeit flawed, emerged like *Runaway Train* it seemed that the *schlock*-oriented Cannon distribution team simply did not know how to handle it. It was here that the much-vaunted selling machine, so famous for their presales campaigns, seized up, for *Runaway Train* ran out of steam after just a few weeks with a desperate $3m in domestic rentals against a $9m budget. Why? Had *Variety* been mistaken in its estimation of the picture? In a way – yes. Although it was indeed a quality movie, the truth is that it never stood much chance at the box office. In a sense it was even unfair to blame Cannon's marketing, although possibly that could have helped it gain better results. The main flaw, however, lay in the picture itself, for heavy-handed allegorical symbolism has never been known to go down big at the box office and Konchalovsky himself would say of the picture, 'It can be Nietzsche, and it can be Shakespeare as well. And it can be Zen. It's just the moment when evil and good are intermingled. And when you put it upside down, it can be Dostoevsky as well!' Some would say with this that he had tried to be far too clever and ended up making a film that was too mixed in style, as *Maria's Lovers* had been before it, to have wide commercial appeal.

'For everyone in the audience who listens, he has his own feelings and images which bring him to a special emotional state,' Konchalovsky continued. 'The symbol should never just have one meaning, because if you are going to build the whole story around it, you can't use it more than once.' Well, maybe, but other things wrong with *Runaway Train* could be listed as Jon Voight's occasionally admirable, but otherwise declamatory and over-the-top performance, the action being constantly interrupted so that he can make an Academy Award nomination-type speech, and Eric Roberts's totally ridiculous and out-of-sight performance, devoid of all subtlety. The occasional use of blatantly inappropriate disco-beat background music and the frequent reminders of Cannon budget restrictions did not help either. (Typically: the faked prison long-shot and the non-collapsing bridge.) Konchalovsky, proving that often those closest to projects are not necessarily the best judges, declared himself 'very happy with the picture' – too close to it to pick out the lapses of tension and outright implausibilities, something the old-time moguls would have noticed for him and put right – but not Golan! Even with these reservations, *Runaway Train* remains Cannon's best movie since their inception in 1979.

When BBC-TV's 'Omnibus' ran an extended Cannon commercial in May 1986 in Britain the only figure they quoted was *The Delta Force*'s first weekend take of $6m. The fact that the following week saw a 42% drop, followed by a further 42% drop in the third week, then a 36% drop in the fourth week, was never mentioned. Nor was the deficit in business terms of the US box-office figure of $17,768,000 achieved by *Delta* discussed, equivalent as it was to net domestic rentals of $6.9m before distribution costs were deducted, against a budget of $9m plus saturation release costs of an estimated $6m. This spelled out bad business for Cannon – and poor reporting by the BBC.

The position now was that their last six big-budget movies had all failed either relatively or completely in the main market in the world, namely the US/Canadian domestic theatrical market, as can be seen below:

Film	Negative Cost	Domestic Net Rentals
Lifeforce	$ 22,500,000	$ 5,000,000
Invasion USA	$ 13,000,000	$ 6,923,802
Death Wish III	$ 9,000,000	$ 6,446,675
King Solomon's Mines	$ 11,000,000	$ 6,000,000
The Delta Force	$ 9,000,000	$ 5,600,000
Runaway Train	$ 9,000,000	$ 3,000,000
	$ 73,500,000	$32,970,477
+ total ad/print costs	$ 29,000,000	
	$102,500,000	

This comes to a staggering $69,529,523 deficit in the US market in one year and that is without Cannon charging themselves any distribution cost – normally distributors charge 30% on domestic net rentals returns and if this is applied here the deficit grows to a colossal $80,519,682. Okay, we know all about cable and video and foreign, and this would have chipped in a fair bit – but $80m or even \$69m? If that had been achieved it certainly was a good trick making 28% of the world market (with the US/Canadian market being reckoned at 72%) not only pay for this staggering deficit but also turn a profit for Cannon as well.

Cannon's box-office share for January 1986 stood at 1.8% and 6.3% for February whereas pictures with legs in 1986, far outgrossing Cannon product, were:

Film	Distributor	Box-office Gross	No. of days released	As at
The Color Purple	WARNER BROTHERS	\$73,631,931	89	Mid March
Out of Africa	UNIVERSAL	\$69,670,271	87	Mid March
Jewel of the Nile	20TH CENTURY FOX	\$59,525,716	61	Feb 12th
Spies like Us	WARNER BROTHERS	\$56,522,595	59	Feb 12th
Down and Out in Beverly Hills	BUENA VISTA/ TOUCHSTONE	\$43,404,701	45	Mid March
White Nights	COLUMBIA	\$39,186,398	52	Jan 29th

Despite their shattering disappointment with *The Delta Force*, it simply had to be onward and upward for Cannon in terms of new projects and just in case anyone thought they were slacking, they announced a further undertaking prior to the AFM opening. In addition to Amy Irving in *Rumplestiltskin* there was now to be no less than an additional eleven feature-length films to be made based on classic children's fairytales, all of the films to be produced by Patti Ruben. When she was interviewed about the undertaking Miss Ruben had this to say: 'The Menahem that I know is a person who gives you tremendous chances. I have worked for the company casting and I've had different jobs and I walked into him and I said, "Look, I really want a challenge. Give me something interesting." He said, "Well, about three years ago I had this idea I'd like to do some fairytales, and I have the whole world and we can do all kinds of things. Would you like to do that?" I said, "What?" He said, "Would you like to go and produce these?" and I said, "Well, sure."

We went to Czechoslovakia, we went to Italy, we went to Switzerland and Spain and finally Menahem called me up and said "Okay, we are doing it in Israel."'

Still Miss Ruben looked on the positive side as she declared: 'I have sets here I could never have got in Budapest. I have total control and people work harder and stronger, more vigorously – these are the Israelis and I have never seen performances like theirs in my life.'

Golan stated at the opening of AFM: 'It is the most important market for us now for overseas placements. It used to be from Cannes to Cannes but starting with the Los Angeles market in 1986, our yearly programme will now be for AFM to AFM.' He declined to state how many of their announced productions would actually shoot during 1986, preferring to side-step this issue, but pointed out that they had placed twenty-two pictures into production in 1985, trotting out yet again the weary 'more than any of the majors'. He recalled that their first stand at the market had been in 1980, where they had been an unwelcome participant as they had refused to join the club at the Westwood Marquis. Golan also took the opportunity to let it be known that the new Cannon Headquarters in Los Angeles would be opened during AFM and that Tom Bradley, mayor of Los Angeles, would open the festivities at a black-tie gala to mark the occasion. More than 2,000 guests attended the event held inside Cannon's new car park – while in the street outside American-Arab anti-discrimination protestors held a candlelight vigil to demonstrate against the *The Delta Force*. Prominent guests at the party were Credit Lyonnais's Frans Afman, Bank of America's Peter Geiger and Lewis Horwitz, a Cannon director and private lender. It was piquantly noted after a perusal of the guest list that lenders came in handy for Cannon – they certainly did! Although Cannon probably thought the world of the new car parks and saw them as the height of opulence, a string of hapless guests were obliged to park their own cars in neighbouring streets without even the benefit of a valet parking service, while the food was, at best, basic and the white wine ran out early in the proceedings. Tom Bradley's speech was a fawning tribute to Golan and Globus which sounded as if it came straight from a Cannon handout. The heads of Cannon wore fixed grins as their achievements were recited to a crowd who looked decidedly cynical.

During the party Golan sounded off about how little he paid himself. 'I get $350,000 a year and not a penny more when I direct,' he boasted. It was in fact clearly stated in the original E. F. Hutton security offering prospectus, under the heading of Golan/Globus agreements, that as of July 1st 1983, the company had entered into employment agreements for terms expiring December 1st 1988 with Mr Golan and Mr Globus on identical terms, *except* that Mr Golan's agreement also provided terms governing his services as a motion-picture director.

'Anywhere else,' Golan claimed, 'I would command $700,000 to $1,500,000.'

When it was pointed out to him that with his bonuses, stock and interest-free advances from the company, he was in fact fully in the league with the majors' moguls whose lifestyle he so detested, Golan protested it was all a matter of accounting. 'I have not withdrawn any money from Cannon over and above my salary,' he claimed, 'even though these additional funds are in my name, it's all working capital for the company.'

One journalist got short shrift when she asked if it was true that both Golan and Globus had purchased corner apartments at Trump Towers in New York, hardly the most modest of pieds-à-terre. A telephone call to the Towers asking for Golan and Globus's telephone numbers there had apparently elicited a 'We do not put out that information' response.

Despite Cannon's claims to have 'bought' their new headquarters, the 72,000 square-foot building, for which they 'paid' $15m had been secured with a down payment of $1m, with the balance financed through the American Savings and Loan Association over fifteen years, with an original interest rate of 11.375%, adjusted semi-annually. It was estimated that a further $3.75m would need to be spent on interior completions.

Golan angrily denied that Cannon still had a reputation for slow payment, and not just with tradesman but with creative artists also. He was supported here by Robert Altman, who seemed to have joined the ranks of the Cannon followers after his *Fool for Love* experience. Always the maverick – and producer of a series of commercially disastrous but artistically valid movies after *Mash* – Altman noted that the love-and-sex saga of Sam Shepard's *Fool for Love* had been rejected by fifteen studios and production companies before Cannon had offered to develop the project – a recurring Cannon theme. Shepard's William Morris agent had counselled against the deal, but both he and Altman had found no fault with Cannon, describing the experience as purely positive, with no artistic interference and all salaries arriving on the button. Altman recalled, 'We would not have gone to them, because of everyone saying how terrible they were, not paying their bills, interfering and so on – everything that can be said has been said about them. Sam had a lot of scepticism, and he still gets told these stories all the time, but so far these Cannon people are the only ones who have shown any respect to us as artists or businessmen.'

Cannon's campaign to gain respectability took a giant step forward with the announcement that they had been invited to show three films in competition at the 1986 Cannes Film Festival – Konchalovsky's *Runaway Train*, Robert Altman's *Fool for Love* and Franco Zeffirelli's *Otello*. Had Gilles Jacob come up trumps at last? Menahem and Yoram were delighted, for this was no small honour and the Cannon publicity machine had a field day with the news. Golan's succession of snubs at Cannes – from being dropped from the jury to having Konchalovsky's earlier *Maria's Lovers* rejected in the official competition – looked as if they were going to be handsomely compensated for, as from three entries a prize seemed almost inevitable. Zeffirelli was rushing to get *Otello* finished in time and declared that he wanted to give Golan and Globus the best possible picture as a reward for their $11m investment. He also joined Altman in his praise of the Cannon duo: 'I'm not an opinionated man, except when it comes down to politics or sport. In work I'm a real whore – I'm like the bankers of the Renaissance who went to the Court of the King of Spain and the Court of the King of Naples, without absolutely questioning what their political ideas were, only concerned with finding someone who'd give them the money and the means to work and to become famous. So this is my attitude. The ways of the Lord are infinite and should not be questioned. Any money, if you really insist, is not necessarily clean, especially in movies. You don't know where it comes from. Let me not mention producers that I know, the money is not clean. Cannon are very clean people – they're special – Menahem and Globus are two surprises. There is no-one like them nowadays in the world.'

Statistics were released covering all US independent production outlets which showed that of total foreign and ancillary sales during 1984, foreign theatrical had accounted for 52% of the total revenue, home video 32% and TV (including cable TV) 16% – the indication was that for these independent companies the total of these revenues was already greater than the US domestic theatrical market.

Cannon announced that they had signed an exclusive seven-year deal with Chuck Norris, of the recently-released *Delta Force* and Cannon's last hit, the 1984 *Missing in Action*. Menahem Golan stated that Cannon's relationship with Chuck Norris has been extremely rewarding, from both a professional and financial standpoint. The indomitable Chuck, blown up to heroic proportions by his stone-faced demeanour and wooden acting in a succession of nasty action dramas before and during Cannon, pontificated on the nature of violence in the world today when interviewed on the subject. He earnestly explained, with a kind of open-faced, boss-minded sincerity: 'The whole thing is that movies are entertainment, but there are two types of violence on the screen that the liberals just don't understand. You have negative violence which provokes violence on the screen and that kind is bad. When a person is retaliating against violence – which I think you would do on the street if you were attacked – I think that is good. You cannot hide your head in the sand and say there is no violence out there. The key point is how do you deal with violence, that's what's important. That's what we try to demonstrate on the screen – not in a negative way but in a positive way and that is not detrimental to our youth in America.' Just in case anyone missed the point, Chuck the hero – obviously confusing his real-life self with his role in the junk he appeared in, added, 'I started at the very bottom and I've reached this level of success. How many countries do you have that opportunity in? So – God bless America as far as I'm concerned.' And God bless you too, Chuck, a spokesman for the redneck community if ever there was one.

Cannon proudly announced that it had captured Dustin Hoffman for Elmore Leonard's *La Brava*, due to shoot in August in Miami. Hoffman had been brought to Cannon by the Mirisch brothers, who would produce the package. Hal Ashby had been signed to direct the movie after his contretemps with PSO on the

Jeff Bridges picture, *8 Million Ways to Die*. (He had filed suit against PSO alleging they had 'caused him to be fired'.)

And still the signings continued. Michael Caine would star in *Surrender*. Cannon had plans to produce two films based on major plays, featuring the stars who had originated the roles. Anthony Quinn would play the title role in *Zorba*, based on the Broadway musical. Principal photography was scheduled for October 1986, for producer Barrie and Fran Weissler, who had produced the stage show. There was also a two-picture deal with Al Pacino, the first due to emerge being *Investigation*, based on the 1970 Italian movie *Investigation of a Citizen Above Suspicion*. Paul Schrader was set to write *Investigation*, Andrei Konchalovsky to direct. Following this Pacino would recreate his Broadway performance in David Mamet's *American Buffalo*.

On March 6th the group disclosed peak earnings for the full fiscal year 1985, together with an announcement that its stock, currently traded over the counter, would be listed on the New York stock exchange from March 18th. Reported profit for the year was $16.6m on revenues of $150.8m, up from $12.4m on $108.7m in 1984. In an analysis of these revenues, film distribution had risen by 30% to $113.2m from $86.8m in 1984 and the income from cinema operations was up 72% to $37.5m from $21.8m a year earlier. Now came the figure that everyone was waiting to see, and on which everyone placed widely differing interpretations – amortisation of film costs for the year stood at $64.8m, representing 57% of distribution revenue – the value Cannon attributed to unreleased product on which it was impossible to obtain a breakdown. Golan and Globus's personal shareholding climbed to $80m.

A trifling annoyance came Cannon's way in the form of a $3m suit against them from plaintiff Glen Hartford, the owner of the picture *Hell Squad*. Hartford had bought the rights from his father Ken Hartford, president of Cinevid Inc. Hartford alleged that Cannon had violated the distribution arrangement with Cinevid by selling the picture to home video without ever having attempted to release the film theatrically. He claimed that per the agreement between Cannon and Cinevid, Cannon had guaranteed that it would release the movie with at least seventy-five prints, supported by a minimum of $100,000 for promotion. Cannon had also guaranteed to debut *Hell Squad* in at least ten cities, including

New York, Los Angeles and Chicago. Cannon also had stated, per the August 1983 agreement, that it would release the picture through MGM, which it had not done – instead the film had been put out on an MGM home video without the benefit of a theatrical window. Another victim of the MGM fall-out!

Variety reviewed Cannon's new release *The Naked Cage*, starring Shari Shattuck, summing it up as 'a dumb exploitation film'. Cannon opened this optimistically nevertheless with 420 prints and collected a dismal $897,589. After a few weeks it ended its brief run with a pitiful $3m at the box office, netting down to $1.2m for Cannon.

Cannon-France claimed four releases, and four successes, after just a few months of operations. Jean Luc Defait was jubilant over the performances of *Invasion USA*, *American Ninja*, *King Solomon's Mines* and *Death Wish III*. He claimed that *Mines* and *Death Wish III* had cornered 20% of the market, *Mines* alone drawing 500,000 admissions nationally in two weeks with 120 prints in circulation. He noted that the films had done more than 65% of their total business in the provinces where Cannon had concentrated a good part of the promotional effort and noted, 'When you don't have a Stallone or a Belmondo, you have to look for your clients ouside Paris.' He added that he was particularly proud of having successfully marketed *American Ninja* in mid-season and with what he termed an 'adequate' advertising budget. Was Jean Luc Defaut's jubilation entirely justified? Dredging up the Paris figures for his four releases, starting with the first to go, we find that with *Invasion USA*, *Variety* had termed its opening figure of $343,000 'Fair' – in the same week *Prizzi's Honour* opened with $468,000. For only one more week would *Invasion USA* appear on the top ten chart, having slumped to $159,200 while *Prizzi's Honour* held at $361,000. In its fourth week *Prizzi's Honour* was still taking $157,000, with *Invasion USA* but a fond memory. By this time *American Ninja* opened with an 'okay' $297,500 – again, one more week in the chart and it was out. *King Solomon's Mines* relatively did the best of the bunch, although during its opening week *Variety* headlined '13 Paris Bows out of luck', noting that *King Solomon's Mines* had led 'the dreary session'. In its second week it dropped to $282,000 then to $150,000, bowing out with $83,000. Now *Death Wish III* debuted, with $387,000, in a week during which *Variety* stated that there was no warmth for film exhibition. In its second week it dropped immediately to $184,000 and then disappeared. Jean Luc Defait's modest expectations of success were highlighted properly when some real successes did arrive on the scene in Paris, *Highlander* opening with $1,324,000 and *Out of Africa* with $858,000, before going on to feature for no less than ten consecutive weeks. Of the four releases only *King Solomon's Mines* could really claim to have made a reasonable impact. Defait averred that one of the advantages of working with Cannon was that distribution calendar and print delivery were set long in advance, enabling them to plan marketing and booking strategies well ahead. Cannon-France was to continue its co-distribution arrangement with major UGC, where Defait had been an executive before joining Cannon. Defait and his sales manager, Burt Mousart, handled the marketing for France's twenty largest cities, while UGC looked after the smaller towns and guaranteed physical distribution. Defait stated that Cannon was expecting to move into production by 1987 and had created a script division, headed by his wife, Line Defait, employing twelve readers to screen manuscripts. 'Since Menahem Golan and Yoram Globus were interviewed on TV here last December we have received over 500 scripts to date,' he declared but added rather sadly, 'Of over 200 we have read only one so far is feasible.' Oh, well, Jean Luc, you can't win them all! He continued, 'We plan to produce or co-produce two to five films annually. We want to work in the same eclectic spirit that has done so well for Cannon Inc, producing more personal efforts alongside bigger commercial productions. One I have in mind is about France's underground rock music culture, which Andrei Konchalovsky is keen on doing.' This sounded like a sequel to Golan's *The Apple*. Defait also stated that a new bureau would start up in May, to be known as Cannon services. They would rent out fully-equipped production and post production offices and facilities, Defait noting that 'This will fill a need and also provide Cannon with the necessary facilities when we find our own cruising speed as a producer.'

Back in the US Cannon's next release was *POW, the Escape* (ex-*Behind the Enemy Lines*), which was destined for an even quicker demise than *The Naked Cage* had experienced. It opened at 476 theatres and took a paltry $1,100,691, then promptly dropped by 52% in its second week. It ended up one week later with a rock-bottom finale of $39,384 at eighteen cinemas and a total box-office gross of $2,162,866, and a net $860,000 to Cannon. Meantime Cannon had rushed out their new Charles Bronson/J. Lee Thompson Cannon-custody-from-Hemdale picture *Murphy's Law*. It opened wide at 1,260 cinemas and did a poor $3,388,907 opening weekend. The second week's decline was 37%, then 51% in its third week. Had it been worth going to court for? In a review of the film, *Variety* had asserted that the 'nasty smeller for Bronson fans should score well in quick, wide release, but fall off quickly'. They had the beginning and the end right, but not the middle, since *Murphy's Law*'s tired opening returns were anything but a score. The US box office in April had taken a general nosedive, reversing the promising upward trend which had been evident earlier in the year. Dollar gross was the lowest in five years, with ticket sales the worst for fifteen years. *Murphy's Law* ended its run with a box office gross of $10m–$4m to Cannon in net rentals, just about enough to cover the costs of the saturation release campaign and no more. Was even the old demand for Cannon shoot-em-ups falling away?

Meanwhile trouble of a different kind was brewing for Cannon. In a terse statment Dustin Hoffman announced that he had terminated his contract with Cannon to appear in *La Brava*. He alleged breach of a clause which gave him personal approval of all uses of his likeness in promoting the film. Cannon had splashed Hoffman's picture over a full page *Hollywood Reporter* advertisement, welcoming Hoffman to Cannon's family. According to a dismayed Yoram Globus on April 1st, 'Hoffman still has a contract with us.' Rather touchingly he added, 'I think the world of Hoffman.' Hoffman was none-the-less furious over this breach of his rights and his Los Angeles-based attorney, Bert Field, denied Globus's assertion, stating that 'The contract was terminated personally by me by letter.' He confirmed the contention by Lee Gottsegen, the New York-based president of Hoffman's Punch Productions, that the actor had walked out on *La Brava* due to the contractual breach over the use of his likeness, adding, 'When someone doesn't give you the rights you bargain for at the outset, you wonder what will happen when you get into the arduous process of making the film.' He would not confirm Hoffman's reported $6.5m salary for the film, plus the apparent 22% profit participation Cannon had reportedly set for the actor.

Meantime a rattled Globus continued to insist, 'We are doing the picture with Hoffman – period. We are sitting now with Dustin's people in our office and we are working with his people.' When contacted in New York Gottsegen denied this outright, stating 'We have no idea what he is talking about.' Field added, 'There is no communication whatsoever. Neither I nor Michael Ovitz, Dustin's agent, are talking to Globus nor discussing a resolution of the ad problem. Dustin still likes the property, but he has terminated his contract with Cannon and we have not been seeking a new contract.' Menahem Golan later appeared on TV and stated that he was considering suing Hoffman. From the Hoffman camp came an on-camera reply giving them the address of the court room. 'We look forward to seeing Mr Golan in court,' the message ended.

Cannon began to close a deal with Warner Brothers in the UK to release certain Cannon films in that market, which many observers felt was further alarming evidence of acute finance shortage prior to the new securities launch. Obviously they would be precluded from preselling to themselves, and it appeared that for the sake of upfront money from Warners, Cannon were fully prepared to bypass their own local distributorship in the UK. While the titles that Warners were to handle were not announced, the implication was that they would be Cannon's prime product, if that is not a contradiction in terms.

Despite the plethora of announced deals and productions, only one solitary low-budget movie was started by Cannon in the entire first quarter of 1986, *Duet for One* with Julie Andrews, under the direction of Andrei Konchalovsky, which had started work in London in February. Speculation was rife that the delay in starting others was due to an acute cash crisis. The securities offering announced in February had in fact been under scrutiny by the Securities and Exchange Commission (SEC) for fully seven weeks, considered by many to be a long spell under review, starting further concern about the solidity of Cannon's underpinnings. When a planned offering is viewed by the SEC with some misgivings, this regulatory office can consider a referral to their investigative committee, a body with wide-ranging powers of authority. As the weeks stretched on while the Cannon offering was being considered, rumours reached fever pitch. Observers felt that Golan and Globus, almost certainly fully drawn on their bank borrowing limits with both Credit Lyonnais and the First National Bank of Boston, were very close to the brink. *The Delta Force* had taken less than a fifth of its hoped-for gross of $100m. *Runaway Train* had run out of steam with a meagre $3m in rentals. *POW, the Escape* and *The Naked Cage* were stillborn. *Murphy's Law* was headed for the fast fold that had become the norm for Cannon action fodder, and five of what Lee Isgur had referred to as Cannon's eighteen efforts at 'going to bat' in 1986 had already gone. No $100m gusher from *The Delta Force*, therefore, but when the long wait for clearance ended and they were given the go ahead by the SEC, a windfall of a different kind still came their way. Clearly they still had not used up all of their nine lives, as they went ahead with an offering of no less than $110m of subordinated debentures priced at 99.5% and due April 15th, 2001 with a yield of 12.95% – *as well as* a $70m offering of convertible senior subordinated debentures with a conversion price of $50 per share. Their statement ran that they proposed to use the proceeds from both offerings to repay bank debt and for general corporate purposes. This total of $180m proved another sell-out for Cannon, yielding $207m, and providing them with the massive capital injection they needed so desperately to carry on – in the opinion of many Cannon-watchers.

The glamour of the motion-picture industry, combined with Cannon's constantly upward-rising quarterly financial statements, had stood them in good stead yet again.

Almost unnoticed in the share prospectus was a 'sinking fund' time-bomb, for one of the underwriters had seen fit to insert an investor-protection clause. In addition to 'sinking fund' payments that required to be made there was a covenant to the effect that if the company's Consolidated Net Worth as at the last day of each of any two consecutive final quarters was equal to or less than $37.5m, then the company would be required to redeem, commencing on the last day of the fiscal quarter following such second fiscal quarter, 1) 10% of the aggregate principal amount of the Convertible Debentures originally issued or 2) if new Debentures were outstanding, 10% of the respective aggregate principal amounts of each of the Convertible Debentures, less Convertible Debentures repurchased by the company and the New Debentures originally issued, at a redemption price equal to 100% of the principal amount thereof, together with accrued interest to date of redemption, and would be required to continue to make like payments semi-annually thereafter until such time as all outstanding securities were redeemed. The consolidated net worth of the company was estimated at December 28th, 1985 as approximately $74,698,000 and consolidated net worth was defined as the total consolidated equity of the company and its consolidated subsidiaries, as determined in accordance with generally accepted accounting principles.

Surely there was no way Cannon's consolidated net worth could sink from $74.6m to $37.5m – was there? This would involve a halving of their April 1986 share price.

It seemed that if they could not get finance from hit pictures, then courtesy of the banks and through their securities offerings, Cannon could still get what they needed anyway. Who needs hit pictures, just so long as the share price is boosted by continually increased revenue and profitability announcements? So now, excluding unspecified advances in cash from foreign distributors, and advances received from the likes of Viacom or Heron or Warner Brothers for future products, Cannon's total cash raised looked like this:

1) 1.28m Cannon Share Float (October 83) (through Hutton & Furman)	$ 24,700,000
2) Issue of 9% Convertible Subordinate Debentures, due 2009 (March 84) (through Hutton & Furman)	$ 34,500,000
3) 12⅜ Senior Subordinated Notes due 1994 (October 84) (through Hutton, Furman and Bear Sterns)	$ 70,000,000
4) 8⅞ Convertible Senior Subordinated Debentures 12⅞ Senior Subordinated Debentures (both April 86) (through Furman & Drexel)	($ 70,000,000) ($110,000,000)
Actual Realisation:	$207,000,000
5) Credit Lyonnais facility	$ 45,000,000
6) First National Bank of Boston facility	$ 65,000,000
Total =	$446,200,000

Meanwhile the 1986 value of Golan and Globus's shareholding had grown from $500,000 in 1979 to $3m in 1980, then $7m in 1981, to $12m in 1982, then $40m in 1983, to $50m in 1984, $60m in 1985 and $80m in 1986 – the sky indeed seemed to be the limit.

Chapter Eight
WINNERS AND LOSERS

In April 1986 after this hiatus their second production of the year, *Number One with a Bullet*, rolled and they also announced that they would release Bobby Eerhart's Dutch-Belgian co-production *Wild Schut*, as *Stronghold* in the US, without mentioning when and by courtesy of which crazy bunch of cinemas. More details were released of the 'Cannon movie tales' being shot in Israel by Patti Ruben. All of the films were being shot using the same sets, including interiors at the old Jaffa customhouse, outfitted with sets by exiled Polish production designer Marek Dobrowolsky.

Morgan Fairchild was set for *Sleeping Beauty*, then later *Puss in Boots* and *Beauty and the Beast* would be directed by Jean Marner. *Hansel and Gretel* with Lainie Kazan and *The Emperor's New Clothes* with Tahnee Welch, both directed by Len Talan, would follow; then *Snow White* with Diana Rigg, to be directed by Michael Bertz. Next would come *Jack and the Beanstalk*, *Cinderella*, *The Frog Prince*, *The Pied Piper* and *Little Red Riding Hood*.

Cannon declared that John Travolta would be joining Anthony

Quinn in *Zorba – the Musical*. Golan stated that he planned to personally direct a TV mini series based on the life of *Moshe Dayan*, the project spanning the entire history of the State of Israel. The script had already been revised by Milard Lampel, from an original story by Dayan's children Yael and Assaf. Director Andrei Konchalovsky would next film *Shy People* in September with Jill Clayburgh top-lined, making this Konchalovsky's fourth straight Cannon picture after *Maria's Lovers*, *Runaway Train* and *Duet for One*.

Cannon announced a deal with Showtime/The Movie Channel, the second largest pay-TV service in the US and Viacom Enterprises, a major independent distributor of feature films and off-network and first-run TV programming – both units of Viacom International – for exclusive pay-TV and pay-per-view rights through to 1989 and beyond, plus syndication rights, to cover a slate of sixty Cannon features. The announcement was made at a press conference in Hollywood by Yoram Globus and Showtime/The Movie Channel's senior vice-president in charge of programme acquisition, Fred Schneier. For Showtime/The Movie Channel's two pay-per-view channels called 'Viewer's Choice' (in addition to its two pay-TV network) the Cannon arrangement was seen as the latest in a series of moves aimed at giving the four outlets more continuity of product and some differentiation from their competitors. Cannon movies were to be exclusive to Viewer's Choice in the pay-per-view field and stated as being among the completed pictures in the deal were *Runaway Train*, *The Delta Force*, *Fool for Love* and *Death Wish III*, with eventually *Death Wish IV* to come – as and when (obviously, this is one horse not yet considered fully flogged). Of the sixty titles involved, Globus stated that thirty were finished or in post production with the rest not yet completed. The first title to be shown would be *American Ninja*, probably before summer 1986.

Variety reviewed Cannon-Tuschinsky's *Maria*, indicating that the most original feature of the film was the way the finance had been raised. A new director, Peter Janren, had asked the Dutch public in press advertisements to buy certificates of 10 gilders ($5) each of which would be accepted at box offices in payment for tickets when the film reached theatres, thereby raising 20% of the film's total budget of $270,000. Unfortunately they then went on to say that the director's 'complete ignorance of filming' prevented the picture from coming to life and they deemed its chances outside Holland as 'less than slim'.

In a 10k annual audited accounts filing that created further anxiety in the financial community – but with the securities offering safely launched – Cannon now reported that the foreign tax shelters it had been enjoying might be in danger because of possible reallocation by the Internal Revenue Services (IRS) and certain tax legislation that had already passed the US House of Representatives. They added that 'the risk existed' that the IRS might seek to reallocate revenues and expenses and subject a greater proportion of Cannon's profits to US tax under Section 482 of the Internal Revenue code. Cannon added that pending tax legislation, which could be back-dated to January 1st 1986, 'may materially increase the amount of US tax on foreign source income' of its subsidiaries. Since Cannon was known to be the most consistent user of this tax avoidance device through its subsidiary companies in the Netherlands Antilles, the effect on Cannon's tax bill looked like it could be very considerable. One industry source noted that if the provision in the 1986 tax bill was adopted by the Senate, it would stop some of the Netherlands Antilles situations completely. Until December 28th, 1985, Cannon Productions NV and its foreign subsidiaries had $22,082,000 in undistributed income, which had been as close to tax free as it is possible to get. They stated that they had no intention of transferring funds back to the US, according to their current foreign investment plan, and that these would be reinvested indefinitely outside the US. Cannon Productions NV had been subjected to substantially lower tax rates than US statutory rates, and revenue from this source had been seen to account for a disproportionate percentage of operating income as compared to their percentage of total revenue, borne out by their payment of a ludicrously low 2% ($254,000) of their $12,489,000 1984 pre-tax income. In 1985, Cannon had made provision to pay 8%, or $1,375,000 of $16,607,000, in pre-tax income. Meanwhile, 72%, or $14,155,000 of Cannon's 1984 total of $19,621,000 in operating profits were claimed to originate from the Netherlands and territory, which included the Netherlands Antilles. The figure had dropped to 34%, or $9,674,000 out of $28,491,000 during 1985, Cannon claiming that the percentage would have been much higher during that period had there not been 'a surge in domestic profits' – as they termed it – to $18,739,000, from $5,033,000 during 1984.

The same 10k filing showed Cannon's debt to Credit Lyonnais as of February 1986 standing at $47,913,000, just over their $45m limit, which consisted of a revolving credit figure of $35m, plus $10m in letters of credit. The 10k also further spelled Golan and Globus's pay compensation for 1985 and put paid once and for all to their protestations – for each had received $835,642 from a base of $350,000 and this base itself was set to increase by $50,000 per annum to $500,000 in 1988. In addition, they were further entitled to 3.5% of Cannon's pre-tax earnings above $7m, as earlier revealed, but not to exceed $1m per annum, by virtue of their having waived all compensation due prior to December 31st, 1984. In the light of this the Cannon duo's open contemptuousness of other Hollywood high-rollers seems to acquire more than just a whiff of hypocrisy. Among the lower echelons Christopher Pearce, executive vice-president and chief operating officer, was paid $110,654 in 1985 and Barry Lublin, executive vice-president and chief financial officer who had joined Cannon in July 1985, earned $84,135. William Steinbach, vice-president and treasurer, earned $68,850. These figures did not include stock options.

Meanwhile, back in Britain, the management buy-out of Thorn-EMI Screen Entertainment (TESE) had run into problems, so the Australian entrepreneur behind the management, Alan Bond, had personally agreed to meet the £110m asking price after Gary Dartnall had failed to raise the money by the March 21st deadline set by the TESE management. Bond stated, 'We are pleased to have this opportunity to invest in the British film industry', and indicated that TESE would 'continue under the supervision of existing management, headed by Gary Dartnall'. The go-ahead was expected to be given for the sale on April 18th, without reference by the authorities to the Monopolies and Mergers Commission – unlike the reference anticipated should Cannon or Rank have emerged victorious in December 1985.

Dartnall made a lengthy announcement in the press, listing twenty-three projects (not dissimilar to Cannon's periodic outpourings). Michael Winner was given space in the *Sunday Times* to pour scorn on Dartnall's list and many felt that in the light of

Winner's well-known connection at Cannon it seemed surprising that he was allowed to go ahead with what amounted to a hatchet job, since his vested interest was obvious to everyone, perhaps with the solitary exception of the *Sunday Times*. He began by stating that 'announcements by film companies are always amusing to those who know the facts' (Golan and Globus must have winced at this one). He referred to TESE being 'exaggeratedly described as half the British film industry' and reported that the £110m purchase price was considered by trade insiders as being between '£30m and £50m too much, not the least reason being an additional £150m needed for film production commitments, including £60m to US producer David Begelman' (described by Winner as 'he of the famous forged Hollywood cheques scandal'). He scoffed at Dartnall's twenty-three films-in-development announcement, defining development as 'a bit of cash to write scripts' (trained in Cannon's ways, he of all people should know the truth of this). Ah, but Winner was in a position to know better as he revealed that Bond already had plans to break up TESE! He had agreed in principle, Winner reported, to a £50m deal whereby the EMI cinemas would be bought by the Canadian group Cineplex in partnership with Northcott Hoare, claiming that Richard Northcott had told him that it was their firm intention to start to modernise the cinema chain in Britain if the deal was concluded. Not if Mr Winner had anything to do with it, as he made obvious when he innocently stated that 'Cannon films: Menahem Golan and Yoram Globus, are also moving back in to see if they can join the fun.'

The next revelation was that Bond aimed to further break up the group with the sale of EMI's Elstree Studio, which according to Winner was the subject of advance negotiations with the Samuelson group. He blithely maintained that a price of £16m had been more or less agreed, then went on to gloat that the strident Puttnam-led group appeared only to have paved the way for a break-up of Britain's last remaining production-exhibition-distribution outlet of any size. Even Peter Noble, a long-time Cannon supporter was moved to write in *Screen International*, 'I wonder if Winner has got his facts right?'

Cannon announced that it had sealed a deal for remake rights to *Born Yesterday* with its creator, writer-director Garson Kanin, who would script the new feature version. Walter Matthau was set to play the role Broderick Crawford originated in the Judy Holliday 1950 version which had won the Best Picture Oscar, and for which George Cukor had been nominated as best director. Kanin had written and directed the original stage version of 1946, which had also starred Judy Holliday. Yoram Globus – of all people – was asked what could be done to improve the original memorable film. He hesitated for only a moment before replying, 'I think we will give it a new dimension that fits the 80s and 90s!' Kanin was already at work on the script and it was to be delivered in a matter of months, for a 1987 shoot.

Globus further announced that Cannon would distribute the Roman Polanski and Walter Matthau feature *Pirates*, with a July 11th release planned on 1,200 screens. Apparently the De Laurentiis Entertainment Group (DEG) and the film's producer, Tarak Ben Ammar, had failed to come to terms for the film's release, originally due August 22nd. Globus declined to specify the amount Cannon paid for domestic theatrical and TV rights for the film, but noted that it involved what he termed a big sum in advance. Cannon had agreed to provide a wide release and a heavy advertising budget. Globus stated that Cannon would mount no less than a $8–$10m campaign utilising TV, print, a treasure-hunt promotion and other ballyhoo and they would be pushing back the release of *Allan Quatermain and the Lost City of Gold* to accommodate the *Pirates* release. Originally *Pirates* had been due to go out via MGM, but this company had decided to pass on the project also. DEG had been in a position to acquire the domestic rights of the picture after Ben Ammar negotiated, with the help of Credit Lyonnais, to buy back the rights from MGM, who had a $10m stake in the $40m production. MGM was reported as retaining a multi-million dollar investment in the film, with De Laurentiis still having a $15m investment in it and the foreign rights to the picture. It seemed that Ben Ammar had negotiated a $6m deal with International Home Video, calling for stipulations in the size of the release and the amounts spent, which De Laurentiis had not been prepared to consider. Rather than jeopardise the home-video deal, Ben Ammar had approached Cannon, who viewed the movie – and were sufficiently impressed with its potential to buy it.

To help their debt position Cannon called for holders of its outstanding 9% convertible subordinated debentures, due 2009, to redeem them for common shares in a conversion plan to become effective on June 3rd. The conversion-right deadline was given as May 19th, with debenture holders able to surrender the notes at the redemption price of 107.20% of the aggregate principal amount, together with accrued interest from March 15th, 1986, to the date of redemption. No interest would accrue after June 3rd, when all rights to outstanding debentures would cease, except the right of holders to receive the redemption price and accrued interest. A conversion rate of 45.45 shares for each $100 principal amount of debentures would apply under the plan equivalent to a conversion price of $22 per share.

Back in Britain Gary Dartnall indicated that he would *not* be happy to serve as an employee in the new Bond-owned TESE set-up, and promptly took himself off on holiday to the Seychelles. This was on the eve of the Cannes Film Festival and the stage was duly set for an announcement which would rock the international film world to its foundations.

Just one week after the completion of the purchase of TESE for £125m ($190m) on April 25th, Alan Bond sold it outright to Cannon for £175m (£266m), as Screen Entertainment Limited. The agreed bid between Thorn-EMI and the TESE Management had been £110m ($167.2m), but the price had changed because of TESE's forward commitments. When the first round of bidding had been going on in late 1985, these commitments had stood at £165m ($248.8m), but as of late April, with projects coming on stream, they were apparently down to below £100m ($152m), with the purchase price correspondingly affected. Bond was reported as having been paid £130m in cash by Cannon, with the rest in Cannon shares, together with the rights to the company's 2,000-odd title library for Australia. He was estimated to have cleared £15m profit from his seven-day ownership of the company and would remain a director of Screen Entertainment Limited (SEL) and also become a director of the Cannon Group Inc. Thus Cannon had after all acquired the company it bid for but failed to get in the original round of negotiations in December 1985.

The deal was seen as massively expanding Cannon's asset base, putting them overnight, per Golan/Globus, in the $1b league. It made them the most important film company in Britain in all areas – production, distribution and exhibition. In the release from

133

Cannon group UK Ltd of May 3rd, it was stated that Cannon would be taking over the management of the properties and all the interests of SEL and its subsidiaries forthwith. With reference to a future referral to the Monopolies and Mergers Commission, Golan anxiously stated that he regarded the settlement as 'a done deal'. Barry Jenkins, MD of Cannon UK, was to become the new MD of SEL. The deal was stated as being subject to Cannon Group shareholders' approval and it was revealed that part of the financing had been arranged by the Standard Chartered Bank of London. Golan and Globus, reportedly tired but exhilarated at the outcome of the negotiations, stated that the merging in Britain of Cannon's 198 screens on seventy-seven sites and SEL's 287 screens on 106 sites with the ABC circuit was calculated to give Cannon 39% of the total UK screens, with Rank well down in second place with 216 screens on ninety-five sites and a claimed 25% share. When added to Cannon's 175 other screens in Europe, the total came to 660 screens. What did Cannon get for their £175m?

1) A video-cassette distribution successfully operating in the US (in partnership with HBO); operational also in Australia/New Zealand, France, Germany, Japan, Scandinavia, South Africa, Belgium and Holland.

2) Elstree Film Studios, one of the UK's top three (together with Pinewood, owned by Rank, and Shepperton).

3) A UK Distribution company shared with Columbia and Warner (COL-EMI-Warner).

4) A library of 2,000-odd film titles.

5) A forward commitment to product from David Begelman's Gladden Entertainment, De Laurentiis Entertainment Group, Kings Road, Silver Screen Partners and Carolco.

6) A foreign sales arm with output deals in all major and most minor countries and third party contracts 'worth $225m'.

Bond justified his quick sale and profit taking by pleading that he was unhappy at ending up with full control of TESE, when originally all he anticipated was becoming a minority shareholder in the Dartnall-led management buy-out. He stated, 'Because of difficulties with the buy-out, the only way for us to complete the purchase was to take 100% of the company – not a position we were happy about.'

Cannon's story was that Globus had called Bond with an offer to chip in with its management to help run SEL, and discussions had begun which led to Cannon's taking over the new set-up completely. At a company breakfast one hour after the conclusion of negotiations, Golan and Globus described Cannon's take-over as 'the biggest deal in the history of the British industry'. They would commence immediately to analyse the company and its deals, to try to get at the root of what they termed its 'sickness'.

'We will try to amend deals where we can,' averred Golan. 'We will not let producers take unfair advantage over the company and we will not seek to take unfair advantage over them.' Barry Jenkins, newly-appointed Managing Director, stated that it would take 'a year to turn the company around'. Golan and Globus indicated that they would be spending much of the next six months in England while the new set-up was being absorbed.

The Dartnall departure, together with Cannon's take-over, was seen as marking the end of the free-reign management style Dartnall had maintained. His ambition had been to create in TESE a rival to the US majors outside the US and he had negotiated numerous deals with product suppliers which he claimed would help TESE reach that position. The first deal he reached in 1983, with Silver Screen Partners, had always looked ridiculously loaded with risk and dubious return compared to the extent of the investment. Trade insiders had depicted Silver Screen Partners as 'jumping with joy' when the deal was concluded. TESE had committed themselves to providing 40% of the budgets for the ten films set with Silver Screen Partners – 40% for the rights to the films set with Silver Screen Partners – 40% for the rights to the films outside the US/Canadian domestic market, often estimated to be worth only an average of 25% with 75% accruing to the US. No content control over the ten films had either been sought or given. The inheritance to Cannon totalled a $30m commitment to the Silver Screen partnership, which had yet to yield a single box-office hit. TESE had apparently tried to renegotiate the deal with Silver Screen Partners, but had met with a flat refusal.

One deal which Dartnall had managed to renegotiate, if only to a limited extent, was a uniquely disadvantageous – to TESE – nine-picture contract with David Begelman and his Gladden Entertainment. TESE had obtained the rights to Gladden films for the world outside the US/Canada, together with video rights for North America, and originally the deal had called for TESE to fork out 55% of the budget in exchange for the rights over a fifteen-year period, before this was renegotiated down to 50%. For a further investment of 25% TESE was to receive a share of US/Canada receipts, with the first project financed in this way (with TESE shelling out 75% of the budget) being *The Manhattan Project*, budgeted at $18m. TESE had donated $13m – reportedly the entire actual cost of making the movie – with the balance of $5m being used up in 'consultancy fees' to Gladden. A curious arrangement. Suspicions were raised. Was the $5m for him alone or was there a deal of a different kind involved here? The next Gladden picture, *The Sicilian*, was to be directed by Michael Cimino of *Heaven's Gate*, and budgeted at $23m. This one had called for TESE – and now Cannon – to fork out $18m on the same 75% basis. This money had not yet been disbursed, and early indications were that it might never be. Begelman's felicitations to Golan and Globus on their SEL take-over were met with a curt invitation to a meeting with them at Cannes to discuss a renegotiation of the deal on *The Sicilian*. When Begelman accepted, one industry wag quipped, 'I'd give anything to be a fly on the wall during that meeting!'

Chapter Nine
$1 BILLION CONCERN

TESE had acquired world video rights to ten pictures being made by Handmade Films, having agreed to put up 40% of the budget on these low-to-medium budget features. As with the Silver Screen Partners deal, TESE had no say in the pictures' content. Paradoxically, it paid for Handmade to make *Mona Lisa*, a project the TESE management itself had earlier turned down as uncommercial! Their deal with Kings Road Productions similarly had called for no right of refusal, no theatrical release commitment, nor any minimum launch spend. The deals included US/Canadian video rights in three films at $1.5m per film; two films at $1.6m per film and two films at $1.7m per film. TESE had managed to re-negotiate an escape clause if the price it put up exceeded 15% of the budget. The deal apparently was re-negotiated so that TESE had to put up $30m for US/Canada video rights in eight films.

TESE had also fully financed several of their own pictures, including two major flops, *The Holcroft Covenant* (£8m cost) and *Wild Geese II* (£11m cost), together with other, lower-budget loss-makers such as *Restless Natives* and *Morons from Outer Space*. Recently TESE had put up all the money ($19m) on the Christopher Lambert/Sean Connery *Highlander*, from Panzer/ Davis Productions. The risk of fully financing the film was seen by some as having been ludicrously high. For their money TESE did not even get the US/Canada theatrical rights, nor did it have the US/Canada TV or pay TV rights, as part of their six-picture deal with Panzer/Davis. 20th Century Fox, who had contributed nothing to the budget, had picked up the US/Canada domestic rights.

Dino De Laurentiis had also been an eager participant in deals with TESE, resulting in their involvement with *Bounty*, *Dune*, *Marie*, *Pirates*, *Taipan*, *Year of the Dragon*, *Cat's Eye*, and *Red Sonya*.

Of all the TESE deals, only *A Passage to India* at Columbia was expected to eventually turn into a theatrical profit-maker. John Simenon had been brought in by Dartnall to handle world-wide theatrical and video distribution, and had decided to move away from territorial presales, instead introducing a 'roll-over' part- nership deal with a number of key distributors, notably AAA in France, who signed a forward commitment to TESE Films. The fault in Simenon's concept was seen as TESE's contractual obliga- tion to refund all advances and distribution expenses not recouped by the sub-distributor – clearly he would have to be one of the first to go.

Theatrical distribution of TESE films in the States had been a left-over from the break up of the AFD US distribution set up jointly organised by Lew Grade (ITC) and EMI (TESE). Universal had agreed in the wake of AFD's closure to release a maximum of ten TESE films annually, but then simply stalled on the projects they were unenthusiastic about – which tended to be almost all of them. TESE paid Universal an upfront contribution towards print and publicity costs to release *Wild Geese II* and *Morons from Outer Space*, but were unable to coax Universal into releasing *Hand Gun*, *Britannic Hospital*, *Second Thoughts*, *Rest- less Natives* or *Scorpion*. Their desire to have these films released theatrically was not purely to wave the British flag – TESE's output deal with HBO stipulated that HBO would fund 25% of the budget of any film that Universal – or even another company –

agreed to release in the US market. Otherwise, HBO's guarantee dropped from 25% to 12.5%.

Considered to have been the jewel in TESE's crown was the HBO partnership in North American video cassette releasing. The two companies jointly represented about 8% of the US market in pre-recorded video sales and was widely believed to be the only significant revenue-earner for TESE, with *Rambo* raking in the shekels.

Yoram Globus's assessment of TESE on day one was, 'It is a very sick company.'

Predictably Michael Winner greeted the news of Cannon's coup with delight, describing it as 'the best thing that's happened in the British industry almost as long as I can remember'; before adding, 'What England has always lacked is management. These chaps have got what we need, a lot of thrust and major international selling power.' Andrew Mitchell, head of Elstree studios and now an employee of Cannon, declared, 'It has to be good for the industry.' Michael Williams-Jones of UIP which handled Universal, Paramount and MGM/UA and released the pictures in TESE's ABC cinemas, stated, 'It's the best thing that could have happened. Cannon put their money where their mouth is. They are building for a future based on exhibition, which is very good for our business. We deal with Cannon in many countries [here he referred to Holland, Italy, Germany and Israel] and we wish them well.' The Association of Independent Producers expressed concern that such a large chunk of the British industry had fallen into foreign hands, adding that the way Cannon was run was also a worry, as it seemed to be a very autocratic set-up. James Daly of Rank stated that if TESE had had to go to somebody, he thought that Cannon was as good as anyone else, for at least they were positive about the film business.

With Thorn Video already being seen as up for grabs, the company with the inside track on it was thought by many to be Gerald Ronson's Heron International, with its extensive video interests via its Media Home Entertainment Company. Heron had of course partnered Cannon in the original bid in 1985 for TESE, when Golan had declared openly that Ronson's fortune would be required to run TESE – not now, apparently. Golan confirmed the possibility of the sale of Thorn Video by stating, 'We probably won't stay in retail,' but added – just in case anyone, ex-partners or not, thought they were in for a quick killing – 'the video side of TESE is the only thing that's profitable.'

Coincidental with the take-over came the news that Heron had concluded a second $50m home-video rights deal, involving the use for the North American market of twenty-three Cannon titles. This followed the thirty-two-picture $50m deal the two companies had signed in 1985, and the films involved included the Norman Mailer feature, *Tough Guys Don't Dance*, *Assassin* with Charles Bronson, two Chuck Norris films, *Missing in Action III* and *Kickback*, and the Jerry Schatzberg vehicle for Christopher Reeve, *Street Smart*. Stephen Diener, president of Heron, stated that most companies in the business had been after the twenty-three-film package since Cannon's output accounted for the largest supply of non-committed theatrical films so far as the video market was concerned. The $50m figure translated to $2m plus per picture in advance of Cannon's average $5–$5.5m budgets, as against current dealer's estimates that it took sales of 50,000 units to cover a $2m advance. Cannon would also receive royalties estimated at around 20% after Heron had recouped these advances, but an important clause in the deal was that each of the Cannon pictures had to enjoy what was termed a 'major theatrical release', a key stipulation in the Heron arrangement. This was becoming a commonplace stipulation with most video companies who immediately felt a property was that much less valuable to them if had not enjoyed a proper theatrical 'window'. Cannon therefore would be obliged to spend at least the advance received from Heron on prints and promotions from each picture, whether they would normally have wished to release it or not, to ensure that it came within the contractual bounds of a 'major theatrical release'. Having done this, however, and having a splashy and expensive release at least partially financed by Heron, the film could do minimum business and the deal would remain valid. Even so, they still required the co-operation of cinema circuits to give their films a showcase and this had been a problem from time to time in the past. There was only one way of alleviating this stumbling-block on a long term basis and this was to acquire their own cinema chain in the States, another stated long-term aim of the company which would shortly be achieved. MGM/UA sources stated that the company had had a chance to match any offer for the first thirty-two-film Heron package, but had decided to bale out at $40m. The first Media Home Entertainment release would be *The Delta Force* in July, backed with a 'seven-figure campaign in anticipation of sales that could reach 200,000 units'.

Norman Mailer was involved in two of the films in the Heron package, *Tough Guys Don't Dance* and *King Lear*, for which he was to supply the script for director Jean Luc Godard. With a major theatrical release for *King Lear* thus guaranteed if Heron was to pay up, this was good news for the project which Golan had talked Mailer into doing by offering him the chance to direct his first movie and realise one of his long-held ambitions. Mailer amusingly described how his initial resistance to the project was overcome: 'I have enough enemies without traducing Shakespeare and to make a screen play out of any Shakespearian work is, I think, a dubious venture. I said I'd love to work with Godard, he's marvellous, I've always been influenced by him and stimulated by him and found him fascinating, found his work fascinating, but how would you do it? I don't think I really want to do it. And then we talked to Menahem Golan who said, "Well, how about if you could direct *Tough Guys*?" Well, I've been wanting to direct *Tough Guys Don't Dance* for two years. And no-one had been willing to take a chance on me, because I'm not a professional director. So I thought about that and said, "Sure, I'll do *King Lear* if I can also direct *Tough Guys*." I'd met Menahem Golan maybe a month later and I must say I liked him. There is absolutely no way in the world I was not going to like him, considering his generous belief in me. I'm very simple. Someone who treats me like a caballero is my idea of a caballero!'

In Britain the tremors from the TESE take-over by Cannon continued, with more bodies welcoming the news now that there was no option. Alan Sapper of the Technicians Union, the ACTT, stated that he was relieved that Screen Entertainment was now in the hands of a company with a proven track record in production and exhibition, adding, 'The future looks positive and we are looking forward to detailed discussions with Cannon on future plans for the studios in production operation.' Regarding Cannon's stated intention to increase production and develop British films, he said, 'We obviously welcome this very much and have no doubt that it is a true intention. We wish the very best to Cannon.' Percy Livingstone of the Society of Film Distributors said he was delighted by the news. It was 'great for the industry that a big part of it should be in the hands of a movie-making company'. On the fact that Cannon would now control 39% of the circuits in the UK he commented, 'It is not a threat, substantially the Cannon chain and the ABC chain are not in competition.' Michael Winner unsurprisingly continued to line himself up with Cannon as he held forth with: 'They've already spent a fortune in England in production and on increasing the quality of the cinemas and I know that in the few days that they acquired the company they've been doing deals with English producers and directors willy-nilly. It has to be an extraordinarily good thing that we have acquired good management, which has been missing in our industry over the years. Film is a mass medium. It is a vastly expensive product. England has gone broke for years making films for people in Hampstead and Kensington that they can chat about over dinner. That's why we have no film industry left, because we have gone broke making films for a few aesthetes. Films have to be popular, that's why Hollywood thrives, but they can also be good and Cannon's range today is absolutely extraordinary!'

Yoram Globus revealed how he now viewed the new Cannon Group as 'a $1 billion concern'. He estimated $245m for SEL's on-the-book assets, $225m in third-party contracts payable to Screen Entertainment, $300m being the book value of Cannon's stock and $430m of receivables owing to Cannon, giving a total notional value of $126b. What had he just revealed? For a company whose total turn-over in 1985 was $150,827,000 the claimed figure of $430m in 'receivables' represented almost three years' revenue. To service the revenue of $150.8m in 1985 the company had ended up with a debt burden of $360m, on which interest payable must have amounted to at least $40m per annum, yet they had still managed to yield a profit of $15m, 10% of revenues – nice going with such a mountain of debt!

The number of current Cannon employees was stated as being 1,600 in the UK, 250 in the US, 225 in Holland, 400 in Italy, 150 in Germany and ten in France, which together with Screen Entertainment's current staff of 3,000 added up to almost 5,500 world wide. These numbers, however, were about to be whittled down, for within a few minutes of the take-over, the ABC cinemas' booking manager, Noel Ford, was fired after forty-three years of service. Numerous others followed, both through forced and voluntary redundancies, including marketing head John Simenon (son of thriller-writer Georges), finance director John Reiss and London-based Far East representative Hanna Medawar. In addition, Cannon closed SEL's Los Angeles office and with it had gone Barr Potter, Michael Bromhead and the rest of the staff. SEL representatives at Cannes had been pruned also, down to about a dozen from the original thirty planned, many of them sacked while actually in transit. Cannon's stated intention was to fit all Cannon Group staff in to SEL's headquarters in Golden Square amidst further substantial job losses. Meanwhile trade rumours put Gary Dartnall's golden handshake figure from Alan Bond at $1.1m.

David Puttnam was still one of the few dissenting voices as he criticised what he felt was the predominantly violent nature of Cannon movies: 'We live in a society which is enormously influenced by film and television and we have a responsibility as film makers to that society. I've said this before and I sound like a cracked record, but I have a very precise notion of the sort of society that I want to live in – and I've got an idea what the triggers are that create violence and the triggers that create social and decent behaviour. I myself make movies which take a position which is humanist – essentially humanist – and I believe is helpful to society. It's quite clear to me that the majority of their work in the past – and I am talking about the past – has been work which appealed to the lowest common denominator in the audience.'

Golan continued to dismiss potential problems with Britain's Monopolies and Mergers Commission, stating, 'We have approached the Commission and we have been advised by our lawyers that there shouldn't be any problem. Everyone is well aware that it will bring a lot of new work to England and will keep the studios busy 100%.' At the same time he commented on his view of Screen Entertainment thus far: 'We believe it needs a shake-up. It needs a very strong management as well as renovation and investment in theatres, but we will heal it and we will make it profitable. It needs more British product and less American – the company has become too involved in American productions. We will check every department, we will check all the offices, we will look closely at the overhead. We will look to rationalise. We don't know who is who in the company and it will take a month at least to find out, but we will not throw out good people.

'Our commitment to the growth of the British Film Industry, in production, distribution and exhibition, now becomes the most important challenge in Cannon's future. With no Eady levy and no capital allowances, the UK needs a company like us. We will now double or treble our previous $50m investment over the years.'

A spokesman for Alan Bond stated that he retained a reasonable sized investment in Cannon, but declined to say how much or how his holding was structured adding, 'We do have extensive media interests, but the more we looked at TESE the more we realised what a headache it would be to run. It is an extremely complex organisation and Bond had not been involved in this business before.' Dartnall meanwhile gave this as his main reason for quitting, although many felt that his would have been the first head to roll anyway. 'Excellent though the Bond corporation is,' he stated, 'it is not in the entertainment business, and after what I have been through with the Thorn experience I don't want to start all over again with a board that doesn't understand the industry.' The Cannon Group had already informed him that his services would not be required even for the ninety days that Bond had arranged. ('He's in the Seychelles? That's a good place to stay,' snapped Golan.)

One prominent London journalist expressed the opinion that the whole thing had been stage-managed from the start simply to enable Cannon to outflank public opinion by using Alan Bond as a stalking horse. He pondered on how a company originally valued at under £85m could possibly now be suddenly worth more than double that sum – echoing the sentiments of many of Thorn-EMI's outraged shareholders. He speculated on how long it might be before Cannon, with a new debt burden, having paid way over the odds for TESE, saw any return on their investment and whether it was possible that the bubble might well burst before that happened. The alarming speed with which Cannon had from time to time been seen to move money from one country to another, operating on the 'roll-over' principle, raised further questions as to the basic soundness of their operation. What if it all should go dreadfully wrong and roll backwards? Could their companies in one country after another go bankrupt? Perhaps luckily for this particular journalist, the Go-Go boys were far too busy anticipating their triumph at the Cannes Film Festival to take too much notice.

Chapter Ten
DAVID VERSUS
GOLIATH

Eighteen Cannon executives attended the Cannes Film Festival in May, 1986, together with the much-reduced TESE contingent, decimated as a result of ticket-tearing scenes at London Airport.

Fourteen features were screened, including the three in competition and the opening night's selection *Pirates*, together with Claude D'Anna's *Salome*, featured in the official section 'Un Certain Regard'. Besides actively preselling the company's roster of approximately twenty-five pictures scheduled for filming in 1986, Golan stated that he would be unveiling Cannon's 1987 roster of planned projects at a May 13th press conference. He added that Cannon would also be looking to acquire product at Cannes, as it had done in 1985 when they had picked up *When Father Was Away on Business* for the US market. Golan claimed that Cannon knew how to distribute specialised films and intended to continue to sponsor art films within their mix of broad-based productions. He credited 'Cannon's growing status in Hollywood' to his results-oriented approach, stating that, 'Cannon are doing movies non-stop. We don't take too long to give answers on proposals, we generate many of the scripts ourselves and we are signing actors and film-makers to multiple picture deals. As a result we are having projects submitted to us earlier and gaining access to the industry's top talent. Instead of setting up our own home-video operation, we prefer to make the deals for home-video rights – which bring in production coin. Overall this allows Cannon's yearly production schedule to have its total costs covered before the films go into theatrical release.'

Stalwart Frans Afman of Credit Lyonnais was interviewed at Cannes and reminisced, 'When I first met Golan and Globus ten years ago, they always shared a hotel room. I thought it was to save money but as they grew more successful I noticed they still shared a room. Finally I asked Menahem about it. "We don't do this to save money," he said. "We do it because we talk about our films until one of us falls asleep."' Afman explained the procedure under which his bank considered applications for loans in film finance: 'We had to lay down some ground rules that would make such a loan operation virtually risk free. Any producer seeking finance is required to submit application, including a detailed budget for the proposed film, a completion guarantee report [except in Cannon's case, per Golan], contracts with the director and one or two leading actors, and proof that distribution and video rights are being negotiated.'

Afman elaborated on the amount of finance Credit Lyonnais had exposed on film-making at any one time, putting it between $300m and $500m for 'dozens of independent producers' in any given year. He was enthusiastic about working with independents, as he explained, 'We could get some of the action with the major studios if we wanted to, but there is no fun in that. It's just a book-keeping transaction. We prefer to work with independents, then you really feel that you are part of the movie-making business.'

A life-long movie-buff himself, Afman averred that he now spent half his time in Hollywood, thinking of his bank as a 'service operation' for his clients. 'We don't just provide loans, we provide advice. We know the best deal makers and tax lawyers in the business and we like to act as go betweens.' It had in fact been Afman himself who had brought the Salkinds and Cannon together on the *Superman* rights deal. Afman claimed he was seeking to fix up another three Hollywood clients, then that would be it for the bank. They would join his roster of Dino De Laurentiis, Cannon, Alex and Ilya Salkind, Hemdale, Gladden Entertainment, Carolco, Empire, TWE and King's Road. Afman claimed that Credit Lyonnais had not lost money financing films over the past year, adding, 'One of the privileges I have is that I don't have to deal with people I don't like.'

Journalists arriving in Cannes quickly dubbed it the 'Cannon Film Festival', as it was obvious that they were dominating the event. Huge Cannon posters were strung everywhere heralding 'The company of the future.' The packed press conference at the Carlton hotel heard Cannon's production plans for the future spelled out, to follow the movies they would be presenting at Cannes in addition to those in competition: *Invaders from Mars*; Dutch film-maker Hans Scheepmaker's *Field of Honour*; a pick-up from Harry Alan Towers, *The White Stallion*; Albert Pyun's *Dangerously Close*; *Murphy's Law*; *The Delta Force*; *POW, the Escape*; *The Naked Cage*; *Dumb Dicks*; *Camorra*; *The Berlin Affair*; *America 3,000*; the Israeli production *The Lover* and Fons Rademaker's *The Assault*. Golan revealed that the Cannon movie tales were planned for release as matinée attractions, to be coupled in bookings with Cannon's main features and that it was hoped to get *Rumplestiltskin* out by Christmas 1986 to inaugurate the concept. Shelley Duvall had made previous versions of these tales for Paycable Showtime and CBS/Fox and Homevideo, but the Cannon versions were to be proper feature length films, it was stressed, and musicals to boot.

After the first quarter hiatus when only *Duet for One* had rolled, Cannon were now in top gear apparently with four more started in April: director John Frankenheimer's *52 Pick Up*, Jack Smight's *Number One with a Bullet*; Sam Firstenberg's *Night Hunter*; and Jerry Schatzberg's *Street Smart*. May was due to see the return to the fold of Israeli director Boaz (*Lemon Popsicle*) Davidson and *Dutch Treat*; J. Lee Thompson's *Firewalker* starring Chuck Norris and Louis Gosset Jr; Tobe Hooper's *Texas Chainsaw Massacre II*; Rusty Lemorande's $10m remake of *Journey to the Centre of the Earth*; and Albert Pyun's *Down-Twisted*.

In June Golan himself would at last direct Sylvester Stallone in the much-heralded and much-delayed *Over the Top*; Placido Domingo would again star for Cannon in Jonathan Miller's *The*

Tales of Hoffman; Gary Goddard would direct the '$15m' *Masters of the Universe*; Joseph Zito would direct *Spiderman*; Godfrey Reggio's non-dialogue movie *North/South* would commence shooting; and Pancho Kohner would produce Charles Bronson in *The President's Wife* (aka *Assassin*).

Other 'summer' starts would include *Superman IV*; *Zorba the Musical* with Anthony Quinn and John Travolta, to be produced in Greece and in Israel on a $6–$8m budget; Peter Medak's *River of Death*; Bill Forsyth's *Housekeeping*; and Al Pacino in *American Buffalo*. Set for September were Andrei Konchalovsky's *Shy People* and Jean Luc Godard's *King Lear*. Described as scheduled for later in the year or perhaps early in 1987 were Marek Hlasco's *The Second Killing of the Dog*; Norman Mailer's *Tough Guys Don't Dance*; Peter Boyle in *Citizen Joe*; and Menahem Golan himself set to follow *Over the Top* by directing *What Do Women Want?*, reportedly 'a comedy'. Start dates had yet to be assigned to two films starring Whoopi Goldberg; *Public Enemy*, to co-star John Travolta and be directed by Bud Yorkin, together with the remake of *Born Yesterday* which would team Goldberg with Walter Matthau. Pacino was then due to complete his two-picture arrangement with Cannon by starring in Andrei Konchalovsky's *Investigation* in February 1987. Cannon stated that with this schedule, together with several foreign productions such as Eric Rochat's *Too Much*, shot in Japan ,the Italian *Sinbad the Sailor* starring Lou Ferrigno, and *The Genie*, starring Bud Spencer, the company would be ear-marking $250m for production in the current year. He added that Cannon Releasing were geared to handle up to two dozen feature releases this year, equal to last year's output. Golan claimed that unlike the industry norm Cannon tended to gross at least as much in foreign markets with each film as in the US domestic release, pointing to the recent and unusual success in France reported by Jean Luc Defait, about which opinions differed.

While conceding reluctantly that Cannon had not enjoyed a big hit in the major theatrical market in the world since *Missing in Action* in 1984, Golan strongly maintained that the $15–$20m level of domestic grosses reached by several releases (but only by *The Delta Force* in 1986) translated into profits, noting that Cannon kept costs of preparing prints down to an average of $800 – about half the industry norm – by using foreign laboratories. To keep

Cannon's volume business, labs in London and Rome paid the cost of delivering prints to Cannon in the US. The position was different from Cannon in the early days, when it paid them to exaggerate the budget, for now that they had to justify how a low-grossing film could still be a profit-earner they were obliged to positively understate the budget, so Golan would claim that *The Delta Force* had been brought in for $8m negative cost (only $2m more than his claimed budget for *The Apple* in 1980!). The cost of the 1,700-plus print launch was given as $5.5m to bring total negative and launch costs up to $13.5m. Golan would state that the film rentals of what he claimed to be $9–$10m (surely nearer $7.2m on box office of $18m), 'paid for the marketing costs and a substantial part of the negative cost, with foreign markets and ancillaries ready to take in their fair share.' Many observers would ask where Cannon's own distribution set-up came in – shouldn't a share of 30% of net domestic rentals be allocated to them? If this was done $7.2m would then be reduced to $5.1m and even marketing costs would not be covered, let alone a contribution to the negative costs.

Still more announcements were produced in Cannon's now sixty-five page *Variety* advert released in time for the Cannes festival. Featured as being forthcoming and among its line up for 1986/7 were: Mikhail Baryshnikov in *Giselle*, John Huston's *Haunted Summer*, *Delta Force II* – to be directed by Michael Winner – and Mickey Rourke in *Barfly*. G & G studios in Israel would also contribute *Shigaon* – otherwise known as *The Wild, the Crazy and the Lunatic* – and *Malkat H'kita* (also known as *Chou Chou*), with another Israeli feature, *K'fafoth* (*Gloves*).

While wooing and winning TESE from Alan Bond, Cannon had been negotiating to buy their long-sought-after US theatre chain and the announcement that this had at last been achieved was made at Cannes, stunning the Croisette crowd yet again. They purchased the 425-screen, twelve-State Commonwealth Theatres Circuit for $25m in cash, together with assumption of Commonwealth's institutional debt of $25m–$30m, per Cannon Group's executive vice-president and chief financial officer Barry Lublin.

The take-over of Commonwealth, which was the sixth largest circuit in the US, was subject to approval by the Department of Justice and the Federal Trade Commission, but Lublin stated that he anticipated no objections from these bodies, citing Cannon's record as a European exhibitor as validation of built-in insulation against conflict of interest – specifically the possibility of preferential treatment at Commonwealth Theatres for Cannon films. Lublin dismissed this idea with the comment, 'We are running a theatre exhibition circuit with the idea of maximising profits in that area. If a major movie comes into the exhibition cycle from another studio, we are certainly not going to have it not play in our theatres because there is a Cannon movie there. The idea of exhibition is to make money!' He asserted that the same policy of non-intervention would prevail in the US as it already did in the UK (never mind that the only bookings *Grace Quigley* could ever get in Britain was on their own Cannon circuit and never mind also that soon the ABC circuit would be loaded with Cannon product). Lublin stated that the Commonwealth acquisition was intended to be consummated by June and described the take-over as 'the first step in an openly ambitious Cannon blueprint to make additional exhibition acquisitions in the US.' He denied, however, that Cannon was actively looking at other circuits at the present time – at least until Commonwealth, which consisted of 140 leased and seventy owned outlets, had been absorbed.

Cannon reported their results for the first quarter of 1986. Net income of $3,037,000 for the first thirteen weeks compared with 1985's $2,121,000, a 43% increase. Total 1986 first quarter revenue had increased 100% from 1985, to $51,734,000 from $25,855,000, and motion-picture revenue accounted for $34,181,000 of the total, 72% higher than 1985's $19,823,000. Cinema operations revenue totalled $17,553,000, an increase of 191% over the $6,032,000 reported in 1985. Was there no let-up?

John Frankenheimer took time off from directing *52 Pick Up* to declare his belief in the Cannon *modus operandi* as he commented: 'When you work with Cannon you are working with the same management that you started the picture with and that you finished the picture with. That hasn't happened to me in ten years. Every company that I have worked with, the management has changed from the beginning of the picture to the end of the picture and I don't have to tell you what that means. [He then proceeded to do just that.] It means that the new management comes in and they dump your movie because they want to discredit previous management. That doesn't happen at Cannon. [Here he was correct: the current management *are* the previous management.] You are dealing with film-makers. Most of the people that are in executive positions in Hollywood today have never made a movie. They have never been involved in the production of a movie – they have no idea what it takes to make a movie. Most of them have no idea what a director does. Menahem Golan *is* a director. You are dealing with someone who does the same thing that you do and who understands what your problems are. You are dealing with guys who know every element of the film business and that to me is terribly refreshing. So far [here John hesitated for just a fraction of a second] it's been a terrifically happy association and I have every reason to believe that it is going to continue to be. [Now it was time for Mr Frankenheimer to turn his attention to Britain, having settled with Hollywood.] Unlike England, where everybody talks about making movies and nobody makes them, here these guys make the movies. And they don't talk very much, which I find terribly refreshing.'

Yoram Globus denied at Cannes that there was any plan afoot for Cannon to purchase part of MGM. A local trade report had started the rumour by alleging that Golan and Globus were headed for Atlanta – homebase of Ted Turner, the new MGM boss for a minute or two – at the end of the festival. Globus dismissed the report with a laugh, stating that he would remain in Europe after the festival to take care of business, while Golan would leave directly for Los Angeles to start pre-production on *Over the Top*. Globus further stated that in any case Cannon was not now in a position to take on another significant acquisition, the company's recent TESE purchase having strained their bank credit lines. Another big buy would require another public finance offering which Globus stated that Cannon was not about to launch. Uncharacteristically he maintained, 'We are not going to take on any more debt.' He conceded that he and Golan had met Ted Turner at a Beverly Hills party in Los Angeles, but 'we only stayed for fifteen minutes', he added.

None-the-less Globus maintained at a separate interview – when asked about the Commonwealth take-over – that the Cannon purchase of both this and TESE would not adversely affect Cannon's debt position. He stated that the two buys, together with the cost of their ten films currently in production, would leave the company with more than $10m in the bank, adding, 'We didn't use one penny of our credit line.' To another journalist he boasted, 'The company didn't have any problems to finance the acquisition and don't need any help from nobody.'

Golan was asked if this would be the end of Cannon's outward expansion, and replied, 'Why should it be the end? The sky's the limit!' Despite their assurances, Cannon's debt-to-equity ratio was still reported as being of nagging concern to some Wall Street analysts, for a study released earlier had revealed Cannon's debt-to-equity ratio at 3.6–1, lower than New World's 5.0–1, but more than double Orion's 1.2–1 or Tri-Star's 1.1–1.

From what the duo had seen of the TESE operation so far, they were unimpressed. Globus commented, 'TESE has not been well run. They paid $13m cash for one movie, *The Manhattan Project*, without a single presale. What way is that to run a company?' Nevertheless Golan chipped in, 'Now that we have had a chance to look at the company we realise that it is an uncut diamond – and we are going to have to cut the corners to make it shine. In six months time people will say, "How come you bought it so cheap?"'

With the shock waves generated in the British film community dying down, the executive council of the British Film and Television Producers Association unanimously adopted a motion 'warmly welcoming' the arrival of the Cannon Group via SEL. The motion was passed on May 8th, the meeting having been called by producer David Puttnam to get the Association on record as being opposed to Cannon. He was absent from the meeting, which came out with the opposite of what he had in mind, and he later telephoned council chairman Oscar Bueselinck to disassociate himself from the motion. Puttnam had been the spokesman for the group opposed to Cannon's take-over of TESE in late 1985 on the grounds of the British firm falling into foreign control. Film critic Alexander Walker had described Golan and Globus as 'two Israelis from L.A.' and there had been talk of anti-Americanism if not downright anti-semitism, which Golan and Globus had been quick to pick up. The council's statement added that it looked forward to Cannon 'substantially contributing through British Film Makers to its world-wide standing.'

Cannon confirmed that they would remain in the distribution

triumvirate in the UK previously known as Columbia-EMI-Warner. The initial idea was to now change this to Cannon-Columbia-Warner, but this had yet to be confirmed. The recent agreement that Warner Brothers would release selected Cannon items in the UK was only to go ahead with *The Delta Force* as a token 'Warner Bros' presentation.

Credit Lyonnais revealed more of the financing details on Cannon's US pick-up of Roman Polanski's *Pirates*, stating that they expected to recoup 'within 12 months' the $22m they had laid out on the $30m production. The video rights as earlier stated, lay with IVE for North America (with $6m shelled out, contingent on a specified 'splashy release'). Cannon through SEL now had cassette rights elsewhere, with MGM retaining a modest but unspecified position in the US theatrical release. Apparently Dino De Laurentiis's distribution involvement, which he took to Credit Lyonnais for funding, after presales territory by territory, had ended when he and producer Tarak Ben Ammar (who put up $8m of the budget himself) disagreed about the US release date, De Laurentiis insisting on bringing his own planned release of *Taipan* forward from December to August, pushing *Pirates* back to October. With MGM also passing on *Pirates*, Ben Ammar had sought out Cannon, who were prepared to bump their own *Allan Quatermain* to accommodate *Pirates*.

What of the prospects of the movie itself? Were they so good that both DEG and MGM had passed on US theatrical before Cannon took it up – or had Cannon discerned something in *Pirates* that those two had missed? The first reaction from Cannes where *Pirates* was shown as the opening film out of competition, was not one of enthusiasm, one viewer commenting, 'It doesn't play.' *Variety* found the film a 'Decidedly underwhelming comedy adventure adding up to a major disappointment.'

In the same week they reviewed two other Cannon pictures unveiled at Cannes. From the 'Un Certain Regard' section they described Claude D'Anna's *Salome* as a 'Pretentious howler, certifiably ranking as the 1986 Cannes festival's first hands-down clunker.'

No credit to Claude D'Anna, then, but at least no reflection on Golan or Globus, surely – except in their lack of judgment in showing such a travesty at Cannes? Sure enough, Golan had a hand in it personally! Elaine Warren, a Los Angeles writer, had been interviewing Golan towards the end of 1985 for an article in *CQ*, when he had a call put through to Henry Lange, *Salome* producer. Golan had been viewing dailies on the movie and found early scenes in the picture 'seriously lacking in erotic content'. He shouted into the phone, 'Henry, I am not asking – I *demand* that he shoot the scene with the queen! [Lange is to pass the message on to Claude D'Anna] I want her to drive the man crazy. I want a very good and beautiful erotic scene. The queen has discovered the man under her – how do you call it? – under her blanket. The man has on the chastity belt that she puts on everybody. She's crazy. And now she's working on his body. He should get an erection inside his chastity belt and this is very painful for him, very painful, and he should, how you call, be like in a spasm. This could be done in a most beautiful way, and a very strong scene should come out of it.'

Lange indicated that he would try to convince D'Anna, but that it would not be easy. Golan then barked into the phone, 'I just want you to *do* it, that's all! And if he doesn't do it, the minute he finishes shooting, we're throwing him out of the movie. I'll take the editing away from him!'

The third and – thankfully for Cannon – last review from Cannes was for *America 3,000*, described by *Variety* as being a 'silly sci-fi pic from Cannon, scheduled for domestic release in August but better suited to home-video use. The film is relentlessly silly – the actors do the best they can, but are made to appear ridiculous in most scenes.'

Chasing kudos, and getting no cash (and, incidentally, very little kudos), seemed to be a continuing obsession for Golan as *Fool for Love* was put on the block. *Films in Focus* thought that it was 'for many reasons, almost a complete disaster. Quite simply, an effective play has been stretched out into a very ineffective movie. Unfortunately, the notoriously pinchpenny team of Menahem Golan and Yoram Globus seemed to have just enough money to enable Altman to take *Fool for Love* out of doors, where Sam Shepard's language and stage craft are scattered in the wind. People who don't know the play will feel pointlessly bewildered.' Altman himself had given a hint of what had gone wrong when he revealed that he had originally asked Shepard what the play was about – and the author refused to tell him. When further pressed as to his relationship with Shepard the actor on the set, Altman diplomatically replied that it was 'about the same as my relationship with Shepard the author'. It seemed that the two men had been intent on making two different films and that the result was an unfocused mess.

The Manhattan Project, inherited from SEL, produced by David Begelman's Gladden Entertainment – and due for US release through 20th Century Fox – was described by *Variety* as 'a warm comedy-laced doomsday story which packs plenty of entertainment for summer audiences, but falls short of its potential as a thriller'. 'The hit of the summer', Golan predicted.

An interview an aspiring English producer had with Menahem Golan at Cannes gave pointers to the future as Golan gave the film-maker a few Cannon hometruths: 'Maybe you have an idea how much your picture will cost to make, then we will evaluate it, and I can tell you right now that unless it is packaged well, I am very reluctant to do English stories, English films. It's very seldom there is an English picture, unless it's really a genius piece of work like *Chariots of Fire* or something like that, that it makes it, understand?'

The producer agreed before Golan pressed on: 'England does not have enough stars for packaging, you understand?' The producer saw his chance and interjected: 'It depends what price you make it for.' This was Menahem's cue, and off he went again in full flight, 'Low budget? You're talking to me low budget? You know what's a low budget? We make – our list of thirty movies – we make at least twenty movies that are budgeted at less than £1.5m. You talking £1.5m – that's $2m, right? $2m is a budget you can shoot a big war picture in the Philippines!' The would-be producer tried to explain that if his film were to be made in England, that the English market alone could cover most of its cost at the box office. Menahem agreed with him, but with a sting in the tail, as he declared, 'Yes, a very commercial British comedy – yes, but it's worth *bobkiss* outside!'

More Cannes announcements were made at the crowded press conference called by Golan earlier at the Carlton Hotel where he amusingly started off by saying, 'I start with some *good* news. We have not bought *anything* today!' But still the signings came thick and fast as he revealed that Sally Fields had been pacted to co-star with Michael Caine in *Surrender*, to be produced by Aaron Spelling and co-produced by Fields's husband Alan Greisman, and now to start filming in Los Angeles in July. Cannon had taken over *The Two Jakes* with Jack Nicholson – and 'possibly Roy Scheider' – but without Robert Evans (the film under Evans's sponsorship having been stalled after running out of finance, with Paramount pulling the plug). According to Golan, filming would start in spring of 1987 on a budget of 'around $20m'. John Huston was now set for an autumn start on *Haunted Summer* in Italy. Norman Mailer was now to *appear* in as well as script Jean Luc Godard's *King Lear*, to be filmed in New York for 'under $2m'. Cannon had also acquired the rights to Mailer's *The Naked and the Dead* and planned a TV mini-series. Mini-series throughout Europe were also in the pipeline – there would be *Call Me by My First Name*, *The Richest Man in the World* and *The Seahawk* (to be filmed in England and Spain). Golan maintained breezily that *King Lear* was already '$1m in profit' and that he was looking at an adaptation of Franz Kafka's *Amerika* by Federico Fellini and later pictures by Roman Polanski and Alain Resnais. He also stated that Al Pacino was now being sought to take over from Dustin Hoffman in *La Brava*, Pacino having reportedly said he was interested, provided Francis Coppola directed the film.

Hector (*Kiss of the Spider Woman*) Babenco had now been signed to direct *The Second Killing of the Dog* in March 1987 while British producers, Lord Brabourne and Richard Goodwin, would co-produce with Cannon *Appointment with Death*, with Peter Ustinov being sought to reprise his Hercule Poirot role in the Agatha Christie thriller. Filming of the opera *Macbeth* would begin in July at Rome's Cinecitta studios, with Shirley Vernet appearing under Richard Cahailly's direction. Charlotte Rampling and Michael Sarrazin would co-star in *Mascara*.

Once again Golan the showman had dazzled the world. According to him they were going to produce more films than had ever been done by anyone in the recent history of the movies. Even for Cannon, many now felt that the whole thing was getting somewhat out of hand. They had seven films completed awaiting release, fifteen more actually shooting or just completed, eleven more announced with a definite starting date, thirty-two more announced, four complete from Holland, four complete from

Israel, two 'lost', twenty Cannon movie tales (up from twelve), together with TV mini-series and 'Movies of the Week' – plus the TESE projects, both completed and shooting, that they had taken over. Excluding TESE and excluding 'movie tales' the total still came to a mind-numbing seventy-three features – sixty-four if the Dutch and Israeli contributions are excluded, *but ninety-three altogether if the movie tales are included*.

Completed & Still To Appear

Dumb Dicks	America 3,000	Pirrates
Camorra	Allan Quatermain	Hot Chilis
Berlin Affair		

Currently Shooting/Just Completed

Over the Top	Duet for One	Texas Chainsaw Massacre II
52 Pick Up	Street Smart	
Otello	Salome	Journey to the Centre of the Earth
No 1 with a Bullet	Night Hunter	
Down-Twisted	Dutch Treat	Sinbad the Sailor
It Ate Cleveland		The Genie

Announced with Starting Date

The Barbarians	Firewalker	Spiderman
Housekeeping	Shy People	North/South
Zorba – the Musical	Delta Force II	River of Death
Superman IV	Tales of Hoffman	

Announced Without a Definite Starting Date

Treasure Island	Kick and Kick Back	Second Life
Who's in the Closet	King Lear	The Yellow Jersey
Citizen Joe	Fellini's Amerika	Barfly
Captain America	Second Killing of the Dog	The Two Jakes
Surrender		The Naked and the Dead
Investigation	Tough Guys Don't Dance	
American Buffalo		Alain Resnais subject
La Brava	What Do Women Want	

The President's Wife	*American Ninja II*	*Appointment with*
Born Yesterday	*Giselle*	*Death*
Missing in Action III	*Untitled Roman*	*Macbeth*
Public Enemy	*Polanski*	*Mascara*
	Haunted-Summer	

Lost Films	**Dutch Contribution**	**Israeli Contribution**
The Nat King Cole Story	*The Assault*	*The Wild, Crazy and the Lunatic*
Give a Girl a Break	*Stronghold*	*Chou Chou*
	Maria	*K'fafoth*
	Field of Honour	*The Lover*

Once again two questions were begged – why? And how? *How* could they possibly control this number of productions in any but the most cursory way? And *why* did they apparently have to?

One upsetting little item surfaced while the festival was in full swing, although it was probably lost and overlooked completely in all the tub-thumping that was going on. *Dangerously Close* had opened at 827 theatres across America after a concerted and expensive Cannon TV/Ad campaign. While Cannon 'admitted' to a remarkably poor opening three-day weekend average of only $1,427 per cinema ($1,180,506 overall), an outfit called Entertainment Data called even these low figures into doubt. Entertainment Data's *six-city* sampling actually presented a lower per-screen average, $1,305, than Cannon's reported *national* total. *Variety* described this politely as a highly unlikely occurrence, even allowing for extraordinary performance in the outlying market, adding that, 'Computed on the basis of the Entertainment Data average, the actual weekend take would be around $755,464 with other sources placing gross as low as $578,900 ($700 per screen average).' *Variety* wryly noted that Cannon distribution executives had failed to return their calls.

Even if someone did over-estimate or misjudge these crucial opening three-day figures, there had to be a catching up sometime or the ultimate gross would be inflated, with all sorts of problems

159

rearing their ugly heads. One way to cool down figures might have been to under report in subsequent weeks, but there would not be much scope for that unless under-reporting then started immediately, since after the second and third weeks there wouldn't be much to under report in a fast-fade situation. The only other way would be to adjust the first full week's (seven-day) figures, which again would look suspicious if anyone stopped to count.

By exaggerating the first three days, then deducting the exaggerated portion from the next four days, the figures might have ended up indicating that 80% of the first week's business was done in the first three days (Friday–Sunday) and only 20% from Monday –Thursday, stretching credibility somewhat. As it was, their second four days' figures netted down to $371,999 – so Cannon were in fact claiming that 76% of the first seven days of business had been done in the first three days and a mere 24% in the next four days (a per-theatre basis of a miserly $449).

As the festival proceeded, *Dangerously Close* entered the second weekend of its run and took $474,260 at 535 theatres – bumped after only seven days in the remaining 292 – an average now of only $886 per theatre and a cumulative of $2,026,765 (officially).

In another piquant aside, *Variety* reported Cannon's claimed sales of $35m in the first six days at Cannes, dubbing it oddly from 'the believe-it-if-you-like numbers mill at Cannon'. If Cannon could have pointed to some sort of theatrical success it would surely have made their Cannes sojourn even sweeter. Press reaction to the 'Cannon' festival ignored their box-office performance in the US theatrical market in two hit-less years, concentrating on the SEL take-over and the non-stop stream of announcements that emanated from the Cannon offices and press conferences.

Of the other Cannon product on display at Cannes, *Variety* judged *Invaders from Mars*, Tobe Hooper's remake of the 1953 B-film, to be an 'embarrasing combination of kitsch and boredom'. They reckoned it would make 'two wipeouts in a row (after *Lifeforce*) for Hooper and his ongoing employer, Cannon'. Harry Alan Towers – an ex-Commonwealth United Stalwart – was next for the chop with Cannon's pick-up of his *White Stallion* production: 'Lame is the only way to describe the proceedings.' Surprisingly, they judged *Dumb Dicks*, although poorly titled, to be 'full of laughs and a general air of freshness and élan that makes for fun viewing. The picture should establish David Lándsberg and Lorin Dreyfuss as a top comedy team.' Although *Dumb Dicks* was due to open in the US on May 30th, the Italian-produced feature, directed by Filippo Ottoni, mysteriously failed to appear. It surfaced later for some West-Coast test engagements as *Detective School Dropouts* before being withdrawn.

It took only until May 9th for Cannon and HBO to 'mutually agree' to withdraw from the deal negotiated with Thorn-EMI. It was thought that the break-up, as it at first looked, may have been over the crucial question of the shared overheads of the US operation, previously agreed. Cannon had felt the tab was too high; HBO could not concede this. Globus stated that Cannon was re-evaluating the video holding acquired from Thorn-EMI and gave his opinion that the recent deal signed with HBO's rivals 'Showtime' might have angered HBO and led to the present impasse. This started conjecture that HBO may have initiated the split, but just as this was going on Golan and Globus held out an olive branch, Globus declaring that 'We are peace people. We are not war people.' This was taken as an indication that Cannon were trying to smooth things out, and gradually it emerged that HBO may indeed have fired the first shot in the fracas. Globus stated that HBO's Steve Scheffer had called Cannon's attorney Thomas Pollock initially to say that HBO wanted to dissolve the partnership. Cannon's response was that if HBO wanted out, Cannon would be only too happy to oblige. 'Yes, why not?' was Globus's response. Scheffer's version was, 'These guys must have this mixed up with one of their scripts. There is not a soul from HBO who met with anyone from Cannon since the TESE deal.' Globus then claimed, 'We will meet with them and talk. If we can agree on good terms, the venture will continue.'

'We informed our banker that we are not putting any money into that picture,' was how Menahem Golan personally announced the hold they were putting on David Begelman's *The Sicilian*, the planned $23m version of the Mario Puzo novel which was to have been directed by Michael (*Heavens Gate*) Cimino. Jointly interviewed, he and Globus stated that they had met with Begelman at Cannes to renegotiate the *Sicilian* contract between Begelman's Gladden Entertainment and Thorn-EMI prior to Cannon's take-over. Golan claimed that he had never met Begelman before this meeting and when it was over Begelman left, promising to get back to the Cannon duo within forty-eight hours regarding the fresh proposals. 'We haven't heard a word from him since,' stated Golan, adding that he thought Begelman had subsequently left Cannes for Italy, then had gone back to Hollywood where Cannon had tried to reach him without success. 'Ideally,' said Globus, 'the picture should cost no more than $10m without stars,' adding, 'in all my life experience I have never seen a contract as bad as this.'

He did not say positively that Cannon were pulling out of *The Sicilian*, but indicated that future dealings with Gladden would be through Cannon's attorney, Thomas Pollock. He then came out with the astonishing claim that Dartnall's files had been removed from TESE's office in London four days previously and had been burned, Dartnall having personally negotiated the nine-film contract with Begelman over a period of four months. Dire implications were read into Cannon's allegation, rightly or wrongly. The first Gladden feature, *The Manhattan Project*, was due for release in June. Two others, *Wisdom*, written, directed and starring Emilio Estevez, and *Mannequin*, starring Andrew McCarthy, were in post production, these being youth pictures with budgets of $7m each, according to Golan. The remaining six pictures in the deal, including *The Sicilian*, were now all on hold. The deal for *The Sicilian*, which was described as being 'unprecedented in modern film trade annals' looked like this:

1) TESE (SEL, now absorbed by Cannon) was committed to putting up 75% of the entire cost of the film in exchange for North American video rights, a share in domestic theatrical release and all foreign rights.

2) Gladden – which apparently laid out $2m for the Mario Puzo book and a screen play would get:
   A. $500,000 producer's fee.
   B. 12½% of the $23m budget ($2,875,000).
   C. A 50% share with TESE in the non-refundable $3m advance put up by 20th Century Fox for domestic theatrical rights.
   D. A 50% share of TESE with 25% of gross film rental until recoupment.
   E. A 66⅔ share, against TESE's 33⅓ share, of profits.

Begelman's next move – which looked like finding another partner (but quick) – was eagerly awaited.

The *Sunday Times* headlined 'Cannon roars in' before breathlessly listing the company's past and current achievements. 'Everything about Cannon is gargantuan,' they gushed. They would be making 'over 30 movies' next year, trotting out the well-worn 'more than any of the major studios'. They quoted Golan: 'We are not philanthropists; the challenge now is to grow in quality and still make money but we are now doing what I consider to be most avant garde, modern film around with the French director . . . er, Jesus, we have so many names! . . .' Back in his stride he continued, 'Alain Resnais we just signed yesterday. And how many companies have ever made a profit on a Godard film? By making movies cheaply and selling them in advance we invented a system whereby in the final analysis, no films lose money!'

None-the-less the *Sunday Times* also reported some doubts from people at the quality end of the film business who remained contemptuous of Cannon's bulk-buying approach. Scepticism was also expressed by some about the apparently limitless funds that Golan and Globus had at their disposal. One 'financial heavyweight' was quoted as saying 'There is something wrong somewhere. I know of no other major company which can spend £175m (the SEL purchase price) without consulting a board of directors.'

A photo session for *Newsweek* with the cousins dressed in identical jogging suits brought the proud boast from Globus, 'This is the first time in Cannes in twenty years that I have been on the beach.' Although some of the British film community were reported as still holding out on Cannon, film critic Alexander Walker seemed like a convert. While lunching with Golan he had described a certain Oscar Wilde story which he thought would make a good film. 'Write it!' Golan had declared drawing up a contract on the back of the menu and handing it to the astonished Walker, together with a cheque for $5,000. Walker, said to favour Sylvester Stallone for the lead in his project, announced that he would return the cheque, but would go ahead and write the screen play.

Puttnam's holdout against Cannon's embrace still bothered Golan, who conjured up a suitably picturesque phrase to describe the British film industry's reaction to his 1985 bid for TESE. 'I think they were spitting in their own bowl of soup by trying to keep us out,' he declared, 'but now they have all changed their minds, except Mr Puttnam. He stood up at a meeting of the British Film Producer's Association, and said everyone should reject us. He says we didn't back the National Film School, of which he is the governor, but were putting up £3m for new young directors from film schools to make films – a thing Mr Puttnam never did.'

Describing Gary Dartnall as 'a loveboy of the industry in Britain', he declared that if the management buyout had been successful, 'they would have been bankrupt within twelve months. The heads of EMI felt they were in a big swamp with all these obligations. Their executives did terrible deals. They paid for product and no-one knew it existed. Every day we are finding more and more.' But now – 'You will still be asking me soon how we got such a bargain – for the truth is that we did the most tremendous deal of our lives. Anyway we have already saved the company $25–$30m by renegotiating existing contracts!'

Golan the statesmen came out in his final *Sunday Times* pronouncement – 'Look what we are doing, something that for 20, 30 years hadn't been done. We are creating a place where creative people can work picture to picture, instead of struggling for two to three years to raise more money for the next film.' The Golden Age of the British Film Industry about to dawn – it sounded like nothing less!

Globus wound up claiming approximately $100m of sales concluded to various territories around the world at Cannes. Although the figure stood below that at the time of his announcement and he was not prepared to go into specifics, he stated that the sales could 'well top this figure once the books are finally closed'. Since Cannon now had their own distribution set-ups in the UK, France, West Germany, Holland and Italy, where had the $100m come from? Japan was reckoned to be number one on the list, with Konchalovsky's *Investigation*, *Otello* and *Superman IV* sold to the importing arm of the giant Shochiku Company. Shochiku declined to put a figure on their deal, but word had it that it was 'substantial'. Motoyuki Kubotani of Shochiku described the deal later as 'very expensive'. As an idea of what it might have been, Shochiku's rival, Nippon-Herald, were reported as paying $1,200,000 for the rights to the Arnold Schwartzenneger picture *Running Man*, and

$1,000,000 to Goldcrest for executive-producer Puttnam's *The Mission*.

On the video side Cannon claimed that they had successfully re-negotiated the deal between Japan's Tohokushinsha Film Company and TESE covering twenty-two titles. Globus declared of Benjiro Uemura, the president of Tohokushinsha, 'He's a wonderful guy!' as *Variety* reported that Cannon's other attempts at renegotiation with American and other foreign companies had been by no means as successful.

Cannon confirmed Otto Plaschkes's appointment as head of Cannon Productions in Europe, perhaps his reward for producing TESE's £8m flop, *The Holcroft Covenant*. Earlier he had been associated with such productions as *The Bofors Gun* and *Georgy Girl*.

As Cannes wound down, *Variety* listed the 1986 market shares to date of various film companies as at May 11th:

Distributor	No. of Pictures Released	Share
WARNER	9	18.2%
UNIVERSAL	6	13.2
PARAMOUNT	10	10.4
DISNEY	5	9.8
COLUMBIA	10	9.5
ORION	8	7.0
MGM/UA	10	5.6
20th CENTURY FOX	9	5.4
TRI-STAR	9	5.1
CANNON	8	4.7

Despite Orion's higher placing on this chart than Cannon, their results for the quarter ending February 28th, 1986, came out as a $22.8m loss, and they cited the main factors as write-down of their unsuccessful theatrical releases. A group of thirty films, stated as being virtually their entire schedule since their formation in 1982, was stated to account for the largest portion of losses, and these were due to be identified when Orion filed the details with the Securities and Exchange Commission (SEC). Orion's loss on revenues of $198.1m for the full year came to $31.86m. Was there a clue here as to how Cannon continually showed a profitable balance sheet – could it be that if they did an Orion exercise and stringently wrote every dud on their books down that the same type of results would apply at Cannon?

As it was, the SEC had spent what many considered to be an unusually long time before authorising Cannon's April 1986 securities offering. Could the delay have been because of some doubts over Cannon's stringency in the area of write-downs? For make no mistake – although estimates of future revenues are freely allowed and accepted in the film industry as standard practice, by the same token, as soon as a film emerges and it becomes clear that it is not performing to expectations, then the company is *positively obligated* by law to revise their estimate immediately. Had the SEC, while authorising Cannon's April offering, taken note of Cannon's future estimates?

David Puttnam decided to elaborate on his campaign of protest over Cannon's take-over of SEL. Describing himself as 'always an implacable opponent of monopoly and duopoly', he stated that Cannon and Rank were now responsible for 72.6% of all film rental in Britain. He recalled that in 1966 the Monopolies Commission had investigated the duopoly of Rank and ABPC, which had then accounted for 61% of rentals. This had dropped to 51% by 1978 when the Commission took another look, but it was decided then that since the duopolist's share was decreasing, that no action would be taken. Puttnam summarised, 'After 1978, the situation got better and when Cannon came in there were three chains and we had something that looked like competition. Now that the situation has reverted to a duopoly, how can I not be opposed?'

He stressed that his dissent was not 'personal' as he produced a letter written on December 2nd, 1985 to Golan in which he had stressed that if Cannon's circuit had been the subject of a take-over by either Rank or Thorn-EMI, then he would have opposed that just as vehemently. He insisted, 'I'm not being critical.' Yoram Globus was clearly upset by this further outburst of opposition from Puttnam – the working breakfast had not apparently mended the fences it was supposed to.

To counter Puttnam's criticism, Golan claimed that 99% of the British industry's reaction to Cannon's SEL take-over was positive, adding, 'I think David Puttnam is a very good and talented producer. But he is very stubborn – or maybe he is looking to score some publicity.'

When he was told that Puttnam had informed the press at Cannes that he had welcomed Cannon's original move to the UK years ago, Globus retorted angrily, 'He didn't support us at the time. He never called us before we bid for TESE. I challenge him to show one article where he showed his support for Cannon.'

Referring to the working breakfast, Puttnam stated that he and Golan/Globus had gone their separate ways 'agreeing to differ', adding that Globus had told him that Cannon's refusal to make a £2,000 contribution to the National Film School had 'been a misunderstanding'. Puttnam stated that when the money had been subsequently sought from Cannon, it still had not been forthcoming. Rhetorically he asked, 'How am I supposed to accept these are benign buccaneers? I have to be sceptical.' Globus conceded that he was not involved in the payout or non-payout of the sum, but added scornfully, 'To pick on an issue involving £2,000 is just silly!'

The new contretemps had arisen just as Britain's new minister responsible for films, Geoffrey Pattie, had concluded meetings in Cannes with Cannon. Pattie would be the one to decide whether or not the report from the Office of Fair Trading on the Cannon take-over of SEL should be referred to the Monopolies Commission. He refused to comment in any depth on what had been discussed, but it seemed likely that he had been suitably romanced by Cannon as Golan introduced his concept of a £10m revolving film fund to be set up, 50% by industry and 50% by the government. He must have been floored indeed as he met the duo, all ready to launch into his stern government-official persona, only to be confronted with Golan's cleverly pre-emptive suggestion. It was a typically cynical Golan offer, designed to win Pattie over and preclude the possibility of a reference to the Monopolies Commission by the Office of Fair Trading going ahead – as was Cannon's further offer of three £1m grants to film school students to make first features. Pattie was flattened – blown away by Cannon and their superior guile.

Meanwhile Yoram Globus stated that Cannon now planned to release a major film 'nearly every two weeks with 1,000 to 1,500 prints', without specifying the time-table for the commencement of this startling event. Two stages that had long been planned for Elstree Studios had now been given the go-ahead, with £2.5m committed and building to start by the end of the year, with completion by the summer of 1987. Menaham Golan stated that all of the British development projects inherited from SEL would be honoured, hedging somewhat by adding: 'All of the company's commitments, both in the UK and in the US, are currently under review.' Cannon, he declared, would be 'looking to put some kind of logic into the situation.'

Yoram Globus confided to Screen International's Peter Noble, 'Both Menahem and I are film buffs at heart,' before adding, 'it has always been our ambition to have a Cannon film in competition in Cannes, but to have three is a dream fulfilled!'

Otello, it seemed, was their most serious Golden Palm entry at Cannes. *Variety* were one of the few who had actually seen it and they had nothing but the most lavish praise for the Zeffirelli production. 'There is nothing in this film,' their review ran, 'that does not serve the purpose of high drama – musical, cinematic or otherwise – to ultimate perfection!' With this film Cannon obviously had a real chance of crowning their triumph at Cannes by gaining the coveted Golden Palm.

By one of those amazing coincidences that do occur in the film industry, the event shaped up as a battle between David and Goliath, with Cannon as Goliath versus David Puttnam, no less, who had taken an astonishing gamble and entered his incomplete *The Mission* for the coveted Golden Palm, against Cannon's *Otello*, *Runaway Train* and *Fool for Love*. The Robert De Niro/Jeremy Irons picture, directed by Roland (*The Killing Fields*) Joffe, and co-produced by Fernando Ghia and Puttnam, was widely seen as the troubled British production outfit Goldcrest's final throw of the dice after the debacle of Hugh Hudson's *Revolution* and the non-event of *Absolute Beginners*. With five weeks work in post-production still to be done and described as 'a work in progress', the collective nerve behind the decision to put the film into competition at Cannes had to be admired, for even if it got a special prize at this incomplete stage, failure to win the top award was going to make it doubly difficult to sell when the picture was completed, for this far-from-obvious natural commercial blockbuster needed to

168

open with a blaze of publicity as an award-winner to convince the public.

In the event *The Mission* took the Golden Palm from under the noses of the Cannon bosses, ruining what had been a festival where they had held sway in royal fashion. Puttnam described the award for *The Mission* as 'a miracle – or a near-miracle' and the press had a field day along the lines of 'Hallelujah, Goldcrest is saved!' which might or might not yet prove to be the case. None of the three Cannon entries won a prize in any category and there were dark murmurings that they had been snubbed yet again, but Gilles Jacob was in a conciliatory mood and tried to pour some oil on troubled waters in his statement, declaring that Cannon having three pictures in competition itself was already a great achievement. He added, 'The matter of prizes is one that we leave exclusively to the jury members. Cannon is a comparatively new company that can be practically considered to have reached the status of a studio. Cannon is making pictures at an artistic level that is of undoubted festival quality, and I consider that the company has a policy that is exemplary to the great directors who are making these films.' (Unquote: Jacob was clearly at the business of mending fences too!)

In *Variety*, *Dangerously Close* was summarised as 'a well-intentioned suspenser which degenerates sadly'. They were still of the opinion that *Dangerously Close* had come surprisingly near to being a good film, but that after a good start it quickly fell away and 'almost from one minute to another, the picture goes utterly flat'. Indeed there were elements in *Dangerously Close* which could have made an exciting picture. In the old days the vulgarian moguls, of which Golan and Globus were surely today's representatives – albeit somewhat diminished – might have intervened and tightened up or reshot some sequences to make what was nearly a good picture into an excellent one. Not so Golan and Globus – Globus couldn't do it anyway, and Golan was far too busy listing new films to bother about the fine tuning of a little item like *Dangerously Close*. Worth noting for the future though, was young director Albert Pyun's visual skills – with a good script and guidance he looked to have the potential to do later films that were really interesting, maybe his current Cannon effort, *Down-Twisted*?

As Cannes was in its closing hours it transpired that Cannon had bought theatrical and TV rights to *Regine* and Golan stated the project would end up a four-hour mini-series. Franco Zeffirelli's contract with Cannon covered two more films – *Young Toscanini* and *Aida*, planned as a made-in-Egypt production. Yoram Globus reached a twenty-picture deal for distribution in Turkey as 'an initial step toward the formation of Cannon Turkey', as he put it.

A joke that swept along the Croisette at Cannes had Steven Spielberg arriving at the Pearly Gates and asking St Peter if Menahem Golan was inside. Assured that Golan had not yet been called, Spielberg entered, spying, as he did, a figure sitting on the heavenly throne before a bank of telephones and barking commands. 'Sign Dustin Hoffman, get me Coppola, buy Thorn-EMI!' A horrified Spielberg beat a hasty retreat back to St Peter. 'I thought you said Golan wasn't here!' he said. 'That's not Menahem,' said St Peter, 'that's God. He just thinks he's Menahem!'

And so two weeks of jamboree in Cannes came to an end, two weeks which had seen the British Film Industry reshaped. Two weeks of triumph for the Cannon team with their three entries, even though they had been denied the coveted Golden Palm and had been forced to come away empty-handed from the competition. Two weeks that had seen the unspooling of full length films, promotional reels and in some cases the discussion of just the germ of an idea, seasoned with a star name or two, with millions guaranteed in advance on the strength of the combination.

Two final comments seemed to sum up the quality of the merchandise which had been on display at Cannes. One powerful Latin-American distributor declared, 'I prefer not to go to the market screenings. If I did, I wouldn't end up buying any films!' A Helsinki distributor offered, 'Cannes is flooded with too much product fit only for the home-video trade.'

Chapter Eleven
THE FLY THAT
CRAWLED

Cannes was no sooner over than the European edition of *Newsweek* hit the stands. In their even-handed article Golan was given the chance to air his claims once more for Cannon's status. 'We are out-performing Paramount, Fox, Disney, MGM/United Artists, Orion and Tri-Star,' he unabashedly told them. 'We had 30,000 playdates [a new use of statistics] in 1985 and our box-office growth exceeds that of any other company. We have a movie for every kind of theatre, from downtown Chicago to New York's East Side. And we are doing it all with overheads that are a fraction of what they are in the major studios.' *Newsweek* then had the temerity to compare Paramount's 1985 earnings of $78m with Cannon's $15m, also to state that Cannon still ranked a distant tenth in box-office receipts in the US. They pointed out that the only validity in Golan's claims were inasmuch as Cannon had been started from scratch, the conclusion being that clearly Cannon were self-promoters *par excellence*.

Newsweek also felt it was an open question as to whether Cannon could deliver on their promise to become the 'seventh major'. They argued that while many on Wall Street had cheered their progress, some analysts still remained sceptical of their earnings reports, while a few had even damagingly likened the Cannon empire to a 'house of cards'. Leveraged to the hilt as Cannon was, they speculated on the fact that Cannon might be too small, too ambitious and too under-financed to weather the set-backs in what was a notoriously risky business. On the other hand they quoted someone they referred to as the Dean of film industry watchers, one A. D. 'Art' Murphy, who seemed to come down firmly on the side of Cannon as he declared, 'Golan and Globus have a passion for pictures. If some markets dry up, they will find new ones. They are in the business to stay.' Those who saw Cannon as a 'house of cards' clearly were not highly reckoned by Mr Murphy, who had served as financial editor, film critic and news reporter for *Variety* for many years up to 1978 and still acts as special correspondent for the 'showbiz bible' while teaching at the University of Southern California's School of Performing Arts.

Newsweek came back to the tantalising doomsday theory, fuelled by the risks Cannon were now taking with salaries such as the $12m to Stallone or the $4m to Al Pacino for *Investigation*. Golan described this as a 'calculated risk' to Cannon but *Newsweek* continued to speculate on what would happen if Cannon's financial commitments, due to fat contracts like these, outpaced their presales. Under those circumstances, would Cannon be able to survive a series of big-budget losers? When Golan insisted that the doomsday scenario would never materialise, *Newsweek* – as if to make up for their temerity in even suggesting such a monstrous hypothesis – proceeded to give credit to Cannon for the successful release of *My Beautiful Laundrette* in the UK, which had in fact been released by Mainline Films and had nothing whatever to do with Cannon, except some bookings on their Classic circuit. *Newsweek* figured that since the Cannon circuit now accounted for 40% of Britain's movie houses with the April buy of TESE and the addition of the ABC's cinemas to their Classic and Star chain, this accounted for *My Beautiful Laundrette*'s almost instant success – ignoring the fact that its distribution took place not only without Cannon's auspices, apart from Classic bookings, but also well before they had acquired the ABC chain! Their disingenuous inference that in any case all one had to do was own 40% of Britain's

172

cinema circuits to make every film released a huge success, was ill-judged.

BBC-TV's 'Omnibus' programme on Cannon went on the air after Cannes and contained its fair share of illuminating and hilarious moments. Golan was seen addressing a meeting of Cannon executives, who all appeared suitably awe-struck as he emotionally explained, 'Cannon today is in a stage – maybe it could be compared to the beginning of United Artists. You'll remember those days. We reached this room, this table, this building, this kind of recognition. For the first time I felt – I was two weeks around the country – and the first time I felt, first of all that everybody knew about us and everybody treated us with respect and the interviews were fantastic. They looked to us and they said, 'You are those guys that conquered Hollywood, you are those – it's like a fantasy and they looked to us with appreciation; they were as if – they *loved* us for what we are and what we did.' Later he would add, starry-eyed, 'We are like those troubadors in the middle-ages who used to go to the market-places and tell fairytales, tell stories to the people who had dreary lives. I believe that all of us are looking for – one of the great things that we are all looking for – is more life. Life – another life, like beyond what we are limited to on our earth. Life beyond E.T. – life up there – and then, what cinema provides us. Its practically a godliest art!'

These outpourings were nothing as he shamelessly played God talking to an agent on the phone about obtaining the services of film director Peter Bogdanovich. The conversation went like this:

MG: Jack! We are talking about a director, eh – No?

JACK: Bogdanovich.

MG: Bogdanovich [pause] I want to *sign* with Bogdanovich – eh, two- or three-picture deal.

JACK: Yeh, but you know, Menahem, let me tell you something, all right? I mean, you and I know each other a long time. If you wanna buy Peter Bogdanovich off the street, okay, just say you had a project you had to roll next Friday, see?

MG: I am not *buying* people, I am giving them opportunities –

JACK: Menahem, he is not going to do it for a $1m, honest to God he's not.

MG: Then we don't have a deal.

JACK: I'd got to tell you, tell you honestly – look, I do respect you, all right?

MG: My friend, my friend – my offer to him is [long pause] a million dollars a picture. With points, fair points. Aaand – to be a member of the Cannon family. He needs a family because he is now without a family. And he is a loser and needs to be in with the winners.

JACK: (Earnestly) I'll get back to you. I *promise* you – I'll get back to you.

MG: I *will* work with him. We are working now with Franco Zeffirelli, Friedkin is signing with us – eeeh, as you know, Zeffirelli will do three pictures here – [prompt] Andrei Konchalovsky. Great director – he should be with the family of great directors. He should appreciate the fact that I consider him a great director.

JACK: I understand [presumably about to scuttle off to comb Beverly Hills for Bogdanovich].

The 'Omnibus' technique of being a 'fly on the wall' watching Golan living out his dreams of mogulhood had only one snag – Golan knew full well the fly was there and played it up for all he was worth. For the BBC, it was the fly that crawled. Any real juicy stuff like their Begelman meeting was strictly *sub judice*. Instead Golan was filmed holding forth on the difficulties of dealing with Christopher Reeve and Jerry Schatzberg as he hilariously pontificated: 'Nobody shoots today in New York when they have a low-budget movie and if they think that they have a big-budget movie here I have a new story to tell them. *Street Smart* is comparatively a low-budget movie. So Jerry Schatzberg – the first thing he does, he calls and complains, giving me pains under my belt and complains to Christopher Reeve. Half an hour later, almost midnight, Christopher Reeve's calling *me*. What am I doing? I am told that I am ruining the picture. Look, Chris is the star of the movie. He should act in the movie, work on the script with the writer, I did everything they wanted, I sent the writer to New York, I did everything. His interference – that we have a kind of axe over our heads from a star – oh, I don't like it, honestly to God, I don't like it. He should – we are doing this movie and he said, you know what he said to me and that I thought is a kind of a way – ah, which I

174

wouldn't like to hear it from nobody. He said, if you don't have another million and a half to do this movie in New York how do I know that you have $30m to do *Superman*? I mean the way he talked to me like that – Where do you take the money? he said, I said from the bank, from the *bank*. You don't understand the world of realities. What can I tell him – that he is only worth a dollar as *Superman*? Can I tell him that and I would be a guy who insults him? I did *Street Smart* because I wanted to please him, because I liked the script, because I think it's a good project, but if we go bananas with the budget, then we will risk our arse. We don't work this way.'

Later he was seen still holding-forth again on the expense of New York location shooting: 'The director is not flexible and he doesn't find that he can shoot the streets of New York in Montreal or Toronto, you know, let me tell you. John Schlesinger is shooting for Orion – it's a New York story, he is shooting it 100% in Toronto. I mean the difference we found in the budget is – to shoot two weeks in New York, well actually less than ten days, second unit, cost $1.5m compared to $200,000 in Toronto. The budget for Toronto for six weeks is as much, practically, as below the line of New York for ten days. You understand? And if you have to go to New York for a couple of days and steal some shots, fine with me. But the main thing you have to be is fast and flexible because the Unions – especially the Teamsters – are killers!'

Golan was also seen at his most amusing as he described an encounter with John Cassavettes back in the *Love Streams* days: 'John bought me a two hours and fifteen minutes movie in *Love Streams*. I had the right to cut it. I told John – John, I think fifteen minutes, the movie can't suffer. Go out and cut out fifteen minutes in the middle and you will see that you will get a much better movie. He said, Menahem, it will be done in the next two days. Two days later he came in and the movie was two-and-a-half hours and I said (laughing) John, you added fifteen minutes and he said, but it's shorter nevertheless! And I said, John, you're a genius, what can I tell you? I will not argue with you and will go on with your cut. We suffered!'

He was also seen taking care of business with director William Friedkin's agent:

AGENT: What is your problem with giving up a percent of the gross deal?

MG: Look, I – we do not want to go to gross deals with directors. We don't want to. I think Friedkin deserves points, I don't tell you no –

AGENT: But he's always had points.

MG: But not gross, I cannot give you gross. I'm not giving gross.

AGENT: Dino is doing the same thing with him . . .

MG: But we've negative costs to pay.

AGENT: Let me ask you something. The Mirisch brothers – how much are they getting for this?

MG: Listen, the Mirisch brothers brought us Dustin Hoffman. You will have to understand that when they brought us Dustin Hoffman they had something to sell us!

All in all 'Omnibus' was an outstanding achievement for Cannon, who were so pleased with the fifty-minute commercial, laced with scenes from forthcoming Cannon movies, that they promptly ordered 500 copies from BBC TV for their own use.

Four weeks after taking over ABC cinemas, Cannon decided to make up for lost time and give themselves something they had never received before in the UK – with the possible exception of *Breakin'* in 1984 – a wide release. Naturally the one to be chosen was Menahem Golan's own *The Delta Force* – what sort of release this might have achieved under normal competitive conditions (without the ABC take-over) is a moot point, for Britain had shown no appetite in the past for Cannon's cheap-jack action movies, but of course Golan would maintain that this was because they had never had a proper chance, due to the ABC/Odeon stranglehold. Now all that was in the past, as ninety-four cinemas across Britain – ABCs of course – were set for *The Delta Force*'s opening. Not even Menahem Golan or Yoram Globus could have been prepared for the result and the Cannon staff at Golden Square must have felt the chill wind of their displeasure as Cannon went on to collect the biggest bloody nose dished out to a film company in many years.

In London it opened at the Warner West End 2 with £5,548

(1986 High: £32,573, Low: £3,180), Cannon 2 Haymarket with £2,788 (1986 High: £9,315, Low: £1,934), Cannon 3 Oxford Street with £1,799 (1986 High: £4,808, Low: £1,824), Cannon 4 Chelsea with £741 (1986 High: £3,005, Low: £453) and Coronet 1 with £599 (1986 High: £7,329, Low: £515) for a total first West End week of £11,475 – compared with Martin Scorsese's *After Hours* which opened at four theatres and took £54,823, while *Down and Out in Beverley Hills* in its second week at one cinema took £48,253, and *Room with a View* took £34,437 in one theatre in its *eighth* week!

The figures round the country were if anything even worse and in ninety-four cinemas *The Delta Force* collected a rock-bottom £69,281 or a pathetic average of £734 per cinema. At ten leading cinemas contacted, the film set 1986 lows at all of them. Together with its first week in the West End, the grand total came to £81,595. Contrast this with the hits for the year at the same time: *Jewel of the Nile* with £2,676,734, *Out of Africa* with £4,787,746, *Clockwise* with £4,073,718, *Spies Like Us* with £2,288,587 and *Jagged Edge* with £1,394,713.

With its second week, before it bowed out for good, *The Delta Force* managed to just top the cumulative £100,000 mark – at least the print costs were covered, but what an unmitigated disaster and another example of Menahem Golan's well-known knowledge of what audiences want, and an instant and devastating rebuff for Cannon product – cinema ownership or not.

As Warner Brothers prepared in the US for the release of their Stallone project *Cobra*, billed as a Golan/Globus production, the Cannon duo watched anxiously for the opening figures, a vital guide to what they could expect from Stallone's next, their long-awaited and all-important *Over the Top*. They had forgone Stallone's services in the immediate wake of *Rambo* and *Rocky IV*, so now it would be *Cobra* they would be following. How strong would Stallone and their $12m investment in him be? (Although Cannon denied it, trade rumours had it that the $1m Warners had paid to Cannon had been added to Stallone's fee to bring it up to $13m.) Warner Brothers carried out one of the most expensive campaigns in their history in the run-up to *Cobra*'s release, put at over $8m. For months before the opening huge posters were everywhere proclaiming 'Crime is a disease. Meet the cure. Stallone. *Cobra*.

The Strong Arm of the Law.' A record 2,131 cinemas were set for Warners' widest-ever opening. Twenty-four-hour 'Cobra-thons' were organised for opening day in key city cinemas, and only one sour note emerged during the campaign as Warners announced that there would be no press showings until opening day. Variety still managed to preview it and was bullish about its prospects, describing it as a violent, exciting police thriller 'destined for paydirt'. The fact of the matter, though, was that Stallone had never before scored without a Rambo or a Rocky and now that he was apparently trying to muscle in on Clint Eastwood's Dirty Harry territory, would the public line up for him in yet a third hoped-for first-of-a-series? When the answer came it was 'not really'.

In the same Memorial Day weekend during which Rambo had opened with a huge $25m box office take a year earlier, Cobra took a relatively lame $15.6m, an average per cinema of only $7,345 compared to Rambo's $20,000. By its second weekend the take was down by 52% to $7,511,542. Warners were nonplussed – although Golan and Globus had only vanity billing, the picture was performing like a Cannon! The third weekend recorded another 33% fall to $5,016,853 or a meagre $2,370 per cinema, then the fourth weekend found the take further reduced by 45% to $2,783,728 ($1,417 per cinema and a $39,226,928 cumulative in twenty-four days). Now there was little mileage left and it would take the first $20m to pay for the huge advertising campaign, let alone contribute to the picture's negative cost. Of course, Cobra remained a profitable picture, especially since Warners were the distributors as well as the producers, but it was no Rambo-type gusher and it posed the tantalising question – how much was Over the Top (written by Sylvester Stallone, to be directed by Menahem Golan) worth now, as the next Stallone feature?

While Cobra opened, Golan and Globus spent a few days in Britain trying to settle the few ruffled feathers that still remained following their SEL take-over. They continued to simmer over what they claimed were the outrageous deals which Gary Dartnall had struck with David Begelman, and it was possible to read all sorts of implications into their statements. They repeated their claim never to have taken $1 out of Britain in all their years of operation (perfectly credible to anyone who knew of their Netherlands Antilles tax haven and the danger of repatriation of any earnings to the US), and Golan stated of London-based Otto Plaschkes: 'I'm sure he will have an open ear to every British Producer.' A new cinema complex, the largest in the UK with seventeen screens, was planned for construction near Piccadilly Circus and an eight-screen site had been optioned for Southampton. A feature on the Falklands war was planned for September – to shoot under the direction of Stuart Urban.

Meanwhile the Office of Fair Trading were considering the referral of Cannon's SEL take-over to the Monopolies Commission. The 'done deal', it seemed, might still be undone – many feeling that Cannon should be made to divest themselves at least of the ABC circuit. Michael Winner's previous hot tip that Cineplex was interested could be put to the test. However, this never did represent much of a probability – Cannon had mounted an effective campaign to win over the British community and government sources, not least with their audacious Pattie-flooring suggestion of the formation of the £10m ($15m) rolling fund, to which the government and industry should contribute 50% each, to be used in the financing of new film ventures, with Cannon's contribution as part of the 'Industry'. In a further attempt to blacken Gary Darnall and his TESE colleagues, Golan and Globus released documents indicating that the management buy-out team had planned to sell Elstree studios and thirty-seven cinema sites. All they actually produced to substantiate this were reports from accountants Peat, Marwick and Mitchell, which had been commissioned by the Standard Chartered bank. The accountancy firm had been asked to review prospects in the event of the management buy-out prevailing and Gary Dartnall denied outright that the documents amounted to an agreed blueprint for the future of the company, averring, 'There were a lot of banks and institutions involved in advising both the buyout and Alan Bond during the sale. For all I know there may have been documents produced by banks not even working for the company. But it was precisely because I was uncertain over what Bond would do with the company if he kept it, that I resigned.' Bond's assistant Simon O'Farrell admitted that the proposal had been a matter of looking at ways of repaying borrowings, adding, 'They were going to be very highly leveraged and if a business doesn't produce enough cash, then disposals have to be made.'

As he left for the States on June 9th to commence shooting on *Over the Top*, Golan was asked to explain his approach to directing Sylvester Stallone and replied, 'I don't have a big ego. I give creative freedom to directors. I'd be an idiot not to respect Stallone's talent.' He revealed that *Over the Top* was now budgeted at $20m and denied again that Stallone's $12m had gone up to $13m. Stallone in fact had just signed a six-year, ten-picture exclusive deal with United Artists, effectively flying the Cannon coop after *Over the Top*. Stallone stated that he had been approached by other companies, but had chosen to go with United Artists, his original *Rocky* backers adding, 'Ten years ago I had a dream to do a film called *Rocky*, and no-one was willing to gamble with me except United Artists.' This did not stop Golan from claiming that Cannon too had been offered the Stallone package, but had been forced to reluctantly turn it down, claiming it was too rich for Cannon's coffers.

Golan sighed, 'There was no way we could protect our downside.' So how had he proposed to cover the downside on the Hoffman and Pacino projects? Goldcrest had failed to manage it with Pacino and *Revolution*, even with Warners taking it for the US.

When Golan had stated that future dealings with David Begelman would be through his attorney Thomas Pollock, he had said a mouthful. Two weeks after Begelman's disappearance from Cannes his Gladden Entertainment sued Cannon, charging in a civil suit that the group had schemed to coerce Gladden into altering a nine-picture contract so that Cannon would gain substantially more money. Gladden claimed damages of $25m, including Cannon's alleged failure to finance $4m of *The Manhattan Project*'s costs. He also claimed that Cannon had cancelled *The Sicilian* and were engaged in a campaign to stop others working on the Gladden project. On top of the $25m damages, Gladden also claimed $75m punitive damages.

Begelman announced that he still had a starting date for *The Sicilian*, however, and had set Christopher Lambert to star, beginning in July. This was news to Christopher Pearce at the Cannon HQ in Los Angeles, who stated, 'Cannon is surprised to hear that the project is looking ahead. I cannot talk about it as we are in litigation now, but we will have an official statement soon.'

Variety continued to report a slump in the US box office with the May figures having fallen to the lowest dollar *and* ticket levels for five years. The cumulative box-office gross for 1986 was now the lowest in four years.

Cannon-Italia's boss John Thompson claimed that their original two-picture programme was now increased to six after the Cannes festival. 'You never know what the annual production programme will be until you attend an event like Cannes where Menahem Golan and Yoram Globus put their seal on new projects day after day,' he stated exuberantly.

Cannon announced they were going ahead with their plan to convert twenty-five of their mainstream ABC cinemas to art film exhibition, concentrating the effort in university and college towns, with Kenneth Rive in charge of the operation.

When Cannon let it be known that they have signed a deal for cable or video rights with a company, they choose never to divulge payment details on these deals, so the trade is left to figure out the details of the agreement based on what someone in basically the same situation as Cannon have managed to negotiate – and divulge. When Dino De Laurentiis and his DEG Company announced a deal with Vestron for six pictures, they not only gave the dollar breakdown per picture, but spelled out how the money would be dispensed to them by Vestron – 25% on commencement of principal photography, 25% on delivery of answer print to Vestron, 25% three months after initial release (memo: if there is a release, or even a 'full theatrical release' per Cannon's agreement), then the final 25% (contingent presumably on the third being triggered) when the film was finally ready for home-video exploitation.

In the ever-competitive world of the film industry, new companies emerged all the time and it soon became evident that there were many laying claim to Cannon's original position of low-budget kings. The names edging to the forefront were New World, Atlantic, Island, Empire and Concorde. New World's stock had quadrupled in 1986 and their chief executives, Bob Rehme, Larry Kuppin and Harry Evans Sloan, confidently predicted no fewer than thirty-five releases in the year, raising speculation that there could soon be a cheap-film glut. They reckoned to get 50% of their revenue from U S theatrical releasing, 30% from foreign and 20% from ancillary.

Some of the other companies reckoned they could get as much as 60% of their total income from video rights, so were less dependent on success from a theatrical release. In spite of this a slowdown in video appeared to be developing, with even major titles starting to perform below expectations.

It seemed that Jerry Schatzberg and Christopher Reeve had emerged victorious over Golan's objections to shooting *Street Smart* in New York, for they moved there in June following initial work in Toronto. As the film started shooting on June 10th, however, Cannon's mid-town offices were promptly picketed by various unions – including Golan's dreaded Teamsters, protesting over the use of non-union crews. Picketer Sam Robert explained, 'Our picket is informational to let people know that Cannon works below area standards. We're only speaking for local unions today, but this could be the start of a national campaign against non-union productions. We plan to follow up with more location picketing.' Another union spokesman stated, 'The Cannon Group has become one of the biggest theatrical production companies in the world and one of the most notorious and flagrant non-union operations.' An embarrassed Euzen Kolar, *Street Smart*'s associate producer, said, 'We would love to work with the unions but for X number of days we have X number of dollars, and can't afford them.' Kolar denied further union claims that Canadian technicians were being used illegally on the shoot, adding that two people American in nationality were on the crew in accordance with regulations. To add to Cannon's troubles on *Street Smart*, Christopher Reeve had to go into hospital for an emergency appendectomy, but filming (albeit picketed) went on while he was briefly absent.

Barry Jenkins, head of Cannon U K, held forth on the prospects for the group and was asked why Cannon's distribution in the past had been so bad. He admitted, 'For reasons of cash-flow, we had to release films earlier than we would have wanted. But we had to do it.' He reckoned that would all change now that Columbia-Cannon-Warner had been formed. 'All of us report to Menahem and Yoram on a daily basis,' he added. 'At Cannon we sink or swim together.' Meanwhile Otto Plaschkes added two members to his staff, stating that his department would give the go-ahead to between six and ten projects a year. 'The word is out on the streets that Cannon is looking for projects,' he stated. Plaschkes, introduced to a meeting of UK film producers earlier by Menahem Golan with the comment, 'Look, the way to make a project happen is to excite lovely Mr Plaschkes, who will excite me', noted that he had known Golan on and off for about twenty years. When asked why he thought Golan had appointed him to his job, he disarmingly replied that he had no clear idea. As producer of *Georgy Girl*, *The Bofors Gun*, *Galileo* and the $8m TESE disaster *The Holcroft Covenant*, there were many other mystified trade observers who also had no clear idea as to Golan's reason for appointing the 'lovely Mr Plaschkes'.

Cannon's *Invaders from Mars* opus opened wide at 1,212 cinemas in the US, to take a grim $2,046,516 ($1,689 per cinema); then in its second week it sank to $926,421 ($843 per), down 55%. Seven days later the take was $365,947 at a severely-shrunk 486 theatres; then the week after it was over and out with a peanut $141,092 at 178 theatres and a cumulative take of $4,768,372 – a major theatrical casualty. The week before this 20th Century Fox had opened Gladden's *The Manhattan Project* – earlier predicted as 'The hit of the summer' by Golan – on which Cannon stood to make 25% inherited profits from the US take – but it too was out of luck, with an abysmal $1,503,545 at 827 theatres ($1,818 per) opening, before dropping 50% the following week. Meanwhile *Cobra*'s take climbed to $44,769,650 – not the top hit of the summer Warners had hoped for, although it was solidly in profit.

The appointment of British producer David Puttnam as chairman and chief executive officer of Columbia Pictures surprised many in the trade, mainly because Puttnam had often stated he would never again work in Hollywood. However, circumstances had clearly changed, mainly due to some fast talking by Columbia Pictures' president Richard Gallop, who for four weeks had been unwilling to take 'no' for an answer. Puttnam recalled that a political friend of his had stated that he had not left his Party, but that his Party had left him, adding, 'I think probably, deep down inside me, there's a sense of that. There was also a sense of going round the track again.' His appointment was to take effect from September 1st and his contract was to run for three-and-a-half years – a compromise between the five years Columbia had wanted and the three Puttnam stated he wanted to gamble.

Again he returned to the subject of Cannon, as he explained for the benefit of American reporters how he now saw the British film industry: 'Three years ago, two chains controlled 60% of net rentals. The Monopolies Commission said that was excessive, and that it would not be in the public interest if that share increased. Here we are three years later and 72.6% of rentals flow through these two companies. What's worse, one of those companies, Cannon, is the biggest single customer of the other in its film division. It's wrong; it's not a serious commercial environment; it smacks of a banana republic. But all the signs are that it will be allowed to continue. It says something psychologically about the state of the country that the Department of Trade would, even for a second, think that a legitimate way to conduct business. For a nation which sees itself too corporately controlled, that situation seems to be an abdication of responsibility.

'If Rolls-Royce closes down its aero-engine division and you know you're a good engineer and someone comes by and says: "You make terrific engines; come work for us," you go. You go to the place where you can pursue your dreams and ambitions and skills. That's the situation I was fighting against; I welcome Cannon in terms of their production programme, employment they will bring and change they are liable to bring to the industry. I'm not prepared to concede, however, that 72.6% of an industry controlled by two companies can ever be a good thing.'

Puttnam thus became the first British head of production of a major Hollywood studio. While many were only too aware of the pitfalls that might be involved in his working for 'a division of Coca-Cola', he none-the-less took the job with the good wishes of the vast bulk of people involved in film production in Britain.

Meanwhile an astonishing series of rumours began to circulate about Cannon's purchase of SEL. The claim was made that, far from having forked out the full purchase price to Alan Bond, Cannon had in fact only paid a token £10m deposit and were now either unable or unwilling to close the deal, so concerned were they about the state of SEL and the depth of the problems they had found. In any case, one story ran that they didn't have the money. The rumours were described by an embarrassed Barry Jenkins as 'absolute rubbish'. He denied that they had paid too high a price, had not got the cash and were seeking to renegotiate the deal with the Bond Corporation. Jenkins added that Cannon had paid £40m on May 1st, the take-over day, then £15m more on June 27th. When it was pointed out that that left a cool £120m, he replied that this would be paid out in two further instalments, one in December 1986, the other in May 1987. 'Our bankers have given an undertaking to Mr Bond that these payments will be met on schedule,' he stated adamantly.

Jenkins further pointed out that Bond also had the right to take shares in Cannon, which at July had gone up to $44 from $34 in May, yielding him a further profit. Yoram Globus reacted with fury to the rumours, describing them as 'absolute lies'. There was no question of renegotiation with Bond, he raged. Adding, 'That's not on the agenda, not ever!'

Chapter Twelve
ENTER THE SEC

Cannon's second release on their recently acquired ABC circuit was *Runaway Train*. It received some favourable reviews, but its takings rivalled those of *The Delta Force* as the lowest of 1986. It opened at the Warner in London's West End to take £6,429 (*Delta Force*: £5,548, High for Year: £32,573) and round the country the story was the same, where it grossed £15,052 at eleven cinemas, to average a disastrous £1,366 per screen. Far from being good, the word-of-mouth in the provinces could not have been worse, for in its second – and last – week at Bristol the film took £362 (1986 high: £3,520) and at Cardiff it took £571 (1986 high: £3,166). At least there was one saving grace, if only a small one – Cannon had at least restricted the number of prints, unlike their big splash on *The Delta Force* – that bloody nose must still have been hurting. Of no comfort, however, was the fact that yet another of their hoped-for big ones had bit the dust – Golan's judgment was again shown to be questionable.

The fact is that Cannon's latest release roster was setting records in both the US and the UK for the lowest openings of all time. If

Cannon were a 'normal' company, they would be folding up their tent and creeping away into the distance. In previous years their record had been bad enough, but at least until 1984 there had been the occasional low-budget hit that lent some credibility to their shenanigans – now all that had gone.

US takings in 1986 had been appalling for *Runaway Train*, *Fool for Love*, *Naked Cage*, *POW, the Escape*, *Dangerously Close*, *Murphy's Law* and *Invaders from Mars*. *The Delta Force* had taken more money, but relative to its negative and launch costs ($14.5m), it had yielded only a paltry $6.9m to Cannon. Eight flops out of eight so far, then, in June, with only their pick-up of *Pirates* still set to open in July – the movie which MGM and DEG had both ominously passed on.

If that failed, their judgment would not merely be suspect – questionable indeed would be the *only* apt description, since here they had at least had the opportunity to see a *finished* film before they bought it, unlike the rest which they developed from scratch, and arguably had contained some potential at that stage. It was not only Cannon who were deeply involved in this one either – Tarak Ben Ammar as producer wanted his money out of it, as did Credit Lyonnais's Frans Afman with $22m of the $30m total budget of *Pirates* committed. Afman was on record at Cannes as having said he expected to get his investment back 'within twelve months'. Ben Ammar must have felt a distinct touch of anguish at the miscreant who had reckoned, 'It doesn't play' after its Cannes showing; then *Variety*'s pithy 'shapes up as a loser' must have caused a further twinge. His only crumb of comfort must have been the secure knowledge of Golan and Globus's unfailing, unerring taste in appreciating just what it was the public would flock to see – or was it stay away from?

The July 11th opening day was postponed for a week to July 18th, perhaps to allow Cannon's claimed $8m–$10m programme of ballyhoo to peak – treasure hunts and all that! Was the US ready to return to a comedy swashbuckler? Well, no – it was far too busy queuing up to see 20th Century Fox's *Alien* sequel, *Aliens*, which opened on the same day with brilliant timing.

Aliens took $10,052,052 at 1,437 screens ($6,995 per screen average). Golan, Globus, Afman and Ben Ammar were collectively rocked back on their heels by *Pirates'* figures, representing one of the worst-ever wide openings in motion-picture history. *Variety* dubbed *Pirates*' totals 'disastrous', as 1,108 cinemas reported an unbelievably low opening weekend average of only $935 per theatre and a grand(!) total of $1,035,447. With a total gross of $1.5m –$2m ($800,000 maximum to Cannon) in the US now seen as the upper limit of *Pirates*' capability, Cannon stood to incur a whopping $8–10m loss on their originally-claimed launch costs alone, with no contribution to their own distribution arm's cost. Precisely *nothing* would accrue to Ben Ammar from the biggest theatrical market in the world – representing about 70% of the total. Had Cannon really gone ahead and spent $8–$10m on 'launch & ballyhoo' – or was all that just part of the ballyhoo in itself? Probably. Once again Cannon's ability to sell a picture through their own distribution arm was called into question.

Pirates from MGM? – Mmm. *Pirates* from Columbia – or Universal, or Paramount? Maybe. *Pirates* from Cannon – never!

As if this wasn't enough, the company found itself in court again in a $20m dispute related to TESE's advance distribution deals made before the Cannon take-over. This related to non-delivery by Cannon of three previously pacted films, *Highlander*, *Link* and *The Hitcher*, to Rome-based Monitor TV and Merchandising, Proper Film and Films Rover Intl. The action was taken to ensure delivery of these pictures by the end of July to enable dubbing and censorship clearance to be completed before their scheduled Italian release. Eighty theatres had been booked for *Highlander*, with Monitor's boss stating, 'The shame of it is that unless the matter is settled now, these films will not come out in Italy this season. We have been completely in the dark about what's going on since the Cannon take-over. We were never notified of the change and now there is no-one left of the people we had contact with.'

Cannon had apparently told Films Rover at the Cannes festival that they wanted a renegotiation of the TESE theatrical deals and demanded minimum guarantees equal to advances already agreed and paid for – in other words, paid double! It seemed that in addition to this Cannon wanted to remove *The Manhattan Project* and *The Sicilian* (itself the subject of Begelman's separate $100m suit) from a larger overall package of sixty pictures also negotiated by TESE. With hearing of the suit set for July 23rd in London's

High Court it was felt that Cannon might be forced to hand over the three pictures to Films Rover pending appeal, since delay would render the suit pointless. Many of those who had welcomed Cannon to Britain must have asked themselves if this was the thin end of the wedge. Could anyone now be sure they would honour agreements – including Alan Bond?

They certainly wanted to rewrite everything else they had inherited, it seemed. How many more companies with whom TESE negotiated were being kept in the dark? It was felt that a lot more would emerge and that the Rome-based lawsuit would be but the first of many in the same vein.

Here's how Cannon's programme of releases for 1986 to date stood, excluding the pathetic *Pirates*:

Widest No. of Cinemas	Film	Negative Budget	Launch Costs	Box-office Gross	Net Rentals To Cannon
(1720)	*The Delta Force*	$ 9.0m	$ 5.5m	$17.76	$ 6.9
(954)	*Runaway Train*	$ 9.0m	$ 3.0m	$ 8.00	$ 3.2
(57)	*Fool for Love*	$ 2.0m	$ 0.5m	$ 0.90	$ 0.3
(420)	*Naked Cage*	$ 1.5m	$ 1.5m	$ 3.00	$ 1.2
(476)	*POW, the Escape*	$ 2.0m	$ 1.5m	$ 2.16	$ 0.8
(827)	*Dangerously Close*	$ 1.5m	$ 3.5m	$ 2.40	$ 1.8
(1212)	*Invaders from Mars*	$ 7.0m	$ 4.5m	$ 4.88	$ 1.9
(1260)	*Murphy's Law*	$ 8.0m	$ 4.5m	$10.00	$ 4.0
		$40.0m	$24.5m	$49.10	$19.3

For how much longer would Cannon be able to get away with their claim that these figures represented a *profitable* operation? They showed a return of a mere $19.3 on an investment of $64.5, representing a loss in the US market of a staggering $45.2m. If Cannon distributors were accorded the 30% others get (and this arm must cost them something) then the net return would shrink to $13.5 and the deficit increase to $51m. Are we seriously expected to believe that foreign and ancillary chipped in $45.2–$51m for these eight projects, resulting in at least a break-even? This would mean the average presales on *each* of these flops to be between \$5.5m and \$6.2m, which seemed highly unlikely.

In another fervid example of their non-stop twists and turns, Cannon called a special stockholders meeting to seek approval for proposals supposedly to protect the company in the event of a 'hostile take-over'. Their main proposals were:

1) That the number of authorised Cannon shares be increased to 40,000,000 from 20,000,000 and that a series of 20,000,000 shares of preferred stock be created.

2) That 80% of voting stock – as opposed to the current simple majority – be required to approve mergers involving Cannon and 'any holder of more than 20% of the voting stock'. (How about Golan and Globus themselves? 'We are *not* a threat,' Globus declared).

The same 80% would be required to remove a Cannon director.

So what of the 20,000,000 new shares? Cannon declared, 'The new shares will be used sometime in the future to be sold to purchasers who agree with the board of directors, to prevent a sufficient vote for certain transactions we believe not to be acceptable, in the best interests of the company.'

Since the new shares would be issued with the full voting and conversion rights, surely that would water-down the value of current shareholders' investment? Cannon conceded that this would indeed be the case in their statement: 'The position of current shareholders may be diluted.' Nevertheless, the motion was passed.

Nine failed releases in 1986 out of a total of nine, Cannon and ABC off to a disastrous start in the UK, writs pouring in, the new share issue providing another hot potato to fuel further financial rumours, the Sword of Damocles hanging over their cosy Netherlands Antilles arrangement – and a hundred projects to juggle in various stages of preparation – Cannon could reasonably be described as being in a perilous condition.

For the film business in the US – and the dreaded and reviled rival majors – things were to look decidedly rosy. The slump seemed to be over and hit after hit was being turned out, even to the extent of making theatre availability scarce for the first time in a while.

The top studio for 1986 emerged as Paramount, regaining the lead they lost earlier to Warner Bros. The main hits at July were:

Studio	Title	Box-office Gross
1) PARAMOUNT:	Top Gun	$ 95,348,936*
	Ferris Bueller's Day Off	$ 43,907,797*
	Gung Ho	$ 36,570,775
	Pretty in Pink	$ 40,366,274
		$216,193,782
2) WARNER BROS:	The Color Purple	$ 94,028,572
	Cobra	$ 47,542,215*
	Police Academy III	$ 42,707,092
		$184,277,879
3) UNIVERSAL:	Out of Africa	$ 83,142,343
	Legal Eagles	$ 36,911,873*
	The Money Pit	$ 30,012,612
		$150,066,828

Compare this with Cannon's pitiful $41.9m from eight releases! Orion had three big ones also – *Back to School* with $58,771,021*, *Hannah and Her Sisters* at $34,984,051 and F/X with $20,550,307. Buena Vista had bounced back with *Down and Out in Beverly Hills* at $60,221,261, *Ruthless People* at $29,815,615* and *The Great Mouse Detective* with $15,152,870*. Columbia was currently riding a winner in *The Karate Kid II* with $61,087,962* and climbing. MGM had a hit with *Poltergeist II* at $38,437,336 as

*still in release at July.

had Tri-Star with *Short Circuit* at $38,206,900. Only Cannon of all these had failed to breakthrough with even one single picture.

Now came flak for something they had next to nothing to do with. Warners' Stallone vehicle was being reviled everywhere it was being shown, and widely attacked as a Menahem Golan and Yoram Globus/Cannon production – even their vanity billing had misfired. The normally laid-back Australians declared themselves disgusted with the way its 'violence was relished'. On July 27th the *Observer* in the UK reviewed the movie, against the wishes of Warners who were holding a press show only the day before its saturation release on August 1st. Adrian Turner reckoned this was 'perhaps because the film's producers, Golan and Globus, felt that *Cobra* does little to help their cause as Britain's principal movie moguls'. He went on to say that the film was not only reprehensible, and as close to a fascist tract as the mainstream Hollywood cinema had produced, but it was also ineptly made. '*Cobra* is grindingly monotonous and offensive, a shameless remake of *Dirty Harry*, but without a trace of Clint Eastwood and Don Siegel's irony and introspection,' he declared. Maybe it was time indeed for some introspection at Cannon.

Their rumoured sources of finance from Israel were increasingly seen to have backed a pair of losers. Although Israeli backing was never confirmed for Cannon itself, substantial government support was known to have been given to build the new G & G studio complex in Israel. In December 1985 they needed Gerald Ronson and his 'fortune' to enable them to run TESE after the take-over. In May 1986 – they no longer needed Ronson.

Sir Gordon Borrie of the UK Office of Fair Trading (OFT) was in charge of the decision whether Cannon's SEL take-over should be referred to the Monopolies Commission or not. It came as some surprise when his decision – that it should indeed be referred – was overturned by Paul Channon, Trade and Industry Secretary, since it represented the first time in two years that the OFT's advice had not been heeded. The significance of the disagreement was played down as it was pointed out that Sir Gordon made more than 200 recommendations a year and most were accepted. Channon's justification for overturning Sir Gordon's recommendation was that a greater anti-competitive concern in the cinema industry was posed by the problem of 'alignment' in UK film distribution – the practice whereby big distributors offer first-run films exclusively to Screen Entertainment or Rank. The DTI made the astonishing claim that 'very little' had in fact changed because of the merger, but sent a rather feeble warning shot across Cannon's bows as they warned that they could order a full-scale monopolies investigation of the industry if they spotted any abuse of monopoly power. The *Sunday Telegraph* found Channon's decision 'a little short on logic' and referred to the baffling statement that 'a merger reference would not allow the commission to consider the more general problem (of monopoly in the industry)'.

Clearly Sir Gordon had observed that in the prospectus for their April securities offering, Cannon had freely noted that 'the company's operation of European theatres enables it to secure desirable playdates for Cannon pictures'; then 'the assured availability of theatrical exhibition of Cannon pictures (in the markets where Cannon has its own theatres) enhances the value of these ancillary rights and offsets the risk associated with no longer obtaining certain foreign theatrical advances and guarantees' – both of which statements the DTI had chosen to ignore. Geoffrey Pattie had apparently passed on the favourable impression he had gained at Cannes, when Cannon had regaled him with their proposals for nothing less than the complete revival of the British Film Industry, albeit at the price of their unimpeded monopoly of UK theatrical exhibition. Channon appeared to have ignored the fact that Cannon's Classic and Star chains, together with SEL's ABC circuit, now accounted for 39% of the UK cinema screens, 43% of box-office receipts – and no less than 48% of the net rentals to distributors.

The Association of Independent Producers (AIP), in expressing their disappointment over Channon's interference, referred to the 1983 Monopolies Commission report warning that 'any further increase in the degree of concentration in film distribution in the UK, especially if it involved one of the three existing groups, should be carefully examined under the arrangements for dealing with mergers in the Fair Trading Act, 1973', effectively stating that any such move had to be referred to the Commission. Although the AIP were not automatically opposed to the deal, 'We feel it should have had careful examination,' they stated.

Cannon now had achieved what they had wanted all along.

Having failed to obtain meaningful presales on their movies in the UK market for years – or what they considered fair distribution – they had manoeuvred themselves into a position where they could guarantee their own product a substantial showing. There was only one problem – with a mere two releases so far the judgment of ABC and Odeon's bookers over the years had been proved correct, as *The Delta Force* and *Runaway Train* had indicated. Were empty Cannon cinemas showing their own product *really* the answer to Cannon's problems?

Still sensitive about their precarious image in the UK as *schlock* purveyors, Cannon were stung by the attacks on *Cobra*. When asked about their new Stallone effort, *Over the Top*, they piously stated that it contained no violence, apart from the arm-wrestling theme. Could it be that Cannon had turned over a new leaf and were now about to eschew the violent themes of their past seven years' output? Hardly. As the *Cobra* reaction intensified, they prepared to release *The Texas Chainsaw Massacre II* in the US. They had not made the original movie in 1974 but had acquired the rights subsequently, and although they had stated in their April securities offering prospectus that their policy was always to go for a rating in the US no more severe than an 'R' (Restricted) – indicating that no unaccompanied children under the age of seventeen be admitted to such a film, they now announced that they planned to release *Massacre* unrated, having failed to get an 'R' from the Motion Picture Association of America's Classification and Rating Administration. The picture had been screened twice in Los Angeles and failed on both occasions to get an 'R', despite trimming of some of the 'bloodier scenes'.

Tom Berman, Cannon's president of distribution, stated that a corporate decision had been made that further cuts could not be made and 'still do justice to the film. In order to get an "R" rating, we wouldn't have been able to deliver the film the audience was expecting and we'd have an unhappy audience,' he explained. Cannon, as a non-signatory to the MPAA (Motion Pictures Association of America), had therefore decided to release the film unrated. Berman noted, however, that the film would bear a company-affixed warning stating, 'No-one under 17 admitted'. And so it did – but first-class eyesight was required to spot this.

The last time a full theatrical release in the US had been

organised for an unrated film had been in August 1984 – for another Cannon picture, *Bolero*.

According to one source close to the production, the refusal of the viewing committee to give *Massacre* an 'R' rating was a 'concept' issue. 'The MPAA didn't go for the cannibalism,' the source indicated. Since the original *Texas Chainsaw Massacre* – considered one of the most horrific and gruesome films of all time – had still qualified for an 'R' in 1974, speculation was rife as to how much more ghastly Cannon's sequel could be that an 'R' rating could not be achieved. If it was a 'concept issue', surely the original would have failed to get an 'R' also?

David Begelman's Gladden Entertainment announced in August that it had dropped its $100m lawsuit against the Cannon group. In their out-of-court settlement, Cannon had agreed to go along with the production and distribution agreements previously negotiated on three pictures – *The Manhattan Project*, *Mannequin* and *Wisdom*. No information was given by either Begelman or Cannon as to whether any cash was paid as part of the settlement. Meanwhile the Italian-originated High Court action against Cannon was dismissed on a technicality, although it would succeed on re-submission and Cannon would be forced to hand over the films and honour the agreement Films Rover had entered into. *Highlander* would go on to do extremely well for them.

In the US 10 Q filings – quarterly unaudited statements – required to be lodged with the SEC (Securities and Exchange Commission) no later than forty-five days after the end of any financial period. Cannon's filing for their quarter ended June 28th was unusually late, although many conceded that since they had to reflect the major acquisition of SEL in these figures, a few days' delay was not unreasonable.

The Wall Street set-back of July had seen Cannon's shares fall from their peak of $44 to $35 – no less than 20% of the value of the company wiped out overnight. Whereas most other companies started to claw back lost ground immediately, Cannon did not, and by mid-August their shares were still languishing at $33, having experienced further erosion since July.

When the quarter's results came, on the face of it all doubts should have been set at rest. Cannon reported net income of $5.69m on revenues of $132.5m for the quarter ended June 28th, compared to the same quarter in 1985 of net income of $3.1m on revenues of $35.98m – an 84% net income rise.

Net income for the first half of 1986 had increased 67% to $8.73m on revenues of $184.3m, compared to 1985's $5.2m net income on revenues of $61.8m.

A closer study of Cannon's 10 Q filing revealed how these figures were calculated and what they included. It seemed that Cannon had already licensed what they described as 'SEL's 2,500-film library (including some Cannon titles)' to VMP (Video Median Pool), for German video cassette and TV release – and included this revenue in their figures. The SEL acquisition had been allowed for in the accounts as a purchase as of May 1st, 1986, and Cannon revealed how this had affected the quarter's results, although quoting six-monthly figures:

1) Gross revenues from 'motion picture distribution' was up for the first six months from $48.7m to $140.7m, SEL having made a $75.2m contribution.

2) Gross revenues from 'film distribution revenue' was up 'for the first six months from $3.4m to $55.2m (including the SEL library)'.

3) Gross revenues from 'cinema operations' was up 'for the first six months from $13.0m to $43.5m – this figure including revenues from their Italian theatre chain (acquired April 1985)', the 'expanded' UK chain (ie, expanded by the acquisition of the 'Star' cinemas in June 1985) and SEL's ABC cinema chain on May 1st 1986.

With results like these, one would have expected Cannon's shares to start advancing again, but there were two major items of concern revealed in the same 10 Q filing. One was a working capital deficit of no less than $105m, then the other was spelled out under 'Notes':

'The staff of the Securities and Exchange Commission has requested, on an informal basis, that the Company provide it with information relating principally to the amortisation of film costs. The Company intends to cooperate with the inquiry and has begun to do so. The Company is reviewing its method of timing the allocation of certain film costs and the impact, if any, on amortisation of film costs and past periods. The Company anticipates that it may take several months for it to complete its review and resolve the issue with the Commission staff. Historically, the Company has as a matter of practice and policy amortised film costs over a three year period, which is generally faster than common practice in the film industry.'

The 10 Q filing was made available to the press on 19th August, 1986 – twenty-four hours later the L.A. *Times* picked up the story.

Chapter Thirteen
THE SLIDE BEGINS

The L.A. *Times* headline ran, 'SEC is Studying Cannon Group's Film Accounting'. They went on to observe that the manner of accounting for the cost of films could have a substantial effect on a movie firm's profit or loss reports. They observed that Cannon's 10 Q filing had not specified when the company had received the SEC request, but that Barry Lublin had now said it was in 'the last few months'. He declined to say what other information, apart from that contained in the filing, the SEC had requested.

The newspaper maintained that Cannon had encountered scepticism at major studios and in 'a segment of the securities industry', the doubts centring on Cannon's own estimates of realisable revenues on individual films, especially now with the box-office failure of so many of them. Cannon's recent amortisation rate, now increased to 65%, meant in effect that the company was expecting to get back $1 in revenue for every 65 cents of expense on a picture.

Jay Shapiro, a partner and specialist in entertainment industry accounting, was quoted as saying that Cannon's amortisation policy had been 'somewhat puzzling'. It had generally been lower than that of other movie studios and some had felt that if their films proved not to be as successful as Cannon had estimated, the company could be forced to take big write-offs in later periods. Lublin's response to all this was, 'We really believe that our numbers are correct and our amortisation policy is one of the top in the industry'. He added that the company had not been obliged to disclose the informal enquiry, but that they had decided to because they preferred to put out the information themselves rather than have it disclosed by others.

En passant the L.A. *Times* observed that some Wall Street analysts and other observers noted that Cannon's auditors were a relatively small firm for a company as large as Cannon and that Lublin had gone to Cannon as their chief financial officer after handling their account for the same accounting firm, Mann Judd Landau of Beverly Hills – not considered in itself an unusual occurrence.

The *Wall Street Journal* was next with the news that Cannon's shares had slumped $3.50 to $31.50 in the wake of the enquiry. Barry Lublin reportedly replied 'We believe we write off movies more quickly than other film companies. We really think this thing can be settled with no material effect [on Cannon's reported earnings].' If a company's revenue estimates were to prove too high, it was pointed out, that company may delay recognising cost for too long and thus risk large future write-offs. Entertainment analyst Harold Vogel entered the fray with, 'Their overall rates aren't really unusual. But there could be questions about whether some of their still-born movies are being carried on the books without write-offs.'

Some analysts noted that they believed Cannon could eventually be forced to amortise their film costs even faster than their present claimed three-year rate, since many of their movies failed at the box-office. Following this, subsequent revenue from other sources could be 'almost completely realised within as little as eighteen months'.

In the *Investors Daily* a chief financial officer for another studio, who asked not to be identified, said of the income forecast method of film accounting, 'These are very individual decisions you make regarding each film separately. You make estimates as the money comes in.' Several other sources, who also asked not to be named, claimed that Cannon recognised profits too quickly by initially making over-optimistic revenue forecasts which tended to overstate their earnings. A high initial forecast would enable the company to report a larger percentage of revenue as profit in the first year. At Paine Webber, Lee Isgur was quoted as saying that the SEC enquiry 'is a non-event to me'.

Although this may have been the case for Isgur, the enquiry was proving to be anything but a non-event for Cannon. On the New York Exchange 517,000 shares had been traded, more than six times their recent daily average, to produce the $3.50 per share loss.

Worse was to come, for a few days later on Sunday August 24th, 1986 the *Los Angeles Times* headlined 'Cannon Bid as Major Studio Is Cliffhanger'. They highlighted that Cannon now had a working capital deficit of $105m compared to a surplus of $32m just a year earlier, despite having raised $207m earlier in the year. They stated that a growing number of observers now believed that 'the long-term success of Cannon is still very much in doubt', given the huge new debt it had taken on to finance its gamble to become a major studio, especially in view of its 'recent lack of film hits'. Of the working capital deficit, they quoted Yoram Globus maintaining in a recent interview, 'We don't have any problems.' He had added that the company had not made any decision on whether or not to raise more money on Wall Street, adding, 'Right now, there is nothing on the agenda, I can tell you.'

'They keep reporting higher earnings on pictures that nobody goes to see,' observed Gordon Crawford, a senior vice-president of Capital Guardian research in Los Angeles. 'They are fortunate to have a very forgiving Wall Street that keeps providing new capital to make films despite their spotty record.'

Some analysts were now astonishingly of the opinion that Cannon must soon produce some hits to retain its credibility. '[Cannon's] argument is that they have no risk [due to pre-selling],' said one. 'But they do. They have huge interest to pay. Movies have to make a profit, they can't just break even.'

Globus angrily countered, 'We *don't* need a hit. If we ever do have a hit, the earnings will jump 120%. Sooner or later we will have a blockbuster – it must come, by the odds. Even when you play roulette, it comes. For us, $20m [in box-office receipts] is a very big success, compared to [the major studios], which think that is a joke.'

Globus conceded, 'We make mistakes. *Pirates* was one of them.' In view of the claimed advance, the cost of prints and the planned $8–10m ballyhoo, Globus nevertheless conceded only the minimum: 'We will lose $1m or $2m and it hurts. It teaches us a very big lesson that we should not even take for distribution a picture for which we don't have all the rights.'

Golan, said to be immersed in directing *Over the Top*, did not have the time for an interview with the *Times*, who returned to the subject of film amortisation in the wake of the SEC inquiry. Short sellers had been blamed by Cannon in the past for their alleged attempt to drive the price of Cannon stock down, short-selling being the method by which an investor borrows shares of a stock and sells them in anticipation of a price drop, at which time he can buy back the shares, return them and make a profit.

One of these major short sellers, Kurt Feshbach of Stockbridge Partners, explained his firm's position: 'Our analysis indicated that [Cannon] couldn't have made money on movies after interest and overhead.' He noted that by writing off less of a film in earlier stages, Cannon may have been able to make itself look more profitable, adding that a company's rapid growth (ie the making of more and more films each year) could mask the effect of poor box-office results.

The *Times* also noted, however, that the movie industry as a whole was often slow in recognising the financial consequences of its flops and that studios frequently took big write-downs, and reported consequent losses, only after a management change. They did not seem to make any connection between this and the regularity of changes at the top in most other movie companies compared to Cannon, quoting Golan:

'This management is already seven years [in office], thank God. You didn't see us in one quarter writing off major things, so how many years we could have, what do you call it, manipulated? Even if we have a mistake, it's cleared in three years.'

Critics, however, still expressed doubts about Cannon's pre-selling methods. They conceded that these may be enough to cover the bare cost of film-making, but that Cannon often didn't receive enough box-office receipts to cover even its substantial cost for prints and marketing. Where, they asked, would the company get the money to cover its administrative overhead, including interest costs on its vastly increased debt of about $400m? Questions were also raised about whether companies who bought ancillary rights to Cannon pictures might grow disenchanted because of the recent mediocre box-office results. Globus insisted this was not the case.

'If they have good money-making pictures and they have them in quantity, it's like a big hit – and better,' he maintained.

Lee Isgur was now apparently off his tack of Cannon's 'going to bat eighteen times and if they just hit one double or triple, wow!' Now he maintained, 'The *real* story of Cannon is basically how much of a jewel is SEL and how fast they can turn it round – no-one else had the audacity to buy it.'

The *Times* characterised Cannon's meteoric rise in Hollywood. Tales abounded among their Hollywood peers of sharp dealing, slow payments and premature ballyhooing of their deals in full-page trade paper ads. Cannon, they stated, had been the subject of scorn and lawsuits – their business methods legendary. Even though an attempt had been made to strengthen their management team in the last year, Golan and Globus *were* Cannon, in the opinion of many who had dealt with them and worked with them, meaning that the opinions of the company within the movie industry nearly always amounted to the opinions of Golan and Globus themselves.

Two high-ranking officers at major Hollywood studios dismissed Cannon as a serious competitor, one calling it a potential 'house of cards' because of its enormous debt, bigger budget aspirations and recent box-office failure. The other executive made the even more damaging assertion that Cannon didn't have a single film project which he coveted.

Globus blamed jealousy for the adverse comments, while adding, 'We are not perfect people. But we are doing everything in good faith and integrity.' He maintained that the 'dozen of suits' filed against the company in recent years were not at all unusual in 'a litigious industry'.

A Las Vegas *Sun* columnist was hilariously quoted as taking Cannon to task several weeks ago for making 'more enemies than even Rambo could handle' while shooting *Over the Top*, recruiting hundreds of volunteers to act as unpaid extras at an arm-wrestling sequence by promising to donate $5 to their favourite charity. The sign-up booths for the charity were at the rear, while the 'free lunch and breakfast' was served at the opposite end of the set.

Some language involved in the recent dispute with David Begelman's Gladden Entertainment summarised a view of Cannon, the *Times* maintained, that cropped up repeatedly, the complaint alleging that Golan, Globus and Cannon 'have become known for bad-faith business practices and the failure or refusal to perform their contractual obligations'. Globus insisted, 'Our track record shows we kept deals even when we didn't like them.'

On Monday August 25th, the day after this article appeared, Cannon's shares fell to a new low of $29, a 34% drop from their peak only two months earlier. There was more to come as America's leading business magazine, *Forbes News*, was due to hit the streets on Thursday, 28th August.

One mitigating factor in the meantime was that Cannon's investigation by the SEC, worrying though it was, fell short of a 'formal' enquiry, which was considerably more draconian, where documents were subpoenaed and share dealings could be suspended while the investigation took place. While the SEC inquiry was under way, however, whether formal or otherwise, there would be no question of Cannon being allowed to raise further cash through public securities offerings – the SEC would not permit this until their investigations were completed. Since this was going to take several months, it was questioned whether Cannon could survive without recourse to disposals, which would be permitted. Another answer would be a hit picture or two, but at the moment that seemed to be out of the question – although this summed up the tantalising appeal of Hollywood and movies generally. *Could* it be ruled out? Might not *52 Pick-up* or *Duet for One* do a *Star Wars*? It seemed unlikely, but Lee Isgur's original scenario of 'eighteen times to bat' remained a persuasive one, even with a track record such as Cannon had.

Cannon had uncharacteristically written off $1.5m from *Pirates* as of the quarter ended June 28th – the very essence of prudence now that the SEC investigation was under way, for the picture was not actually released until July. If their earlier statements about the promotion they were going to give it had been even half carried out, surely a higher write-down still was required? Not according to Globus with his estimate of $1m–$2m in total.

Forbes News pointed out that, as of July 15th, 1986, 10% of the company's 7.9m shares were sold short. It was not that the sceptics didn't like Cannon's movies, rather that they didn't like its book-keeping. Now Tatiana Pouchine of *Forbes* courageously revealed that, on her own reporting, she had reason to believe that the sceptics were on to something and were of the opinion that Cannon might be carrying as assets a 'very big number of sunk costs that it may never recapture'. A movie, they pointed out, was not a hard asset like a pair of shoes and that all a producer had for his money at the end of shooting was exposed film that could turn out to be worth a fortune – or nothing.

Forbes charted Cannon's previously-claimed amortisation rate as the reason why so many people found Cannon's shares an attractive proposition. In 1985 Cannon's rate was 57.2%, compared to Tri-Star's 77.6%. It looked therefore as if Cannon were only spending $572 to get $1,000 in revenues, while Tri-Star was spending $776. Maybe, *Forbes* conjectured – just maybe – Cannon was not more efficient than Tri-Star, merely slower in writing down its inventory of released films.

Forbes then traced the economic progress of twenty Cannon films released in 1985 and discovered that they took in about $9m each on average from all markets – theatrical showings, video, television, foreign – the works. The films had averaged about $5m each for negative costs and $2.4m in marketing costs – advertising, prints and promotion. Overhead and interest added about $1.2m per film, totalling $8.6m per release – just under the $9m *Forbes* claimed the films took. So where – they asked – was the profit? They conceded that Cannon made something from running theatres, but nothing like the $16.6m they had reported as pre-tax profit for 1985. In fact revenues from cinema operations improved from $18m to $37.5m between 1983 and 1985. Operating profit? Down from $1.4m to $418,000 before a climb back was reported in the first quarter of 1986. Where, then, *did* the profit come from? According to the sceptics – from under-amortisation of film costs.

Cannon's inventory, they went on to say, was mounting fast – from $121m at the end of 1984 to $213m at the end of 1985, some of this bulge resulting from Cannon making *more* films each year than the year before. Even allowing for this, the bulge was felt to be excessive. While inventories of films already released were mounting by more than 60%, film revenues – including TV – had risen by only 30%. A $50m plus increase in releases had produced only a $26m increase in revenues.

Further – at $213m, Cannon's total inventory was actually higher than Paramount's $199m, even though Paramount had no less than *eight* times Cannon's revenue.

The suspicion was unavoidable – that Cannon were booking revenues faster than they were recognising costs. Anyone guilty of this was 'a candidate for a fat write-down somewhere down the line'. Was Cannon ripe for such a write-down? Although the short sellers and other sceptics clearly thought so, Globus retorted, 'A lot of people have been hurt trying to short Cannon.'

Financial Accounting Standards Board rule no. 53 stated that management's revenue projections had to be reviewed 'periodically' – the question was how 'periodically' had Cannon been doing these reviews? And in the first place, of equal importance – how *realistic* were these original projections? Jay Shapiro, a partner in the big, prestigious accounting firm of Laventhol & Horwath, expressed doubts on this as he said, 'I can't explain why Cannon's amortisation percentage is so small. There is something very puzzling in Cannon's numbers and as a member of the public dealing with their numbers, I can't explain it.'

Globus and Golan were reportedly adamant that it was all a matter of operating efficiency, Golan stating further that, 'We have the same chance to hit a big movie as any other major. We haven't done it but in the meantime we are making profits.' Granted – *Forbes* conceded – but were they at the expense of a future write-off?

On a visit to London Yoram Globus was interviewed by *Screen International*. He told them that the inquiry was 'only concerned with 1983/84 figures' and would *not* be looking into any more recent accounts. Although Cannon had not been obliged to disclose details of the SEC inquiry, they had decided to do so – even against the advice of their corporate lawyers – 'because we have nothing to hide and didn't want any secrets,' as Globus maintained. When they were cleared by the SEC it would be 'an even bigger victory.

We are ready to challenge any other film company in the industry over amortization of films. It is history they are attacking us for – our library is fully amortized, whereas Hollywood studios choose to keep value in theirs.' *Screen International* also noted that 'doubts centre on Cannon's own estimates of realisable value on individual films, especially since it has had a notable lack of box-office success since last year.'

When the trade paper noted that the second quarter figures just revealed had been boosted by the 2,500-title sale to VMP (Video Median Pool), Globus asserted that the figures represented proof of the value Cannon was already getting from TESE.

A week later *Screen International* printed the following letter from Globus:

> With reference to the article about Cannon, I should like to point out two misleading quotes which appeared and are not as I quoted them to you.
> 1: You wrote about our 'reasonable revenue . . . especially since it has had a notable lack of box office success last year'. I don't know from where you got this information. First of all Cannon do not rely on a box office success for their earnings for Profit or Loss since Cannon are pre-licensing the movies to distributors around the world in all media and thereby covering the negative cost. Naturally it would also be nice to have a success in the US which would reflect even more on the earnings. In other territories in the world, if you look at where the figures are printed in your magazine, you will find that in every territory Cannon have a hit movie.
> 2: When you wrote 'It may take a few months for the review to complete its findings, "but we will bury them", he said' – this is a very incorrect quote. What I said was that my belief is that the shorter is a part of the whole problem and once the enquiry has satisfied the proper authority then 'the problem will be buried' and this is not clearly understood from your article.
>
> I hope that you correct these two points both to be accurate to your readers and to state the facts.

In all the wars of words it was left to Jack Valenti, President of the MPAA (Motion Pictures Association of America) – to which organisation, it should be noted, Cannon had chosen not to belong – to give a cool judgment on the concerns being voiced about the state of Cannon's health. 'I know nothing about their balance sheets,' he stated, 'so I don't know if they're making money or not. But I don't think bankers are dumb and they go on lending them money. The stockholders seem to approve of what they're doing. I don't know where the dissenting voices come from. Certainly, if they get into too many high-budget pictures they're going to have to capture the favour of audiences. Eventually, it isn't the bankers, the studio heads or festival juries who give the verdict. The standard to which Cannon, like any company, must be summoned is to make pictures which a sufficient number of people find engaging and entertaining.'

There it was – and although it had been put in different ways before, it had seldom been better put. Cannon should have had this framed and plastered all over their office.

There was a degree of puzzlement over Cannon's claimed sale of 2,500 titles to VMP (Video Median Pool) in Germany, first revealed in its 10 Q filing for the quarter ended June 28th – the same one which had disclosed the SEC inquiry. Some portion of the sale had already been included as revenue in these accounts, which spelled out that in the identical period twelve months earlier the same activities yielded only $2.4m. In this quarter – largely, it would seem, due to the VMP deal, revenue from this distribution source was no less than a whopping $54,469,000.

A Cannon executive maintained that the deal involved an up-front payment, with the balance to come over a four-year period, and that the total involved was 'some $100m'.

This seemed a surprisingly large purchase for a company of VMP's size and when Dieter Kasper, VMP's boss, was contacted early in September, he was asked if the deal had in fact been signed. The answer was 'no'. What *had* been signed apparently, was what Kasper call a 'clear approved option'. Full explanatory details would be forthcoming in a joint press release compiled by Globus and him 'within a few days' – which never materialised. One thing is for sure – without the inclusion of revenue from this 'deal' Cannon's quarterly figures would have lost their sparkle.

Cannon's reconsideration of their decision to abandon the TESE/HBO deal had several implications, as had their change of heart about 'going into the retail trade' in other countries as well. The first implication for cash-flow purposes was a good one, but the snag was that they were saying goodbye to many presales with money upfront for the future. Their change of heart and subsequent formation of HBO/Cannon Video prompted speculation whether the eventual profits from their home-video involvement would outweigh, and justify giving up, the millions of dollars in pre-financing that their previous output deal had provided. Perhaps cash-flow ruled the day in their decision.

While in Paris in early September for the *Otello* launch, Golan and Globus called in financial correspondents for a breakfast press conference to refute reports emanating from the US and Britain on their financial status.

'Cannon has become a controversial company for two reasons,' Globus explained. 'Firstly, we are successful, and secondly, we have constantly to fight short sellers who acquired about 10% of the stock when the price was around $18 to $22. So far, they have lost about $8,000,000.

'The shorters are trying to force the share price down by rumour and innuendo.'

'Cannon is the strongest and most stable film company. The reasons are that the management is unchanging and the cash-flow is in good shape and getting better,' said chairman Golan.

'The banks are with us. We have a terrific relationship with the banks in the US and the Credit Lyonnais Nederland considers us one of its best customers.

'When you run fast you leave behind lots of casualties. We have made enemies. Now there are lots of shaky rumours and some newspapers have been blowing bad winds against us, based on shorting the stock.

'We are going through a war with shorters of stock and we have learned that the best way to fight that war was to continue on our way and produce our films.

'The US financial community has had a very difficult time understanding the concept difference between Cannon and the major companies.'

Globus added, 'Evaluation of the company should be based on

its asset base. The shorters are beginning to realise that Cannon does not need big hits. They have seen the red light and they are beginning to panic.'

Referring to the SEC investigation into Cannon's method of amortising film costs Globus said, 'This is the first time in history that an important film company has voluntarily disclosed full information.'

With regard to a newspaper suggestion that the hole in the balance sheet could be filled by the sale of assets, Golan said nobody had asked Cannon to sell assets. There had been no such demand from the company's bankers.

Globus said adverse press comment was written by people who understood neither film accounting nor the difference between Cannon and the Hollywood majors, who distribute their own product world wide. Presumably he included America's leading business magazine *Forbes News* under this heading in the light of their recent report. As regards the suggestion that Cannon's balance sheet hole could be filled by the sale of assets – made first, in August, in Britain's *Observer* newspaper – well, only time would tell.

In London for the Royal Premiere of *Otello*, the Cannon team announced that planning permission had been granted by Westminster City Council for their planned £7m seventeen-screen multiplex in London's Piccadilly Circus. Their multiplex in Rome had just opened – the first in Italy – and it was anticipated the London opening would be in May 1988.

With the SEC enquiry still going on, *Screen International* noted the growing concern in the industry on what they still termed the 'losses sustained in the company's distribution activities'. They also maintained that 'It is a widely held opinion that even when Cannon has a good film it does not have the expertise to exploit it fully,' quoting the example of *Runaway Train*.

Meanwhile – how were Cannon's new releases performing? In a word – badly. *The Texas Chainsaw Massacre II* opened – unrated – at 1,474 cinemas and took only $2,882,439 ($1,915 per cinema). By the following weekend it had dropped 38% to $1,737,561, then a horrendous 69% plunge in its third and mostly final week to $534,981 ($1,061 per cinema). Never mind – reinforcements were on the way in the shape of Michael (*American Ninja*) Dudikoff's

Avenging Force. *Variety* reported that it 'continued Cannon's streak of box-office duds' with only a reported $1,131,502 at 500 theatres. Second weekend – a 38% plunge to $698,033 before another sickening drop of 50% to a paltry $210,461 in week three. Even *Otello* was performing way below its obviously more limited expectations – it accumulated less than $200,000 in total in its first month of US release, and *Link*, inherited from SEL, was proving to be a complete non-starter.

The top ten films emerged at the end of September, 1986 as:

Ranking	Film	Box-office Gross	Distributor
1)	*Top Gun**	$150.7m	PARAMOUNT
2)	*Rocky IV*	$123.9m	MGM/UA
3)	*Karate Kid II**	$109.5m	COLUMBIA
4)	*The Color Purple*	$ 94.0m	WARNER BROS.
5)	*Back to School**	$ 87.6m	ORION
6)	*Out of Africa*	$ 83.1m	UNIVERSAL
7)	*Aliens**	$ 76.3m	20TH CENTURY FOX
8)	*Ruthless People**	$ 68.5m	BUENA-VISTA
9)	*Ferris Bueller's Day Off**	$ 67.3m	PARAMOUNT
10)	*Jewel of the Nile*	$ 65.5m	20TH CENTURY FOX

(No sign of Cannon here – what about the next ten?)

11)	*Down & Out in Beverly Hills*	$ 60.2m	BUENA-VISTA
12)	*Spies Like Us*	$ 59.5m	WARNER BROS.
13)	*Cobra*	$ 48.2m	WARNER BROS.
14)	*Legal Eagles*	$ 46.2m	UNIVERSAL
15)	*Police Academy III*	$ 42.7m	WARNER BROS.
16)	*White Nights*	$ 42.2m	COLUMBIA
17)	*Short Circuit*	$ 40.5m	TRI-STAR
18)	*Pretty in Pink*	$ 40.2m	PARAMOUNT
19)	*Poltergeist II*	$ 38.8m	MGM/UA
20)	*About Last Night**	$ 37.7m	TRI-STAR

*still in release.

So apart from their claimed 'net profit position' in *Cobra* Cannon were totally unrepresented. In fact, their first entry, *The Delta*

Force, grossing $17m, appeared no higher than no. 42 on the list. Interestingly, what Paramount saw as their two failures of the Christmas 1985 season, which had been written down in early 1986, were *Young Sherlock Holmes* and *Clue* – with gross box-office figures at $18.1m and $13.4m respectively.

Here is Cannon's full list of box-office performers for the period:

Film	Box-office Gross
Delta Force	$17.0m
King Solomon's Mines	$15.1m
Murphy's Law	$ 9.7m
Runaway Train	$ 7.7m
Texas Chainsaw Massacre II	$ 7.7m
Invaders from Mars	$ 4.8m
*Avenging Force**	$ 3.8m
Dangerously Close	$ 2.0m
POW, the Escape	$ 1.9m
The Naked Cage	$ 1.7m
Pirates	$ 1.0m
*Link**	$ 0.7m
Fool for Love	$ 0.5m

*still in release.

Halfway through the period – in May 1986 – Menahem Golan had told *Newsweek*, 'We are *outperforming* Paramount, Fox, Disney, MGM/United Artists, Orion and Tri-Star.' He neglected to say which extraordinary yardstick he was using. Cannon's feeble total from thirteen pictures of only $73.6m compared like this with the people he was *'outperforming'*:

Box-office Gross Nov. 22nd '85 – End Sept. '86

PARAMOUNT :	$412.6m
FOX :	$236.7m
DISNEY :	$235.8m
MGM/UA :	$223.8m
TRI-STAR :	$187.1m
ORION :	$156.1m

Warners at $307.3m, Columbia at $291.2m and Universal at $225.7m didn't do too badly either – at least, compared to Cannon's $73.6m. But who needs hits? Cannon did – as their shares plummeted from $29 to below $22 before slowly edging back up from the brink.

The rosy picture continued throughout October to grow for the majors. Paramount, without doubt the 'glitz' studio, had yet another smash hit with the Paul Hogan Australian import *Crocodile Dundee*, while director Martin Scorsese's *The Color of Money* had opened to great business for Buena Vista. Columbia's low-budget *Stand by Me* was the sleeper of the year. Francis Coppola seemed to be back on form with *Peggy Sue Got Married* for Tri-Star, while there seemed to be no stopping the holdovers from summer – *Top Gun*, *Ruthless People*, *Karate Kid II*, *Aliens* and *Back to School*. US box-office had now rebounded with a vengeance and it began to look as if the final tally for 1986 might be at least up to 1985's level. The revival that had begun in late June had gathered momentum. At that time cumulative box-office was 1% down from 1985 – but 7% down from 1984.

Now September had shown an 11% increase on the previous year and October seemed to be heading for a mighty 25% increase – proof again that there was plenty of life left in exhibition, given good product.

The Cannon saga took a further turn with the news of a stockholders' class action suit against the company, alleging misrepresentation of financial status and failure to comply with proper accounting procedures. This action followed those of two individual shareholders a few weeks earlier, reported in the *Wall Street Journal*. Those individuals had bought Cannon stock at $44 and seemed to be claiming they had been misled by financial information Cannon had put out.

In the class action suit, announced in October and being brought by Laurence Walner and Associates L.A. Defined Benefit Pension Fund, they charged that Cannon's 1985 annual report failed to properly amortise production costs and further alleged that similar misrepresentations were made in a filing with the SEC and in the prospectus offering of convertible debentures of April 1986.

David Puttnam's installation at Columbia had taken place in September while the launch of *The Mission* was going on and he was fully *in situ* early in November. Interviewed in Europe in October, he was asked about Cannon. Emphasising that he would rather be wrong, he nevertheless stated, 'I don't for one second believe that the Cannon organisation as presently constituted will still exist this time next year.' He repeated that he sincerely hoped he was wrong 'because the effects of that on the British film industry could be extremely damaging'. He reckoned they had been guilty of *folie de grandeur*, growing too fast and overstretching themselves. Their lines of credit were long – and in his opinion, extremely unhealthy. Their major error was to have entered the field of distribution, which he likened to Napoleon choosing to invade Russia in the winter – 'If you make a flop you no longer lose 20% or 30% of your original investment, you may now lose 200%. Suddenly you've got the chance of losing the cost of your prints and advertising as well.' He then criticised their ability in the distribution field and gave his opinion that the likes of *Runaway Train* could have done a lot better if released by someone else.

The Cannon chiefs were stung – and hastily despatched an open letter to the trade paper who had published the interview. It read:

> Mr Puttman,
>
> In response to your bizarre commentary in 'Screen International', especially to your 'prophecy' as to where we shall be one year from now, we were amused, and decided to invite you to a gracious dinner in a year's time to review where we *both* are (meaning you and us). However, in our generosity, we are prepared to extend the date to 24 months from now.
>
> MENAHEM GOLAN, Chairman
> YORAM GLOBUS, President
> The Cannon Group Inc, Los Angeles.

Predictably Michael Winner's contribution was there as well, piquantly printed under Cannon's letter and the headline, 'Cannon chiefs respond to Puttnam's prophecy'. He saw Puttnam's statement as an 'unwarranted and disgraceful attack'. It was amusing to note, he reckoned, that one of the first films Puttnam had acquired for Columbia was Bill Forsyth's *Housekeeping*, 'which he bought from Cannon', as he put it – perhaps more accurately it should have been 'rescued from Cannon', following Puttnam's claim on BBC-TV's Film '86 that the project had been floundering for lack of money. 'Doubtless,' Winner concluded, 'another early project [from Puttnam] will be a remake of *The Bitch*. Starring David.' Now there definitely was something wrong here! *Chariots of Fire*, *The Killing Fields*, *The Mission*? Yes. But *The Bitch* – no, no, surely a remake of this was far more up Cannon and Winner's street?

Prior to Mifed, Cannon announced the following film release schedule for the remainder of 1986 and for 1987:

1)	Ready for release	:	*52 Pick-up, Duet for One*
2)	November 1986	:	*Firewalker*
3)	Christmas 1986	:	*Allan Quatermain*
4)	January 1987	:	*Journey to the Centre of the Earth, Number One with a Bullet*
5)	February 1987	:	*Over the Top, Street Smart, Mascara*
6)	March 1987	:	*African Adventure*
7)	Cannes 1987 Showing	:	*Missing in Action III, Death Wish IV, Surrender, Giselle, Shy People, Tough Guys Don't Dance, Hanoi Hilton, Spider's Web, King Lear*
8)	June 1987	:	*Masters of the Universe*
9)	July 1987	:	*Superman IV, Cannonball Run*
10)	Fall 1987	:	*Investigation*
11)	Christmas 1987	:	*Born Yesterday, The Merry Wives, Guardian Angels, Haunted Summer, Barfly, North/South, River of Death*

Despite their financial difficulties, Cannon's top priority was clearly to keep on making more and more pictures than ever before – in other words, business as usual. As an introduction to their own Elstree Studios, before *Superman IV* moved in, they had filmed a low-budget 'romantic thriller' there (as *Variety* put it: 'read sex and violence'). *Three Kinds of Heat* was directed by Leslie Stevens and starred Robert Ginty, Victoria Barrett and Shakti. With Victoria

Barrett Cannon appeared to have moved into the talent-spotting business, as she had now been identified with Cannon for several years. Menahem Golan himself had cast her as Elliott Gould's dream girl in his *Over the Brooklyn Bridge* and she had also appeared in *Thunder Warriors* (aka *America 3000*), *Hot Resort* and *Hot Chilis* before *Three Kinds of Heat*. A star in the making, perhaps.

Other film starts, despite the hiatus many claimed was going on internally due to the balance sheet deficit, were *The Barbarians* in Rome, *Ben and Bonzo* in Kenya, *Superman IV* in Britain, *Surrender* and *Hanoi Hilton* in California, *Gor* and *Kitchen Toto* in Zimbabwe, *Shy People* in Louisiana, *Giselle* in Bari, Italy, *Blood Sport* in Hong Kong, *American Ninja II* in South Africa, *Tough Guys Don't Dance* in Provincetown, Massachusetts and *Business as Usual* in Liverpool, England – together with the continuing fairytales in Israel.

At the Mifed film market Golan and Globus were not surprisingly said to be 'ired' by Puttnam's statement, but Golan was reportedly beaming about favourable reports from insider screenings of *Over the Top*. Globus shrugged off the continuing rumours about their financial status. 'We've been smeared since we came to Hollywood,' he stated. 'We were smeared when we were small and we're smeared when we've become big. I'd rather be big and smeared.' 'They'll keep saying what they want,' Golan added, 'but we'll go forward. We've never been in better shape!'

Chapter Fourteen
POSTSCRIPT

To their credit both Golan and Globus gave rousing performances at Mifed despite the gathering gloom.

'I'm a filmmaker.' Golan declared. 'I have to see if what I do works. It's part of my life. I go to Mifed to hear and learn from each country. I want to know the buyers' feelings and their ideas, what kind of pictures they're interested in and what's happening in their countries.'

For the first time Globus announced that Cannon would not be giving out dollar totals of their sales. 'I'm telling everyone they should read about it in the company's financial report,' he uncharacteristically explained. Oddly they were not so reticent with any figures it suited them to reveal, like the $2m weekly gross from their British circuit. Did this represent a 'for sale' sign? Certainly not! Nor was there any truth in the rumour that they were set to sell their Italian cinemas on which more statistics were revealed – 25,000 tickets per week sold since their Milan multiplex opened. Golan firmly denied the sale with a little parable: 'My grandfather always told me if you have orange groves, never sell them. They will grow oranges for ever. We will never sell our Cannon Italia circuit. Cinemas will sell tickets forever and you can always go to the ticket window for some of the cash and eat.'

Meantime Globus announced what many interpreted as his most desperate cash-raising measure yet, a three-year output deal requiring distributors to commit to an upfront payment together with a monthly guarantee in return for video and theatrical rights to the Cannon library, plus their new feature output.

In this way, Globus reasoned, Cannon would be assured of a regular cash flow from the foreign market, levelling out what he poetically described as 'the peaks and valleys of income' that would facilitate forward financial planning. He claimed the suggestion had been taken up by ten distributors, describing the deal as a 'marriage of interests', while stressing the whole thing was all part of Cannon's ongoing policy to ensure their customers survived and prospered. In line with this, he explained that the upfront money and monthly contributions 'had not been exaggerated'. The ten? Well – distributors in Australia, Spain, Brazil, Mexico and Argentina were five at least.

What about a rumour that Cannon were going to be forced to sell their US Commonwealth theatre chain to raise much-needed capital? Following his 'orange groves' address, Golan added that owning a stake in US exhibition gave Cannon power, standing and cash flow. That seemed like a 'no'. However, another spokesman for the company privately stated, 'Cannon bought cinemas when everybody said we were crazy to do so, now everybody is buying cinemas. Cannon can be relied upon to go against the trend again if it makes sense financially.' Sounds like an almost definite 'yes' – how about Globus? 'The circuit is not for sale,' he stated adamantly, adding, 'but we have had a number of offers'. A faint 'maybe'?

The rationale behind any sale was that there had been a rash of theatre acquisitions in the States which precluded Cannon's adding to Commonwealth. Universal through MCA had a 50% position in Cineplex; other majors buying into exhibition were Paramount through Gulf and Western's acquisition of Mann Theatres and Tri-Star's buy of Loews – so why not cash in their chips now and take their profit?

Golan claimed another forty films were planned for 1987 – four higher budget pictures, sixteen medium range and twenty low-budgeters, but that Cannon's aim now was to bring the average budgets down from 1986's level of $5.5m average to somewhere between $4.5–$5m. 'We must stretch ourselves,' he declared, 'we have that obligation to our company.'

Perhaps as a result of Cannon's own box-office performance over the last two years, Golan now indicated that he expected the market to change with cheapo exploitationers being released directly to video, at least in the States. Obviously aware of the inroads New World et al were making into this market, Golan convolutedly announced that Cannon, while having a preference in low-budget items for art films, and without wishing to get involved in 'purely exploitational films', would nonetheless themselves be entering the made-for-video market of under-$2m budgeters.

So now their policy was – what? Big budget prestige pictures like *Otello*? Big budget commercial projects like *Over the Top* and *Superman IV*? Low budget art films like *Fool For Love* and *King Lear*? Low-medium budget art/commercial combinations like *Tough Guys Don't Dance*? Medium-budget *Captain America*s, *Masters of the Universe* and *Spiderman*? Low-budget martial arts *American Ninja II* and *Avenging Force*? Continuing medium-budget exploitationers like *Deathwish IV* and *Assassination*? Low-budget soft porn like the newly-announced Sylvie Kristel *Desires*? Medium-budget romance like *Surrender*? Or just anything and everything they could lay their hands on regardless?

'We will continue to seek outside investments for prints and advertising,' Golan declared, admitting that outside investment was required to even allow Cannon to *open* their pictures. 'And we have managed to take $5m out of the budget of *Superman IV*,' he added, causing industry wags to wonder if in Cannon's cut-rate version Superman would be unable to fly.

A date was set for the world premiere of *Over the Top* of February 12th, 1987. But surely that was a Thursday and out of step with industry practice? Golan explained that the unusual launch day was specified by Stallone himself, who had been advised by astrologers that this would be the best day to open. Globus contributed, 'Stallone works by astrologers. He doesn't start shooting until they tell him the day and the date, but with anyone who can gross $300m at the box-office in one year, you can be very patient!' Golan maintained that Stallone wanted to make another picture with him and that he was currently looking for a property. Had he and Stallone got on while shooting *Over the Top*? By the end of it, Golan claimed, he and Stallone were getting on well. Two items were overlooked in Stallone's choice of opening day. One was this would give the film a first-weekend's gross covering four instead of three days, the other was that by opening on the conventional day *Over The Top* would have run into Black Friday the thirteenth!

In Britain *Private Eye* had a look at the disputed 'contract' for the licensing of SEL and Cannon movies to Video Median Pool which Dieter Kasper of VMP had stated only constituted a 'clear approved option'. Cannon's claim of a '$100m deal' had to be taken with a pinch of salt, the 'Eye' reckoned, adding that a reliable source in Cannon's office had sight of the contract and that it was for $50m. They also took issue with Cannon's claim that the deal was for 2,500 titles, reckoning that the total number of titles from the combined library was in fact below 2,000 and that in any case, a substantial part of Thorn-EMI's library had already been licensed for German exploitation in all media, as well as for TV exploitation in European fringe territories, to another German distributor, Taurus Beta Film of Munich. Could it be that Cannon had inadvertently licensed product that had already been sold? The licences, it seems, had been granted to Taurus Beta until the year 2000, then later extended in a separate deal to 2020.

'Perhaps,' the *Eye* conjectured, 'Cannon is a little confused as to the availability of titles from (its) library. Perhaps VMP has been led to believe it will have access to titles that have already been licensed. Certainly it looks as if Cannon's decision to book the revenue from this licensing deal in their last accounts was decidedly ill-advised.' From the Cannon camp – silence.

With Cannon's US box-office market share at a lowly 2.6% for 1986 as of end-October, what of the majors Golan had reckoned they were outperforming in May? Paramount had 18.5%, Twentieth Century Fox 8.8%, Disney/Touchstone 9.8%, MGM/UA 5.4%, Tri-Star 7.7% and Orion 6.9%. Others well ahead of Cannon – Columbia with 11.3%, Warners with 10.7% and Universal with 8.7%. Maybe Golan had meant 'outperforming' in a different way, perhaps referring to debt and leverage. Or maybe he meant film starts, for at the same period as the market share was revealed Cannon had started an incredible 41 films – compared to Columbia's 5, Orion's 10, Fox's 7 and Universal and Paramount's 9 each. If market share and 'outperformance' was measured in these terms, then yes – Cannon *was* number one and outperforming everyone in sight!

Top Ten Film Companies in Terms of Film Starts	Number Films Started in 1986	% of Total	% of Box-office for these Companies in Terms of 1986 Released Films
1) CANNON	41	29.0	2.6
2) NEW WORLD	18	12.8	1.8
3) HEMDALE	15	10.6	–
4) TRI-STAR	15	10.6	7.7
5) ORION	10	7.1	6.9
6) WARNERS	10	7.1	10.7
7) UNIVERSAL	9	6.4	8.7
8) PARAMOUNT	9	6.4	18.5
9) DEG	7	5.0	2.2
10) 20TH CENTURY FOX	7	5.0	8.8

TOTAL = 141

John Frankenheimer's *52 Pick Up* was due to open during the first week of November, so maybe that would halt their non-stop run of flops. The reviews were generally good and the film in fact was a remarkable return to form for Frankenheimer. Attractive performances by the two leads, Roy Scheider and Ann Margret, were supported by three of the best-written and acted villains seen in a while. The authentic Elmore Leonard flavour was there in full measure, not surprisingly as he had co-written the screenplay.

The one sequence that marred the picture was an unnecessarily graphic murder scene. *Variety* was one of the few publications to give the picture a downbeat review, dubbing it a 'thriller without any thrills', with a box-office outlook that was at best modest. As often happens *Variety* was correct and Cannon's hopes of a break in the pattern were dashed as *52 Pick Up* opened at 730 cinemas across the US to take a tepid $1,654,835 – $2,267 per cinema – in its opening weekend. Determined to reverse the almost inevitable trend the following week, Golan authorised a massive press campaign that quoted some of the many favourable reviews, to boost the film. Two-page advertisements appeared not only in trade papers like *Variety*, but also in the Sunday edition of the *New York Times*. Whoever chose the heading for the advertisements should have spent a few minutes pondering the implications. No doubt what he meant to convey was 'The best film of the season – and it's from Cannon'. Instead the heading ran 'The best film of the season from Cannon'. The public reaction predictably was that the claim did not amount to much and a 30% drop occurred in the second weekend of release despite the ads. Worse was to come – a 57% drop to only $504,613 in the third weekend – $4,275,848 cumulative for a film with a negative cost of around $8m and release costs of around $3m. *52 Pick Up* deserved to do better, but maybe with the graphic murder scene excised it would have made a better 'TV movie of the week' than a theatrical release – a fact of life concerning the changing film business.

With the continuing SEC enquiry and Cannon's rumoured acute cash shortage, the company shares were under continual pressure. By the end of September they were just above $22 each on the New York Stock Exchange – less than half their July peak of $45.50. During October there was a recovery to around $25 until the revival peaked in early November at $31. There were two reasons for this recovery – the first was Cannon's finally admitted intention of selling the Commonwealth chain, which was boosted to yield about double the $50m equivalent they had paid for it, and secondly – a $200m 'private placement' that junk bond specialist Drexel Burnham Lambert was rumoured to be about to make on their behalf. The word from Cannon was that this was almost a given thing and on this basis hope returned once more. Just around the corner, however, was a devastating one-two punch.

The first came in the form of an admission from Cannon – but only on October 30th – that the SEC investigation had in fact turned 'formal' on September 15th. Not only that, but together with the SEC's now established formal powers of subpoena – not confined now to Cannon themselves, but also any other source they cared to tap – the scope of their investigation had been broadened

221

to take in almost every other single conceivable aspect of the entire Cannon organisation, on top of amortisation, including:

Reported earnings,
Licensing transactions,
Tax liabilities,
Internal Accounting Controls,
Book and Record Keeping,
Use of proceeds from public offerings,
General financial condition.

The announcement of the formalisation of Lee Isgur's 'non-event' caused an immediate plunge again in Cannon's shares, back to $22. Worse was to come.

The company's quarterly results were due 45 days after the September 27th period end and for the second quarter in succession they were late. When released on November 19th, they told a sorry tale. Despite soaring revenue, up 125% to $77m from $34.3m a year earlier, Cannon announced the unthinkable – **a whopping loss of no less than $14.5m**, enough to wipe out the gains for the nine months of 1986 and register a cumulative $5.82m loss for the whole period.

There were some interesting revelations in the unaudited 10 Q quarterly filing that announced Cannon's first reversal since their formation in 1979. One concerned the video deal with VMP: now it was admitted that, 'the company agreed to modify the payment schedule of a contract for the licence of certain SEL and Cannon library film rights, which had the effect of reducing income by $8,666,000 primarily because of the *effects of discounting*'. Without the inclusion of the $8,666,000 in the June quarter's accounts, Cannon would have had to declare a loss in September – and start the share slide earlier that now followed. Had *Private Eye* hit the nail on the head?

The next revelation – Cannon's long-established auditors Mann Judd Landau were out, in were British-based Arthur Young and Company. Their first assignment – an audit of the disastrous nine month period.

'As a result,' the report stated, 'of the company's investigation of a number of issues relating to the company's accounting policies and practices and financial statements (including its method of estimating the amounts of ultimate revenues and costs and the

222

impact, if any, of such estimation process on the amortization of film cost), the company is reviewing certain items with others yet to be reviewed, the resolution of which could cause *material differences* in the financial data presented herein.'

Next: 'the results of operations for the interim periods of the company's financial year are not necessarily indicative of the results to be expected for the entire year, due to the seasonal nature of the company's business'. Here indeed was a new wrinkle.

The company's losses, the filing went on to state, were largely attributable to major increases in selling, general and administrative expenses and to increased expense resulting from higher overall levels of interest-bearing obligations. The production activities had required the hiring of additional administrative, financial, accounting and marketing personnel as well as increased general overhead expenses, including substantial legal and accounting expenses relating to shareholder litigation and the SEC investigation.

The company had 20 pictures complete and awaiting theatrical release with another 20 in production or post-production, per the filing, and 'the company's first priorities continued to be the structuring of improved and expanded financing to meet the company's immediate and long-term requirements'. (Read: more debt, stress-immediate.)

The company, the report continued, had intensively reviewed its asset base, current financial obligations, financing sources, financial and accounting policies and current liquidity issues – and reached several conclusions. One was that, because of the dramatic escalation of prices for theatres in the US, it should sell Commonwealth theatres and 'continue to rationalise' the combined Cannon/SEL chains in the UK 'by selling selected overlapping sites'.

Second, they had reviewed the Cannon and SEL film library (the titles *Rambo* and *Amadeus* were wheeled out) and had come to the conclusion that these had not been exploited to the full. So now they were proposing to use what they termed the 'substantial unexploited value in ancillary markets' as the foundation for 'asset-based borrowings to supplement existing bank lines'. Yes – more debt!

Third, despite their presales ballyhoo, the company, the report continued, 'has not yet licensed valuable video cassette and significant other rights to a number of its completed pictures and other in production or post-production, including *Surrender*, *Masters of the Universe* and *Hanoi Hilton*. They were 'aggressively pursuing the licensing of these rights to such pictures'.

Could anyone sense a 'fire sale' – firstly of Commonwealth and the unfortunate 'overlapping UK theatres', secondly to unsold video rights – always assuming they were genuinely available and that more demand for *Rambo* had yet to be satisfied – and thirdly, to movies still in production always before claimed to be pre-sold before a single foot of film was exposed?

The report conceded that 'the theatrical performance of the company's pictures has been disappointing over the past 39-week period, but heralded an "unparalleled variety of motion pictures" to come.' Chuck Norris in *Firewalker*! The first fairy-tale – *Rumpelstiltskin*! Richard Chamberlain in *Allan Quatermain and the Lost City of Gold*! In 1987 – Sylvester Stallone's *Over The Top*! *Superman IV*! *Surrender*! And 'throughout 1987 the release of such motion pictures could have a substantial positive impact on the company's financial position'.

For the quarter, Cannon had increased its amortisation rate from 54% a year earlier to no less than 70%, admitting now that they were having to spend 70 cents for every dollar of revenue. The cumulative figure for 1986 was now 66% compared to 58% for the first nine months of 1985.

Bank facilities were listed as:

Credit Lyonnais	$25,600,000 drawn out of their $35,000,000 revolving credit facility, plus $10,000,000 in the form of a letter of credit facility.
FNNB (First National Bank of Boston acting as agents for Bank of America, Chemical Bank and Wells Fargo N.A.)	$64,876,000 drawn out of their line of credit and letter of credit facility for $76,000,000. In addition the company had an additional 'short-term' FNNB credit facility – unspecified – to be repaid from 'additional collateral collections'.

Not mentioned was a Standard Chartered loan of $50m. TESE management had formed a separate company to hold the cinemas and studio property, mortgaging this with Standard Chartered to raise $50m. Bond had inherited the arrangement first, followed by Cannon.

Cannon further revealed that they were reviewing their amortisation policies in conjunction with Arthur Young 'to determine whether, in the light of their proven ability to generate continuing earnings in ancillary markets and the opening of new markets for such product, the company should increase its estimates of ultimate revenues and extend periods for film cost amortisation'. Some observers felt that this took the biscuit for sheer nerve and chutzpah – in the same report that Cannon had admitted a speeding up of their cost amortisation rate from 54% to 70%, they were putting up a kite for Arthur Young that perhaps they were being too quick to write off film costs! What *were* they carrying on their books still, even with the acceleration to 70%? Here's what:

	Sept. '86	June '86	December '85
FILM COSTS (NON-SEL)	$333.5m	$267.7	$213.1
FILM COSTS (SEL)	$144.8	$149.9	Nil (pre-takeover)
TOTAL FILM COSTS:	$478.3	$417.7	$213.1

$478.3m, up from $213.1m in December '85, when Forbes had compared their total with Paramount's $199m – and eight times Cannon's revenues!

How about debt? The total had risen from December '85's $215.2m to $595.7m:

	Sept. '86	June '86	December '85
LONG-TERM DEBT	$433.8m	$391.2	$200.3
SHORT-TERM DEBT	$161.9	$166.8	$ 14.9
TOTAL DEBT:	$595.7	$558.0	$215.2

How about assets over liabilities? Current assets were shown as $177.4m, current liabilities at $299.7m, resulting in a working capital deficit of $122.3m, up from $107m in June '86.

An interesting item surfaced towards the end of the report – the revelation that 'producer and participant costs' for the quarter had gone up from an almost non-existent 1% a year earlier, to 18%. Since Golan and Globus were the producers of the vast bulk of Cannon movies, were they now paying themselves a producers' fee – something they had said they never did? If not, who were these participants who had suddenly emerged to claim a staggering 18% of Cannon's net motion picture distribution revenues? Normally one would expect deferred and residual payments to emerge in a quarter containing hit pictures, but it was considered strange that 18% should be payable in their most unsuccessful quarter since their formation. So was this a catching-up payment? Some of the increase was explained as 'being caused in part by SEL-produced or acquired films which have a higher participation rate than the company's rate excluding SEL', but that 'in addition, certain motion pictures which generated revenue in the thirteen weeks of 1986 were subject to participations and the increased film production in the United States increased the number of pictures subject to residual payments under various collective bargaining agreements'. This statement only served to deepen the puzzle – were deferrals becoming *de rigueur* on so many of Cannon's current productions that a reserve was being created to cope with them?

The revelations in the 10 Q were enough to send the share price on a downward spiral. From the $22 they had settled at after the 'SEC goes formal' announcement, they slumped below $15 on heavy trading.

More shocks were in the pipeline as Alan Bond's resignation was announced, together with the bombshell that he had dropped plans to buy Cannon's stock. He had been given an option when the SEL deal was struck in May to accept part-payment in Cannon shares, then trading at $33. With the climb to over $45 in July it looked certain he would take the stock option offered rather than cash, and pocket yet more profit. Now with the decline he was taking the cash option – $30.6m, due in May 1987. However, if Cannon defaulted on the third instalment of cash due to Bond on December 15th, of £53.3m, then the convertible note for $30.6m was also due to mature on December 15th.

When contracted to confirm Bond's resignation on November 21st, Globus was asked exactly when this had taken place. He answered that it was 'a long time ago', but stated he could not remember exactly when.

Another resignation came from Thomas Pollock, part-time Cannon board member and senior partner in the law firm of Pollock, Bloom and Dekom. This came in the wake of his accepting the posts of vice president of M C A Inc. and chairman of the M C A Motion Picture Group (Universal), replacing Frank Price. Described as one of Hollywood's most influential entertainment lawyers, Pollock had been due to join Universal on October 15th. Among the clients his firm represented – the ubiquitous Sylvester Stallone. While Pollock was said to subscribe to William Goldman's 'nobody knows anything' theory on the movie business – something the Harry Cohns, Jack Warners and Darryl Zanucks would have found amusing, many industry insiders clearly applauded Pollock's appointment, citing his knowledge of the film business internationally and his creative talent connection.

By this time the Ivan Boesky scandal had broken wide open, rocking Wall Street and turning the spotlight on Drexel Burnham Lambert, junk bond kings, who had masterminded Cannon's April '86 securities offering of $207m, partly in junk bonds. Was the given thing that Cannon had leaked concerning Drexel's $200m private placement still in place? Globus declined to comment.

Could there be more? There could. US credit-rating agency Standard and Poor's announced on November 24th that they were putting Cannon's single-B subordinated debt on their Credit Watch surveillance list, with negative implications, affecting $240m worth of debt. The agency referred to the 10 Q's potential 'material adjustment' – clearly S&P's interpretation of this was not favourable. 'Quite frankly,' the agency stated, 'the company has been very secretive about its problems.' Recent developments raised what they indelicately described as 'the spectre of insolvency'.

Now the shares dropped further to a new low of $12 before rallying to $13⅞ before the New York Stock Exchange closed on the evening of Wednesday, November 26th for Thanksgiving. They had dropped 69% since their peak in July. Despite the brave face they put on it, even Yoram ('We don't have any problems') Globus and Menahem ('We've never been in better shape') Golan must have been feeling buffeted by cruel fate.

The hint of the sale of overlapping US sites started rumours in the US that the A B C circuit itself was up for sale. Cannon's British

MD Barry Jenkins issued a firm denial, without referring specifically to A B C: 'There is absolutely no truth in the rumour that our UK chain of cinemas is up for sale. Although previously we have announced that a few selected cinemas will close, these are the ones which have proved to be totally uneconomical. It is possible that in the future a few more closures may occur in towns where the community is served by two of our cinemas in close proximity, but no decisions have yet been made and I stress we are talking about a very small number indeed.'

In any case, the question of an A B C sale was seen as less likely when it was considered that Cannon would get only any excess from the sale over and above the $50m mortgage held by Standard Chartered. Besides, was A B C theirs to sell? In resigning from the Cannon board, Bond had in fact removed some restrictive covenants on the debt used by Cannon to acquire S E L which it was believed might assist in Drexel's proposed $200m private placement. This was hardly an altruistic gesture on Bond's part, since he would be the first beneficiary of the $200m – assuming it was raised, as December 15th loomed.

Golan declared that Cannon were now considering no fewer than seven bids for Commonwealth theatres. His first forecast was that a sale would be completed within two weeks, then he reconsidered and came up with the end of the year as a more likely scenario. He would not comment on whether a major studio was involved in the bidding, nor if a bidding was taking place.

The new Chuck Norris opener, *Firewalker*, had debuted alongside Universal's *An American Tail* and Disney's reissue of *Song of the South*. The hope was that with the addition of Lou Gosset, Chuck could regain some of the box-office sparkle lost since Orion's *Code of Silence*. Another added ingredient was humour – but would his fans accept it and could Chuck cope? Not according to most critics, who did not reckon Chuck's comic touch highly. *Variety* saw the movie as 'a clumsy comic adventure', deeming it 'devoid of suspense'.

It still managed $4.1m at 1,120 cinemas, trailing just behind *Song of the South* at $4.2m – but way behind *An American Tail* with $5.2m. Never mind – the second weekend was Thanksgiving, which could be relied upon to boost figures – couldn't it? For *An American Tail*, the boost was 42% to $7.4m. For *Song of the South* a 24% increase was registered to $5.2m. For *Firewalker*? A 29% *decrease* to $2.9m – and another crapshoot gone. Was Lee Isgur still hanging in there? Or was he still enthusing over what a wonderful buy S E L had been?

The S E C investigation of Drexel Burnham Lambert, in the wake of the Boesky scandal, continued to cause financial shock waves, particularly with regard to entertainment-related stock issues. Scepticism was expressed over offerings from Dino De Laurentiis D E G and from Carolco. 'It will be tougher for the film companies to raise money,' declared John Tinker of Bear, Stearns, specifically excepting well-capitalised companies from his comment. *Variety* reported that 'One Drexel client cited frequently in discussions of the Boesky/Drexel impact on future showbiz offerings is Cannon, which some observers feel will have to take the stock issue route to raise money'. Rumours to that effect were unfounded, Yoram Globus insisted. *Screen International* reported that 'Wall Street's insider trading scandal looks set to severely damage the fund raising efforts of several major film production companies, Carolco Pictures and the Cannon Group among them. For Cannon, the implications of the current crisis may prove particularly serious.'

Now Standard and Poor's entered the arena again, downgrading Cannon's credit rating from single B to single-B minus. S&P's rating specification indicated that 'a company has a greater vulnerability to default but currently has the capacity to meet interest payments'. Ominously it continued, 'Adverse business, financial or economic conditions will likely impair capacity to repay interest'. So S&P's 'spectre of insolvency' was seen as one step nearer. Back down went Cannon's shares to just over $11.

Sumner Redstone of National Amusement blew the gaff on Cannon's hopes of a quick profit from the Commonwealth theatre chain sale when he revealed that Cannon had received bids of no more than $22m – against the $25m it had paid and the $27m debt it had picked up, plus the $4m it had since spent on the chain.

As the December 15th deadline for Bond's $76.9m repayment passed, it transpired that Cannon had been given an extension, but only to December 19th. The $30.6m due in May 1987 was to be converted into four-year senior subordinated notes – in return

Bond was to get 500,000 warrants to purchase Cannon stock at $16 per share.

Hal Vogel of Merrill Lynch commented, 'Cannon's not going to be a strong company, but I think a financial arrangement will be worked out'. Lee Isgur pointed out that the $16 at which Bond could buy Cannon stock represented a premium of 30–40%. If the stock climbed back up to $40 again – which Isgur thought was realistic, Bond would be more than $10m to the good! Isgur continued to insist, 'I think what is wrong with (Cannon's) accounting practices – if anything – is what is wrong with accounting practices at all studios'. Nothing less than an organized conspiracy had been behind the adverse news coverage on Cannon, he maintained, adding that unsigned letters had been received by some members of the press, like the *Los Angeles Times*, about Cannon's accounting practices. A spokesman at the *Times* dryly commented that, unsigned letters or not, the point was the *legitimacy* of Cannon's practices.

Now came whispers of a deal in the offing with Warner Communications Inc. Warner was cash-rich, analyst John Tinker of Bear, Stearns and Co. pointed out, and they had the closest relationship of any major with the Go-Go boys. Even as the parties were seen to be in a huddle, a spanner was flung into the works as Hemdale re-entered the scene. Having lost the *Murphy's Law* court battle to Cannon, they were determined to lose nothing else. As speculation about a Warner deal and the future of the Cannon Group raged, Hemdale obtained an order in the London courts freezing Cannon's UK assets. They claimed they were due $1m from various licences granted to Cannon, the sum having been outstanding since December 1st. All was flung into confusion – there was no question of a Warner deal proceeding until the court order was lifted. Hemdale were far from being alone in their anxiety to be paid, although they were the first to take such drastic action. *Screen International* was supposedly owed a 6 figure sum, and in the normal course of business Rank were owed $2–$3m at any one time.

It was then confirmed that a deal with Warner had been discussed and Cannon were left with no alternative but to repay the debt to Hemdale. It was either that or being unable to pay Bond and facing insolvency. Cannon indeed seemed to have acquired

Murphy's Law in every sense, but with the unfreezing of their assets Warner's rescue operation became official – at a *very* considerable cost. In return for enabling Cannon to make the $76.9m repayment to Bond, Warner wanted their full pound of flesh – a two-year option on a 50% interest in *all* of Cannon's European theatres – Golan's veritable orange groves – for $50m. They would purchase 2 million shares of Cannon convertible preferred stock at $12.5 per share, yielding $25m, together with $25m worth of notes secured by Cannon assets, the theatres included – the transaction to be completed by March/April 1987. Until then Warner would guarantee a $50m bridging bank loan to Cannon, the guarantee to be withdrawn as soon as the stock and note deal was concluded. The estimated value of the European cinemas, A B C included, was $183m, including debt.

In addition, Warner paid $25m in cash for North American video rights to 21 Cannon movies, yielding a meagre $1.19m per movie to Cannon. Since Cannon's last video deal with Heron had been for $50m for 23 pictures, Warner had saved themselves almost a cool $1m per picture – at Cannon's expense. More – Warner was to get warrants to purchase 750,000 Cannon shares at $15 per share – 500,000 immediately and a further 250,000 when the stock and notes deal was concluded. As for Commonwealth – not interested!

Did someone say 'fire sale'? Just one week earlier, in the *Hollywood Reporter*, Martin Grove had spoken to John Tinker, Bear, Stearns analyst, who informed him that Warner actually had $900m in cash available for acquisition, without having to tap the troubled post-Boesky junk bond market.

'It's ironic that someone else's problem may be Warner's opportunity', he had remarked. 'Particularly when you see a company such as Cannon having problems, Warner could be in a very good position. The old story is when you don't want to sell, people will offer to pay a lot for your assets. When you do [want to sell] fire sales get very little'.

He went on to praise Warner's film division, Warner Brothers, noting it was 'one of Hollywood's most successful major studios – profits have advanced over the last four years, without having to recourse to dubious accounting practices'. If Warner exercised its option to buy 50% of Cannon's theatres, there was an irony (apart from being the quickest turnaround ever, since Bond had held them for just one week), in that Warner themselves had at one time owned 25% of the ABC circuit and the Associated British Picture Corporation, before selling out to EMI in 1968 – for £9.5m. One way and another, Warner had done well on both deals.

They had injected just about enough to get Cannon off the hook with Bond – and given them time, by guaranteeing the bridging loan, to restructure their corporate debt. The deal was finalised in New York on December 22nd – on December 23rd Bond received his $76.9m. The Cannon 'Runaway Train' had wobbled into the sidings for the time being. It was a question now of who was doing the driving, as it appeared that Arthur Young's representative had been appointed chief financial officer at Cannon and that Barry Lublin had been 'promoted' to the post of 'executive vice president of the office of the president'. Speculation was rife as to the origin of Arthur Young's entry – had the 'special audit' and the eventual CFO appointment been at the *insistence* of Cannon's bankers?

Were there more strings to the Warner deal, involving domestic distribution rights to certain pictures, leaving Cannon's US distribution arm with the dross? The canny Warner team had certainly given themselves the inside track on any future Cannon pickings.

A steady stream of Cannon executives began to vacate the company's Los Angeles headquarters in January 1987, the departures attributed by Yoram Globus to 'normal ebb and flow', although it seemed to be all ebb, no flow.

Between their banks, Arthur Young and the SEC staff – Cannon were surrounded. Law suits continued to fly from disgruntled shareholders, one alleging 'fraud', and professionals like director Ted Kotcheff, claiming Menahem Golan had denied entering into a contract with him. Incredibly, for anyone unfamiliar with their history, they started production in 1987 with *Death Wish IV*, *Missing In Action III* to follow. 'They put everything on the line for their passion', one of their colleagues had said of Golan and Globus' early days in Israel, 'and when they went broke, knew only one way out – make another film'. Just like their allegorical Runaway Train, would they simply disappear into some misty wasteland, or could we look forward to *Cannon II – The Sequel*?

Remember what Golan's mother said: 'If you throw Menahem out the door, he will come back in through the window!'

Many felt that the developments at Cannon, with their potentially damaging implications for the benighted British film industry, could have been foreseen. If the new custodians had been given even a cursory scrutiny, they would have been seen to be hopelessly overleveraged.

The quality of their release programme in 1987, either through their own organisation or through Warner's distribution, will be one deciding factor in their survival, leaving aside the result of the SEC investigation, Arthur Young's findings and the possibility of insolvency. With all the wheeling and dealing, flim-flam and hype in the world, it all comes down to just one thing in the end, whether displayed theatrically, on video or on television. 'The standard to which Cannon, like any company, must be summoned is to make pictures which *a sufficient number of people find engaging and entertaining*' – Jack Valenti, president of the Motion Picture Association of America, had said it all.